Turning Points

Observations from Life in the Real World

For Brenda

A Good Realtor and Friend.

C.V. Kroeger

Carroll V. Kroeger

Strategic Book Group

Strategic Book Group
P.O. Box 333
Durham CT 06422
www.StrategicBookClub.com

ISBN: 978-1-60976-819-5

Typography and page composition by J. K. Eckert & Company

For my wife, "Amazing Grace," who followed me all over the world without complaint.

A loving wife, a caring mother, my best friend, my companion, and my business partner.

Two roads diverged in a wood, and I—
I took the one less traveled by, and that
made all the difference.

—Robert Frost, *Road Not Taken*[1]

Contents

Introduction

There are times in life when something hits you, something that comes out of nowhere when you least expect it. I was sitting at a sidewalk café on the Avenue Champ-Elysees in Paris drinking a glass of wine, watching people go by, when it hit me. *What was I doing here?* By all the odds I should be in that small town, Trenton, Missouri, working in a drug store. Instead I was in Europe, a member of a small multinational team negotiating contracts in Belgium, West Germany and France for the export of natural gas from the world's largest natural gas field in the Netherlands. I was working in a joint venture of two of the largest corporations in the world, Shell International and Standard Oil of New Jersey! The reality started to sink in. I was several thousand miles from that Midwestern town of six thousand people. What strange journey and circumstances brought me here? What were the turning points along the way?

A letter from R. M. Crockett, Vice President of Esso Europe Natural Gas Organization, reads:

> During the past five years you have made a major contribution to Esso and indeed many European companies and nations. Your valuable advice, assistance, and creativity were key factors in helping bring about a major expansion of the natural gas industry of Western Europe.

A.E. Vizard, Group Director for Natural Gas of Shell International, wrote:

> It was really the existence of that small band of dedicated pioneers in The Hague and in London, of whom you were a leading member, that converted the political will to use gas into the technical/eco-

> nomic reality...In all of this, again, your expertise and many patient presentations won the admiration among all your colleagues and customers alike.

Over the years several people told me, "You should write a book." It was only after receiving a message on Facebook from a former student at Belmont University, Jud Rietdorft, that I decided to write it. I have Jud to thank for the turning point:

"I cannot tell you how much you have influenced my life with your teachings and wisdom. I have a beautiful soon-to-be seventeen-year-old daughter. She has one tattoo, which I gladly paid for, which reads 'Don't wait for the last bus! Catch the next to the last one!' You were definitely my favorite instructor at a fabulous school and your wisdom has stayed with me DAILY."

Some may wonder why I chose *Turning Points* as the title for my book. The answer is that my major at Vanderbilt University was Mathematics, not by choice but by necessity. Why not by choice? That's part of the story. In Math a point of inflection is "a point on a curve where the curvature changes." For the layman it's a "Turning Point" in life.

1

Surviving the Great Depression

The first memories I have are "It was cold!" I remember snuggling down in the bed while my dad struggled to remove the ashes from the pot-bellied stove in the dining room and tried to get a new fire started. Our house had one bedroom, a living room, and a kitchen. There was no bathroom. We had an outhouse (sometimes called a "privy") in the back yard. The only water in the house was a cold water tap over the sink in the kitchen. The kitchen was not big enough to eat our meals in. A table and four chairs were in the dining room. The only heat was a coal-fired stove in the dining room. Dad would stoke the fire before we went to bed and hope it held until morning. Very often it didn't and it had to be started again the next morning.

After it got started I would get up in my long underwear and get dressed. I would relieve myself in the slop jar, which was emptied in the outhouse later in the morning. My mother would help me get my clothes on and try to divert my attention from the weather by saying, "Look at the beautiful windows. Jack Frost came during the night and painted them for us." Condensation froze on the inside of the windowpanes in crystal patterns. This was before the days of double and triple pane windows and insulation. I cried when the ice melted and the beautiful paintings disappeared. "Son, the beautiful things in life do not last very long. You have to learn how to recognize them and appreciate them while you can. Beauty is something you can see and admire. You can't hold it, own it, or save it. Remember that and you won't be disappointed in life." My mother always saw beauty in the most austere circumstances.

Our routine was always the same. Monday was "wash day." We had no water heater or washing machine so mother would heat water on the gasoline stove in the kitchen. It would go into a washtub and she would scrub our dirty clothes with yellow soap on a wash board. Dad's clothes were always dirty and greasy because he worked on the railroad inspecting and repairing railroad cars. It was an all-day job washing, rinsing, and hanging the clothes out on a backyard clothes line to dry. It was not unusual for the clothes to freeze in the winter when they were put out to dry. Tuesday was "ironing day." This was before drip dry and everything had to be ironed. Saturday night was the time for baths. The procedure was the same as "wash day." Water had to be heated on the stove and I would sit in the washtub for my bath. Sunday was the day we always went to church in the morning.

I got very sick and developed colitis. The doctor said I could not have anything to eat. I cried I was so hungry. When my mother pleaded with the doctor to give me something, he said, "If you want to kill him, give him some food." Sometime later as I started to feel better, he allowed me to have "milk-toast." To this day I hate the taste of anything resembling it. Eventually I got better and my mother was thankful. I was an only child and she was told she could not have any more children.

We lived on the north side of town two blocks from the railroad tracks to the south and two blocks north to the Brainerd Elementary School. When I was four years old I watched other children walking to school and cried when told I was too young to go to school. My mother went to the public library to get books to read to me, but I wasn't satisfied. I wanted to be with the other children at school. When I was five, she went to the school and was able to get the principal to agree to let me start school early. When I graduated from high school at age seventeen, it proved to be a profound decision.

We had a piano in our living room and our home was always filled with music. It was before the time of radio and television so everyone provided their own entertainment. My mother played the piano and we all sang songs. The railroad had a band and my dad played the trombone in the band. It was decided I should learn to play the piano so I took lessons. I went through book after book of exercises, earning gold stars on each page, and hated it. Finally I refused to do it anymore. I wanted to play real songs. My folks reluctantly got me a clarinet and I became a member of the school band.

Trenton was a railroad town. It was the division point for all of the Rock Island trains that ran from Chicago to Kansas City and beyond. The engines were powered by coal and required a fireman to shovel the coal and maintain proper temperature for the steam to power the engine. The engineer operated the steam engine and kept the train on the tracks. It took several hours to make the run halfway and the crews changed in Trenton and a new crew took the train on to Kansas City. There was a Roundhouse and Repair Shop. It was a labor-intensive business. The Depression created a need to reduce costs and the invention of the diesel engine made the trains run more efficiently and faster. A crew could go straight through from Chicago to Kansas City. This resulted in the laying off of a large number of people in Trenton, and the tearing down of the Roundhouse and Repair Shops. Trenton would never be the same.

It had a great effect on our family. My father lost his job and joined the ranks of the millions of unemployed throughout the country. The freight trains that rolled through Trenton were covered with "hoboes" who were looking for work. They would come to our back door and ask, "Do you have some work I can do for a bowl of beans and piece of cornbread?" They never asked for a handout. As little as we had, my mother would give them something to eat. My dad looked for and took any kind of labor work he could find for a dollar a day. We barely made it to the end of each month. We stopped using electricity and depended upon a kerosene lamp for light at night. There was a government program called "Relief," which gave cheese and margarine to those who applied. My parents were proud and independent people. They never asked for help and didn't believe it was the role of government to help them.

It became clear that the few jobs my dad could find were not going to be enough to pay the mortgage and put food on the table. He said we were going to lose everything. My mother said, "No, we aren't. You go down to the office of the Electric Company and ask them for work." Dad said, "They aren't hiring anyone. It would be a waste of time." My mother was insistent. "You aren't going to find anything by sitting and feeling sorry for yourself," she said. "You put on your best clothes and go to the Missouri Public Service office and ask them for work!" Dad reluctantly did what she asked and a miracle happened. They told him they didn't have anything, but in Chillicothe, a town twenty-five miles away, they were going to change over to LP-gas and they might have some temporary work there.

He drove to Chillicothe and got full-time work for three weeks. He learned how to adjust the gas ranges and other equipment to operate on the new gas supply. In the process he made friends with other men who had been moving around the country doing this kind of work. They told him in two weeks there was going to be another job in Iowa. This became the saving grace for our family. It was not steady work and required my dad to go where there was a job. It kept the wolf away from our door and we did not starve to death.

Every summer we had a garden and my mother grew our own food and canned vegetables and fruit to store for the winter. It was hard and hot work in the kitchen preparing the fruit and vegetables, putting them in Mason glass jars, sealing them and boiling them on the stove so they would not spoil. I learned how to help making pickles, jams, and jellies. Mother would bake our own bread and cornbread.

Dad learned that a man had been building a house across the railroad tracks on the south side of town and had died. The house had been vacant for some time. He went to the bank and asked for a loan to buy the house and the materials to finish building it. We were lucky when the bank approved the loan. When he was not working on gas jobs, he finished building the house. It was a Godsend for my mother. It had two bedrooms, a real bathroom, coal-fired central heat, and a kitchen with electric stove and ice box. I now could have my own bedroom. Even though there was what is now called the "Great Depression," our family found a way to survive through hard work and not feeling sorry for ourselves. My mother said, "We may not be able to buy soap, but that is no excuse for being dirty." All the while I was growing and learning.

> It's mighty sultry today, my mother used to say when the August temperature would exceed one hundred degrees. No TV weathermen explained why it was so hot and humid. We just knew that we had to bear up under the heat. There were few remedies: sit in the front porch swing and hope for a breeze or mix up a pitcher of lemonade and combine that with the motion of a handheld fan. We didn't know about barometric highs and lows or weather fronts in the 1930s and 1940s. If it was unusually hot, we were told that 'It's a hundred and five in the shade.' I don't know where the weatherman keeps his thermometer today, but back then if the temperature was measured in the shade you knew it was a really hot day. I never thought too much about the heat when I was growing up. It got hot in the summer and there wasn't much anyone could do about it. You wore as few clothes as possible and still remain decent. A great treat was to put on your

bathing suit and dance in the water from the lawn sprinkler. Or sometimes you went swimming to cool off. I've always said that nomads in the desert survive because they do not know there is any other way to live.

I guess that's how we got by, because we didn't know we had any choice. Or as my mother used to say, 'because we didn't know any better.' Why didn't we know any better? Well, everyone around us was undergoing the same hardship. If we were hot in August, everyone we knew was hot, too. Sure, if you were rich, you could go lay by the pool at the country club, but anyone could go to the public swimming pool. And so, life went on without air conditioning, without TV weathermen, without refrigerators, etc. Some folks say we're not as tough and durable as we used to be. That's because we're exposed to so much information that we didn't have years ago.[1]

As I was getting an ice cube out of the refrigerator the other night, it suddenly dawned on me I was witnessing a modern day miracle. Ice is something we take for granted. My mind flashed back to the summer of 1934. I was eight years old and the August temperature was above one hundred degrees. Time seemed to stand still and yet it was only a little after 10:00 a.m. I had performed my daily chore of checking the pan under the icebox to see if the water from the melting ice needed to be emptied. My mother had turned the blue and white card in our front room window to indicate to the iceman we would need ten pounds of ice that day. *This day will never end,* I thought, and then I heard the bell. The iceman was coming! I ran into the house to wash my hands.

The black model "T" truck was only a block away and I could see the reflection of the sun on the cake of ice as it was carried into the neighbor's house. Finally the truck chugged into the block where our house was. I couldn't wait. My mouth was parched. 'Well, young man,' the iceman said. 'It looks like you have been waiting a long time.'

'We're just about plum out of ice,' I said. He reached into the sheath on his belt and took out his ice pick. It flashed in the sun as he deftly set out to chip a cake of ice into separate smaller blocks. Small chips flew onto the canvas bottom of the truck bed. 'Don't suppose you would want any of those,' he said with a smile. 'They're too little to be much of any account to me.' I scampered into the truck and collected the small diamonds. I thrust them into my mouth and then the most wonderful sensation began to creep along my tongue toward the back of my mouth. 'I bet heaven is full of ice,' I sighed. That icebox

1. Article written for the "Nashville Eye" Column. *The Tennessean*, July 6, 1988.

> was a miracle for my mother. Her mother had stored the milk, butter, and eggs in the storm cellar to keep them cool. Today we take the refrigerator for granted.[2]

We survived "The Great Depression" because we had to. There was no other choice. We did it by hard work and believing it was our responsibility to take care of ourselves and family. If there was no work where we were, we went where we could find it. I learned we lived in a big country. I spent my summers in Vinton and Ames, Iowa; Baraboo, Wisconsin; Elwood and Marion, Indiana; Mt Vernon and Centralia, Illinois; and Flint, Michigan. I went to high school for a half a year in Pontiac, Michigan and East St. Louis, Illinois.

Like most young men I grew up full of questions. Over the years I compiled them into a list. It was headed "Things I don't understand." This is the list:

1. Why doesn't pleasure last?
2. How can something hurt and feel good at the same time?
3. Why is it girls you like don't like you and the girls you don't like, like you?
4. Why do people say one thing and do something different?
5. How can you hate someone you love?
6. How can you feel hot and cold at the same time?
7. Why do people want something and when they get it not want it anymore?
8. What does growing up have to do with understanding?
9. How can you feel glad and sad at the same time?
10. Why isn't life fair?

Looking back I find there are some questions for which there are no answers. Life is full of contradictions.

Our founding fathers were very wise in framing our Constitution and Declaration of Independence. They had a good understanding of human nature when they said we had a right to the "pursuit of happiness." My mother said, "Beauty doesn't last." Pleasure doesn't last either. We are humans with free will. Life is a series of choices. The choices can be positive or negative depending on whether we chose the path of least resistance or the one less trod. We never know when

---

2. Article written for the "Nashville Eye" Column. *The Tennessean*, November 22, 1987.

a choice will be a turning point in our lives. We need food and liquid to survive. Sex is a powerful drive. It's that way to perpetuate the species. Almost everything in life is good if taken in moderation. The challenge is to have enough will power to resist the temptations that can take you down the paths to excess. The last question on the list is one that has been asked for generations. As Bill Gates, co-founder of Microsoft told a high school graduating class, "Life is not fair. Get over it!"

2

Winning "Wings of Gold" in World War II

I was a senior in High School in 1943 working at night as a bellboy at the Plaza Hotel in Trenton. Work in a hotel is a learning experience. You see a dark side of life, but once in awhile the sun breaks through. It was such a night when two Navy officers checked in. Lt. Lee Mercer and Ensign Ben Underwood from the Naval Aviation Cadet Selection Board in Kansas City walked into my life. I took their suitcases to the elevator. The Lieutenant looked at the Ensign, and said, "He looks like the type of young man we're looking for." He looked at me and said, "We're here to attend your high school assembly and conduct physical and mental exams for seniors who meet our qualifications. You must be seventeen years old, but not reached your eighteenth birthday before enlistment, be in the upper half of your school class, be unmarried, and agree to remain unmarried until completion of flight training, agree to remain on active duty for a period of four years, and pass the mental examination and flight physical examination."

I was impressed with the way they looked and the idea of flying a Navy plane intrigued me. "Why don't you come see us tomorrow?" they said. The more I thought about it the more interested I became. A little voice said, "Wait a minute, remember what Dr. Cullers said when you had rheumatic fever and the heart murmur? He told your mother she would never have to worry because you never could pass the physical exam for the Army." The Navy exam to fly a plane will be stricter. I might not be able to pass the physical but I was curious how I would stack up against the others on the mental exam. "I'll be there tomorrow," I told the officers.

I was surprised to find boys from other schools surrounding Trenton were there: Bethany, Mercer, New Hampton, and Gilman City. The officers said they would give the complete mental test and a preliminary physical exam. The mental test took three hours. The math section was hard, but the verbal section wasn't bad. The hard work under Opal Cox and Gladys Grimes in English class was paying off. The three years of Latin under Jesse Helen Brannon helped identify the roots of many words in the vocabulary section. Looking back, one of the things that probably made a difference were classes in electricity and physics I took at Pontiac Michigan and East Saint Louis, Illinois High Schools. When the time came for the preliminary physical, I was surprised to find I passed! An angel landed on my shoulder!

A few days later I received a postcard, which read, "On the basis of your preliminary application conducted at your high school, you are qualified to complete your application for naval flight training. Because you are one of a select group of men from your school, we urge that you follow up your initial step to win your 'Wings of Gold' and complete your application before our quota is filled." According to an article that appeared in the Trenton newspaper, "Five senior boys passed the preliminary exams; Bob Ellis, Leon Sawyer, Jim Whitten, Carroll Kroeger and Jim Kemp."

"I don't care if you passed the exams," my mother said. "You are staying home until they come and get you."

"I don't want to be in the Army," I told her.

"It doesn't matter what you want, you can't go anywhere without our permission." I knew my mother meant what she said. She never changed her mind about anything. I had to do something, so as soon as I graduated from high school, I got permission to go to Kansas City to get a job and work. I thought this would help her get accustomed to the idea of me being away from home.

I had been working for about two months when a letter arrived from the Aviation Cadet Selection Board stating that "beginning July 1 there will be a reduction of seventy-five percent in the number of men we will be permitted to enlist each month. If you are serious in your intention to enlist in naval aviation and get started in training that will bring you a commission as a flight officer in the United

States Navy, we urge that you act at once to complete your enlistment."

I went home and confronted my dad. "You have a choice," I said. "You can sign these papers or I'm going to sign your name on them. One way or the other I'm not going to be deprived of this opportunity."

"Do you know what you are asking me to do? You know how your mother feels about this."

"I don't care," I said. "I'm not going to wait and be drafted into the Army!" Reluctantly he took the papers and signed them.

"Your mother will never forgive me for this." he said. I went back to Kansas City, turned over my enlistment papers, and was ordered to report for the flight physical examination.

About one hundred young men showed up that day. It was intense; 20/20 vision, eighteen sound vital teeth, whispered hearing voice at fifteen feet, both ears, chest expansion at least two inches, normal pulse rate, blood pressure within normal limits, ability to distinguish clearly primary colors; height minimum 5'4" and maximum 6'4," weight in proportion to height at least 115 pounds. After meeting the basics we were required to step up and down off a stool fifty times to develop physical stress and pass blood pressure and pulse tests again. We were tested for hemorrhoids, social diseases, visual depth perception, night vision, and every possible physical ailment. The final test was to sit in a spinning chair with our head between our legs and at a quick stop raise our head and allow the doctor to observe our sense of balance and eye movement.

After two days of probing, blood, and urine testing, ten names were called out and told to go into the next room. After a short wait, an officer came in and called out the same names to make sure there were no mistakes. "Men, you have just undergone the most thorough physical examination in the world. Congratulations, you are now a part of the Navy's elite!" We looked at each other. Over a hundred had started out two days ago. Now there were only ten. I couldn't believe it. I was one of them. *I wonder what old Doctor Cullers would think about this?,* I thought. The angel was sitting firmly on my shoulder.

I was issued an ID card that read "This is to certify that Carroll Vincent Kroeger, Trenton Missouri has enlisted as a V-5 Apprentice Seaman in the United State Naval Reserve." As soon as I told my parents I passed, they told me to come home to be with them until I received my orders. My Statement of Income Tax Withheld on Wages for the Year 1943 shows wages of $503.37 earned at Wilcox Electric Company in Kansas City. My dad had to go to work on a natural gas conversion job at Anderson Indiana, so mom and I went with him. I was beginning to wonder if I ever was going to get orders to active duty. A war was on and people would look at me. I was an able bodied young man. Why wasn't I in service? Was I "4-F" unfit for service or a draft dodger?

Looking back, I know what was going on. The Navy was skimming off the top young men before they became eligible for the draft, but did not want to order a seventeen-year-old to active duty. So they waited until we were almost eighteen before they issued the orders. My orders finally came. I was to report to the Naval Aviation Cadet Selection Board on November 23, 1943 for further transfer to the U.S. Naval Air Station at Hutchinson, Kansas for Tarmac duty as a seaman second class. I was happy. I knew there was the possibility that I could have been ordered to go to college for eight months in the V-12 program. In my mind this meant that as soon as I completed the Tarmac Duty, I would become an Aviation Cadet and go to Flight Preparatory School. I was on my way to earning those "Wings of Gold!"

It was a cold November morning at the Anderson, Indiana railroad station that I said goodbye to my parents. My mother stood with tears in her eyes. I shook my dad's hand and thanked him for all they had done for me. "There's only one way you can ever thank me," he said "One day get married and have a family of your own." I got on the train, looked out the window, and waved as the train pulled out of the station. *What in the world did my old man mean by that?* I thought. Soon my thoughts were drowned out by the 'clicky-clack, clickty-clack' of the train. It was only after about thirty years I began to understand what he meant.

The orders issued at Kansas City were for the 109 men to proceed to Hutchinson, Kansas and report to the commanding officer at the Naval Air Station. Hutchinson Kansas was out in the middle of nowhere. The terrain was flat as far as you could see. We reported in and found they had no uniforms for us, so we did close order drill in civilian clothes. I wore out the soles on my shoes before Navy clothes arrived. When they did, we looked like a motley crew. We were issued skivvies (underwear), black watch stocking caps, denim shirts and pants, and cadet gray-green winter coats.

A war was on and everything was in short supply. The first two days we policed the base, picking up trash and putting it in gunny sacks. When the sack was full, you got another one. The lesson was:

you don't litter and throw trash on the ground, not even a cigarette butt! Then, it was close order drill all day long until we got it right. At the end of the day we ran around the drill field. I mean we ran and ran and ran. You go until you think *"I can't make it around another time,"* but you have to keep going. Slowly some started to pass out and fall down. The Boatswain's Mate wasn't satisfied until at least five had gone down and were taken away by the ambulance.

Next we were introduced to the runways. In Kansas in the winter it snows. The runways had to be shoveled clear before we could open the hanger doors and push the aircraft out onto the flight line. Then it was time to gas them up, crank the engines to start, and warm up the engines. The planes were Stearman bi-winged, open cockpit, N3N training planes. Some called them the "Yellow Peril." It took two of us to crank the engine to get it started, then we would sit in the cockpit and warm up the engine until the instructor and cadet came out to fly.

It was cold, I mean really cold! It felt like the wind started at the North Pole and came blasting down across the Great Plains and there was nothing to slow it down. (I now understand why they say there should be windmill farms out there to generate electricity.) There was a double whammy. When you sit in the open cockpit of an airplane, you get what is called the "prop-wash" created by the propeller. I wrote home and asked my mom to send me some long underwear. After they arrived I was still cold.

Soon things settled down into a routine; up at six a.m., calisthenics, breakfast, and then out to the line. Even in a snow storm the Commanding Officer seemed bent on setting a record for the most training flights. They would send up a "weather flight" to see if it was clear enough to fly. Not once did they say it wasn't clear enough. The flights would go out for about an hour. Then we would gas up the planes, check the oil, crank the engines, warm them up until they went our again.

Finally some uniforms came in. We were issued enlisted dress blues, flat hats, new black shoes, and Navy enlisted men's pea coats. Wow! We felt like real sailors! We were issued liberty cards, assigned to a duty section, and allowed to go on liberty on Saturdays. There were three duty sections. In the Navy it is standard practice to keep two-thirds of the crew on station at all times. The duty cards were three different colors so that those on duty at the gates only had to look at the color to know if you could leave. Before I knew it, it was almost time for Christmas. The favorite song on the radio was "I'll Be Home for Christmas." I've never liked that song since.

Hutchinson wasn't a great place to go on liberty. They had an USO, movie theatre, and that was about it as far as recreation was concerned. I found it was better to stay on the base and go to the Recreation Hall. I tried drinking a little beer. Kansas was a dry state so the only beer was called 3/2 beer. Low alcohol content. It tasted like rusty water so I settled for Cokes. Tarmac Duty was a real coming of age for me. I led a very sheltered life. Suddenly I was thrown in with a bunch of very "worldly sailors."

We were required to attend VD lectures. Back then they called it Venereal Disease. Today it's—Sexually Transmitted Disease, STD. We were told the dangers of contracting VD. First, you didn't receive your pay for the time you were under treatment. Second, they showed photos of people who contracted some of the most horrible things you can imagine. And third, you were given a package of condoms and told by the Chief Petty Officer, "When you go on liberty, don't do it, but if you must, use a condom."

My next lesson in life was gambling. Navy Regulations said that gambling was not allowed on Navy Stations or Navy Vessels. As soon as a flight would go out a group would huddle in the corner of a hanger and shoot dice. I was getting paid fifty dollars a month and was shocked to see guys lose a month's pay in a few minutes. I watched, didn't understand the game, and decided it was too expensive for me to learn. Later at casinos in San Juan, Puerto Rico and in Monaco in the Mediterranean, and in Las Vegas, I've watched as people waged and lost what to me are small fortunes. I didn't understand it in Kansas in 1944 and I don't understand it now. The house always wins!

I learned a lot in the three months I was on Tarmac duty. I learned there were different types of people, some who were trustworthy and some who were not. We were a group of young men from all walks of life, some very worldly and some like me, very naïve. We were from many different ethnic backgrounds and cultures, but we were bound together by a common goal. We wanted to fly a Navy plane and we wanted to go out and help win the war.

I was a seaman second class, which was about as close to the bottom of the totem pole as you can get. I swabbed decks. I cleaned toilets in the heads and served on mess cook duty. I learned to make my own bed and to pass personnel inspection, to keep my few possessions neat and clean in my locker. I found it strange that we would work like hell to make everything spic and span because an Admiral was coming the next day on a "Surprise Inspection."

There were two types of planes at Hutchinson NAS: the Stearman N3N, and a few all metal low wing enclosed cockpit SNJs. We were required to attend a parachute lecture and learn how to use a parachute. I still have my card dated 8 December 1943. I heard that if you put in a request it was possible to get a ride in one of the SNJs with instructors who wanted to get in extra flying time. The time came when my request was granted. I donned my flight gear and parachute and climbed into the plane. The pilot revved up the engine, checked all of the instruments and shut it down. He called a mechanic who discovered a fuel leak in the engine. We changed planes and soon I was in the air on my first time in an airplane. I loved it then and I'm still thrilled every time the plane is thundering down the runway on take-off.

It was March and I was getting itchy. I learned about all I was going to learn and was ready to move on to being an Aviation Cadet. I watched the Cadets get in the planes and go flying off into the wild blue yonder. I wanted to spread my wings and fly. After all I was now eighteen years old and could do anything!

There was a great commotion in the barracks and everyone was crowding around the bulletin board. "It's new orders," someone shouted. I crowded up to look. I couldn't believe it.

My class was to report to the Navy V-12 Unit at Washburn Municipal University in Topeka, Kansas. I was being busted down from seaman second class to apprentice seaman. I now was going to be at the very bottom of the Navy totem pole. We were told, "The Navy has found that men with some college training have a greater success ratio in the flight program. Everyone henceforth would complete two semester of college before they were eligible for flight training." I was going to be wearing bell bottom trousers for another eight months before I became an Aviation Cadet.

Looking back, the Navy found it did not experience the loss of pilots in the Pacific War that had been estimated. We were the "Ace in the Hole." The Navy would keep us in reserve in college in the event they needed us. There was an angel sitting on my shoulder I never saw. I was devastated. I didn't want to go to college. I wanted to fly a Navy fighter plane off of an aircraft carrier. At seventeen and eighteen you are a little bit crazy. I wanted to wear those "Wings of Gold." Looking back, how lucky can you get?

There are times in life when we become frustrated because things are not going the way we planned. Learning how to overcome disappointment and adversity is one of the greatest lessons in life. The earlier you learn it, the better off you are. It has been said that opportunity comes disguised in work clothes. It was a great disappointment when I didn't become an Aviation Cadet. Looking back it was the best thing that could have happened to me. Sometimes an intervening force enters our lives for a reason we don't understand. This turning point prepared me to go places and do things I never could have dreamed of!

3

Never Wait until the Last Bus!

It was the summer of 1944. I was a U.S. Navy Apprentice Seaman V-12 (a) at Washburn Municipal University in Topeka, Kansas. The (a) was the designation for "Aviation." My class was transferred from the Navy V-5 flight program at Hutchinson Naval Air Station to complete two semesters of college before going to Flight Preparatory School. I was imbedded in eighteen semester hours of Math, Physics, Engineering Drawing, Naval History, Geopolitics, Elementary Strategy, and intense Physical Training.

Carl T. Rowan describes the program at Washburn in detail in Chapter Three of his book, *Breaking Barriers*. Carl was one of the first black sailors to be enrolled in the Navy V-12 Officer Training Program. I arrived on campus in March 1944 about the time he was transferred to Oberlin College. My experience at Washburn was very similar to Carl's; The V-12 unit was composed of 335 sailors under the command of Lt. Bontrager and a staff of Junior Officers and Chief Petty Officers. I was competing against "honors guys from high schools and colleges" far better than Trenton, Missouri High School. "Guys who had high school courses like analytic geometry and spherical trigonometry." In high school I barely made it through Algebra, taught by the football coach C. F. Russell. If I failed, half of the football team failed! (Today the football stadium bears his name.)

Since neither of my parents went beyond the sixth grade I couldn't look for help at home in Math. Gladys Grimes and Opal Cox, my English teachers, and Jessie Helen Branam, my Latin teacher, were strict, demanding, and hard! Many of my classmates hated them. I loved them because if you performed, you were rewarded. They didn't care a whit about socio-economic background. Their grading system was based on merit. As a result of the Journalism class taught by the principal, Gerald Munday, I became the Feature Editor for the Trentonian school newspaper. If there had been no war, my dream was to go to the University of Missouri and major in journalism.

The Navy didn't ask what my dream was and ignored the fact that I had enlisted in the V-5 program because I wanted to fly a Navy fighter plane. So here I was, immersed in Math, Physics, and Engineering courses and subjected to Chief Petty Officer Montgomery's meanness in what the curriculum called "Physical Education." He delighted in torturing everyone in calisthenics, wrestling, boxing, and strength tests. We hated getting up each morning at six a.m. to run a mile come rain or come shine, Friday afternoon close-order drills, Saturday inspections, and having to improve in sit-ups, pull-ups, push-ups, and squat thrusts at each strength test.

If you want to develop your abs, try lying flat on your back, lifting up both feet with legs straight three inches off the ground and holding them there forever. At least that's what it seemed like when Chief Montgomery yelled if your feet dropped to the ground. Naively I was willing to undergo all of this because at the end of eight months I would be rewarded by getting back into the V-5 flight program and eventually wearing those "Wings of Gold."

Lt. Bontrager was strange. He had been a Psychology Professor at Ohio State University and somehow ended up as Commander of the Navy V-12 Unit at Washburn. His interpretations of Navy Regulations were weird. For example, we were supposed to wear a nametag at all times. I guess this was because everyone looked the same in enlisted men's uniforms and it would help identify anyone who was violating the rules. The Lieutenant had some domestic problems, but we weren't privy to the details. All we knew from scuttlebutt was his wife took all of their gasoline ration coupons and ran off to Florida.

From that time on it was hard to know when he might show up prowling around the dorms and campus. One evening my roommate emerged from the shower and was startled to look the CO in the eye. "Sailor," growled the Commanding Officer, "where's your name tag? You're on report!" From that time on whenever we took a shower, we stuck our name tag on our bare chest. I concluded the CO was not able to forget his psychology classes at Ohio State. He systematically went through the roster of 355 sailors each semester, giving each a personal interview and evaluation. This struck fear in the hearts of everyone, because all it took was for him to decide you didn't have officer-like qualifications and you were "washed out" and on the train to Boot Camp at Great Lakes Naval Training Station in Chicago.

The Rules and Regulations stated that personnel could not go beyond a fifty-mile limit when on weekend liberty. Kansas City was sixty miles away. This was important because after I graduated from high school and enlisted in the V-5 program I worked in Kansas City. Bob Hopper, a friend from school, helped me find a job at Wilcox Electric Company, which made Radio Ground Stations for the Army Air Corps. I started out tying cables. This required over one hundred wires to be laced together and metal connectors soldered to the end of each wire. It was a job that took more than a day to complete. Later I worked on the assembly line where I installed the cables and connected them to rectifiers and various meters. Bob also helped me find a room at a place where he was living. In high school I was a "late bloomer" and living in Kansas City was where I came of age.

Most of my high school classmates probably considered me a nerd. I started school when I was five years old and had just turned seventeen, the youngest member of my graduating class. Looking back, the girls I dated must have considered me immature. All of my friends were immediately drafted into the Army upon graduation, but I had to wait until I was almost eighteen for orders to active duty. Saturday nights were the fun nights and the place in Kansas City was the Play-Mor Ballroom. This was the big band haven where everyone went to meet, dance, drink cokes and have a good time.

I was fortunate enough to meet a beautiful girl named Lucille Grey. Lucille was a fabulous dancer and was kind and patient enough to teach me how to "Jitterbug" and dance the "Lindy." We kept in contact by letter after I reported for active duty and now I was only sixty miles away at Topeka. All I had to do was keep my grades up, get no demerits, and get a pass to allow me to go beyond the fifty-mile limit. The time came and I was showered, shaved, dressed in my liberty clothes, and ready to go to Kansas City. Every Saturday before going on liberty at one p.m. we had to pass personnel inspection. I was ready and as we were about to be dismissed, Chief Pappas called out, "The following named men will report to the Commanding Officer." My name was on the list. It was time for my interview.

It did not go well. As soon as I walked into the office, Lt. Bontrager sniffed the air and said, "What's that I smell?"

"I believe that's my 'All Spice' after-shave lotion," I replied. It was the wrong response! The CO launched into a lecture about how I didn't take my duties seriously. He looked at my record and said, "How do you explain this 'C' in Math?" I had worked my butt off to get that "C" because I had to learn everything I had missed in high school Algebra, catch up, and try to compete with those guys who had gone to big city technical high schools.

The instructors graded strictly on a curve. It was a zero-sum game. For every "A" in the class, there was an automatic "F" for the lowest grade. Obviously I couldn't say I considered my "C" the same as an "A." I had to listen to a tirade about how I was just a playboy interested only in having a good time and not in studying. In retrospect, the CO probably had struggled getting his education during the Great Depression and resented we were getting a free ride with the Navy paying for our education. The interview concluded with my being confined to base, my liberty cancelled, and instructed to have on his desk Monday morning evidence I had spent the weekend studying.

So much for my fifty-mile pass to Kansas City! I spent the weekend studying and I went overboard documenting the weekend work. Eventually, I became eligible for another weekend pass, and made it to Kansas City. Lucille and I had a fun time dancing to the music of Sonny Dunham's Band at the Play-Mor and her mother was kind enough to let me sleep on their couch at their apartment. The next afternoon I was reluctant to leave and waited until the last minute to run to the bus station. Just as I arrived I saw the bus pull out. It was four hours until the next bus to Topeka. I was late reporting in Sunday evening and to my chagrin Lt. Bontrager was there waiting. He listened to my excuse and then chastised me, saying, "Young man, you never wait until the last bus, you take the next to last bus! You are restricted to base indefinitely and if I see you with another infraction you will be shipped out to Great Lakes!"

This had a lasting impression, which carried over into all aspects of my life. Much later I learned about Murphy's Law; "If anything can go wrong, it will." Procrastination is a very bad habit. Over time I learned the best way to avoid problems was to not put things off, attack the difficult problems first, and then coast to the finish line. I must have passed this on in some of my lectures at Belmont University. Little did I know the effect it would have and twenty-eight years later the seventeen-year-old daughter of one of my students would have it on her arm as a tattoo! My wife still thinks I'm strange when I want to allow a lot of time going to the airport. But we never have missed a flight by being late!

4

The Washing Out Machine

My arrival at Washburn Municipal University in Topeka, Kansas was different than Carl Rowan's. He said he saw a lot of sailors and girls hugging and kissing. When my group of disgruntled V-12(a)s arrived, we were blinded by indignation. We felt betrayed. We didn't want to be here. Several said, "To hell with this. This is not what I joined the Navy for!" We were joined by another group of sailors who had been serving aboard ship and saw this as a way to get away from sea duty. They were here because it gave them the opportunity to drink beer and chase broads.

I was assigned a room in the dormitory called "Yorktown." My roommate, Richard Relph Jr., was one of those from the fleet. He received a commendation from the Acting Chief of Naval Personnel for "his courage and determination in the line of duty." In November of 1943 his ship was torpedoed in the Pacific, tearing a hole almost directly under his twenty millimeter gun and throwing him to the deck. He immediately got to his feet, manned his gun, and opened fire on the enemy. He remained at his station until ordered to abandon ship. What a difference between two roommates. At the time of his ship going down, I was moaning about not being called to active duty!

Washburn was founded in 1865 and the campus occupied 160 acres in a residential area of Topeka, the state capital. The administration was happy to have the Navy V-12 unit since the civilian students were not enough to sustain the operations during the war. In fact, the only civilian students were young women. The schedule of prescribed V-12 curricula for the first two college terms required five hours of Mathematical Analysis, three hours of English, two hours of Historical background of World War I-II, four hours of Physics, two hours of Engineering Drawing and Descriptive Geometry, one hour of Naval Organization, and one hour of Physical Training. This totaled to eighteen semester hours. It was a heavy load.

I was shocked to receive a letter from a navy enlisted man in the Pacific, which said he was engaged to Lucille Grey and they were going to be married. He had been home on leave and discovered my name and address in her purse. I was shocked because I thought I was in love with Lucille and that she cared for me. We had known each other for about a year. I spent half of a month's pay to buy her a Christmas gift and she sent me a St. Christopher's medal to protect me from harm's way. Although I was not a "hugger," she found her way through my personal space and I enjoyed her hugs and kisses. I never tried to go further because I believed she was a "good girl" and only "bad girls" engaged in heavy petting and sex. Being young and naïve, I thought being engaged was almost the same as being married. I felt betrayed and wrote her a letter telling her to stop writing to me and why. Looking back, I should have asked her if it was true and let her decide if she wanted to stop writing to me. I didn't see how being engaged didn't make a difference to her in our relationship. To me it made a big difference.

The first semester at Washburn was hard. I had a lot of ground to make up in Math and Science. It was starting to take its toll. The men from the fleet didn't study. At night after "Lights Out" there was a steady procession up the stairs to the roof and down the fire escapes and off to the closest beer joints. My roommate had to go to sick bay for a case of the "crabs" he contracted from an encounter with an unknown female. I'm sorry to say that by the end of the semester he and many like him were on their way back to the fleet. The men from the fleet weren't the only ones leaving. Mathematical Analysis and Physics were taking their toll. One "F" or two "Ds" and you were out of there.

I got an education watching others try to cheat their way through exams. Writing Physics and Math formulas on different body parts was one of their favorites. There was an honor code and I observed it. Those who didn't observe the code got caught and were "washed out." I learned the hard way who I could trust and those who were not trustworthy I found time to submit an application for membership in the American College Quill Club. My manuscripts were accepted and I was initiated at a candle light service at Mulvane Museum on May 10, 1944.

I was pleased at the end of the semester to have survived with "Cs" and an "A" in Engineering Drawing. As things settled into a routine, I began to notice the girls at Washburn. Everyone seemed to congregate at the Student Center. They had cokes for sale and a jukebox. Nat King Cole and his Trio were gaining popularity with songs like "Route Sixty-Six," "It's Only a Paper Moon," and "Sweet Lorraine." I was fortunate to meet Dixie Parker there. I never knew her real first name because everyone called her Dixie. She lived in the residential area near Washburn and her home was within walking distance of the campus. Dixie and I hit it off. She loved to dance and it wasn't long before we were hugging and kissing.

Topeka was one of two locations in the nation where Army Air Force Bomber crews shipped out for overseas service. Saturday nights were nights filled with fun and dancing. My second roommate's name was Bigham. He was a native of Topeka and our source of information of where to go and what to do. He was going with a married woman whose husband was overseas. She was tough and played catcher on a female baseball team. Bigham was bright, didn't have to study, and was an entrepreneur. He always was thinking up ways to earn some extra money. Bigham was running his own little laundry. All sailors wore white uniforms that needed washing. He charged fifty cents per uniform washed and ironed.

One day he said to me, "How much money do you have?"

"Why?" I asked warily.

"This is a dry state," he said. "A bottle of bourbon goes for fifteen dollars. That same bottle sells for five dollars across the line in Missouri. We can hitchhike there and back after inspection on Saturday afternoons and make a fortune." It sounded like a good business proposition so we pooled our money and went into the bootleg business. We found that the liquor dealers in Missouri required you to take a bottle of rum for each two bottles of bourbon purchased. Our business venture was a success. We sold the bourbon at the dance hall and kept the rum for ourselves. Dixie loved rum and could hold her liquor without getting tipsy or sick. She was a good dancer and a lot of fun.

My parents came to visit, met Dixie and her family, and everyone seemed to get along very well. The second semester rolled around and I began to sweat blood and tears. The first semester weeded out those at the bottom of the curve. The competition was getting tough. It still was a zero sum game. For each "A," there was an automatic "F" for the one with the lowest mark. I was struggling because Math didn't come easy for me. I was being forced to develop the left side of my brain.

The war was progressing and the Navy needs for officers were declining. The officers were starting to look for more ways to "wash out" more sailors. One day we were told to report for a night vision test. We went into a darkened room and had to look into a machine and tell which way a red arrow pointed. Five men didn't pass and were sent off to Great Lakes. Near the end of the second term, Lt. Bontrager announced effective July first the V-12(a) students would be required to take a third term of college.

I made a "D" in Math, a "B" in English and History, and "Cs" in the rest of the courses. We were given a series of screening exams and many were told we no longer were under consideration for flight training. I had invested too much now to quit. If I couldn't earn those "Wings of Gold," at least I could become a commissioned officer. We were given a choice of the different V-12 programs and I chose the Deck Program because it was the shortest to get to be an officer. I received a certificate from Washburn for satisfactory completion of two terms of study and meeting the curricular requirements for admission to the Deck Candidate Curriculum. The certificate was dated November 10, 1944. Dixie told me she was going to go to school at the University of Texas in Austin.

Orders arrived and I was one of fifteen former Tarmacs ordered to report to Lt. J. W. Lawson, CO of the Navy V-12 Unit at Peru State Teachers College in Nebraska. My academic schedule was five hours of Differential Calculus, four hours of Inorganic Chemistry, three hours of Elementary Heat Power, three hours of Elementary Navigation and Nautical Astronomy, three Hours of Naval History & Elementary Strategy, and two hours of Physical Education. The load totaled twenty semester hours. I was assigned to a room in Dezell Hall.

I thought Kansas was cold. Nebraska is farther north than Kansas. There was no "prop wash" but there was snow. It started in November and didn't end until Spring. The weather didn't deter the Navy Chief from making us run. There was the "Burma Road" with the obstacle course. The wall was ten feet high. You had to run, jump, grab the top and pull yourself up and over. The monkey bars made your arms twinge and you better not let go! Every morning the Chief Athletic

Specialist K.M. Armstrong would get in his car, drive down the highway a mile, stop and check off names as we ran up. Then we would turn around and run back to the school in the snow. That was how we started off our day.

The academic side kept getting more competitive. The "washing out" system continued. On the first day of the semester the Chemistry Professor, Clyde Barfield, said, "Look at the person on each side of you. One of you will not be here at the end of the semester." He was serious and four months later the class was one-third smaller. Looking back, I believe he had worked his way through college and wanted to make sure we worked hard to get ours too. His exams were hard! When we came to valences we had to memorize all of them. On the exam I missed two and got a grade of "zero." On the retest I made a hundred and received a "C" because I didn't get them right the first time. I was not alone. "In chemistry you can't be just ninety percent right," he said. "If you're not one hundred percent correct, you could blow up the building!"

Peru, Nebraska was really in the boon docks. It was a small college town. There was a one block commercial district with a drug store, and movie theatre. To get a haircut you had to hitch a ride to the highway then another five miles to the next town Nebraska City. There was really no place to spend money. It was the only time in the Navy when I had some of my fifty dollars left at the end of the month. I was feeling good. I would have only one more semester of college, and then I would go to Midshipman's School. After that I would be an Ensign in the Naval Reserve. Twenty semester hours in college is a huge load.

When I taught at Belmont, students complained how hard it was to carry fifteen hours. I told them they didn't know what hard was. I was doing okay in everything except Elementary Navigation. Actually it was a course in Spherical Trigonometry. When we asked how relevant this was to navigating a ship, we were told that we had to learn how people navigated before they had the modern methods. It was difficult to remember all of the formulae, use the tables, and arrive at the right answer. In Navigation like Chemistry there is no room for error!

Since there wasn't much to do with the little spare time we had, I listened to the radio. I played the clarinet in the high school band and Artie Shaw and his big band caught my ear. Wow! What a great sound. I began to collect his records, "Dancing in the Dark," "Any Old Time," "Take Your Shoes Off Baby," "Stardust," "Saint James

Infirmary Blues" and a twelve inch record "Concerto for Clarinet." How neat it must be to lead a band and play like that. I decided I would get a fifty-mile pass and go to Kansas City one weekend. I hadn't been dancing in quite awhile. I missed seeing Dixie. We corresponded, but it wasn't the same.

I hitchhiked to Kansas City. I couldn't call Lucille Grey anymore, so I decided to call Martha Owens. We had grown up together in Trenton and lived only a block apart. We never dated but we always were good friends. I knew she and some other girls from Trenton were working in Kansas City. I looked her up in the telephone book and gave her a call. Martha shared an apartment with two other girls. She invited me over, shared dinner with me, and we talked the night away, reminiscing about the good old days at Trenton. They invited me to stay overnight since I had no place to stay. There was nothing romantic about our relationship. I slept on the couch and Martha loaned me her pajamas. I never saw her again until many years later at the twenty-fifth reunion of our high school class. She took great delight in telling everyone that the last time she saw me I was wearing her pajamas!

The end of the semester rolled around. I was happy to squeak by in Navigation with a "D." I made "Bs" in Naval History and Elementary Heat Power and "Cs" in the rest of the courses. One day everyone was excited and gathered around the bulletin board at the dorm. "It's new orders!" someone shouted. I pushed my way up to the bulletin board and read, "The following named men have been selected for further training in the Naval Reserve Officer Training Program." There were five names and mine was one of them. We were to proceed and report to J.E. Cooper, the Commanding Officer of the NROTC unit at Rice University in Houston Texas.

There are times when life is not fair. The rules were changed again. Learning how to roll with the punches, handle disappointment, and overcome adversity are important lessons in life. I was starting to learn! You don't sulk and feel sorry for yourself. Whatever happens, you don't quit. It was snowing in Nebraska and an invisible angel was sitting on my shoulder.

5

Competing with the Best and the Brightest

When I left Nebraska there was a foot of snow on the ground and the temperature was twenty degrees. When the train pulled into the railroad station in Houston, I had to take off my pea coat. The temperature was eighty degrees and the sun was shining. Houston in 1945 was different. It was hot and humid and it was before air conditioning. There was only one hotel in Houston, the Rice Hotel. I took a bus to Rice Institute (Now called Rice University.). The campus was located on the edge of town. The school was endowed by William Marsh Rice, a wealthy man who left the school a lot of land, which turned out to be oil-producing.

He was eccentric in his will. The school was limited to Caucasian students; there could be no concrete sidewalks, and the school was to be tuition-free with no social fraternities or sororities. He was buried on the campus with a brass statue over his tomb. In 1945 the entire Rice student body was about nine hundred students. Since it was a non-tuition school, the admission requirements were very strict; a grade point average in high school of 4.0 was almost mandatory. The emphasis of the curriculum was on engineering and science. The campus was surrounded by hedges of gardenias. The aroma was overpowering. The architecture was of Italian and Spanish character, with a Sallyport entrance and Campanili tower at the engineering building.

The attitude of the administration was different than Washburn and Peru. The school had an endowment and wasn't dependent on the Navy during the war. The Navy was accommodated because of the war. I was thrown into a lion's den with the best academic students in Texas and the survivors of the Navy V-12 programs. I checked in with the Officer of the Deck at the administration building. We were assigned rooms, issued new uniforms, and given a copy of the station regulations.

For the first time in fifteen months I wasn't going to be wearing bell-bottoms. The uniforms looked like a Navy Officer's uniform except there was no gold braid. There were gold anchors everywhere. The pants had a fly and pockets. For everyday the shirts and pants were khaki with a black tie. The dress uniform was Navy blue with gold anchors and gold buttons. It was quite a change. No longer would I have to carry my pack of cigarettes in my sock or put my handkerchief on my shoulder. When it rained, there was a rain coat. From the uniforms we really looked like officer candidates! The NROTC program was different than the V-5 and V-12 programs. The first two programs were developed during the war and had the objective of turning out Navy officers who could be thrust into the war as soon as possible.

The normal Navy Officer training program required all commissioned officers to have a college education. There were only two ways to do that: The Naval Academy at Annapolis and going through the NROTC programs at selected colleges and universities. The Commanding Officer at Rice was Captain J. E. Cooper. This was his philosophy:

> Can you climb down a rope fifty or sixty feet without burning your hands? Are you an expert swimmer, and if so, have you built up an endurance that will enable you to stay afloat for ten or twelve hours? How long can you throw shells into a five-inch gun without becoming totally exhausted? If all the officers on your ship should be killed or incapacitated, would you be able to navigate the ship to port? If in charge of a gun director, will you get your shells out faster and with more accuracy than the enemy? Have you developed in yourself the qualities of initiative and self-confidence that will make you a valuable asset to the ship or station on which you will serve?

There was to be no kissing or hugging on the Rice campus. The regulations stated that "undue affection" was not allowed and even hand-holding with members of the opposite sex was against regulations. The routine was: reveille at six a.m., calisthenics at six-fifteen a.m., personnel inspection at seven a.m., shoes briskly shinned, all clothes pressed, clean and neat, hair trimmed with no long sideburns, or beard. Brass belt buckle shiny. After inspection, platoons double-timed to the mess hall for breakfast.

Classes began at eight a.m. with room inspection during the morning. The rooms had to be spic and span with no dust or lint anywhere on top of the doors or window frames. The bunks had to be made tight enough to bounce a quarter off the sheets, all clothes folded neatly in the drawers and drawers opened so all contents were visible. Any infraction gave the Room Captain five demerits. Room Captains rotated every week. I was assigned to a room with two roommates, Bob Smader and Lynn Musgrave. Bob and Lynn already had been at Rice one semester. We each had a desk and a bureau with a stack of drawers for our clothes. There was a closet to hang clothes in. The beds were bunk beds and I had the top bunk.

Bob was from Wisconsin and I was surprised to learn that Lynn was married. It was against regulations but he had come from the fleet and to him regulations were something you could take or leave. He spent every weekend with his wife and her family At the end of classes in the afternoon, all men assembled for either strength test development, close order drills, or swimming. There was no swimming pool at Rice so everyone was loaded on a bus to go to the Houston YMCA. The drill was climb a rope to the roof hand over hand, then down hand over hand, swim two lengths of the Olympic pool underwater, and swim two lengths with an artificial rifle without getting it wet. Jump in fully clothed, remove your pants, tie a knot in each pant leg, and blow them up to make a life preserver.

The NROTC General Curricula called for four hours of Chemistry and Engineering Materials, five hours of Calculus and Analytical Mechanics, three hours of Seamanship, three hours of Piloting and Navigation, three hours of Naval Administration and Law, and two hours of Physical Training. It added up to twenty hours. So what else was new? If the Navy said that's what I had to do, that's what I would do. I had invested too much time and energy to quit now. No matter what they threw at me, I was going to make it!

The food in Texas was different. A civilian, Mrs. Hardy, ran the mess hall. The food was "hearty" that is filling. In the Navy I adjusted to beans for breakfast and a lot of vegetables I never ate before. When you are hungry, you will eat almost anything. There was a war on and most food staples were rationed. But at Rice it was grits for breakfast, grits for lunch, and grits for dinner. I never had grits before. They came for breakfast like cereal with sugar and milk, at lunch they were fried and with syrup, and for dinner they were like mashed potatoes with gravy. I ate them because I had no choice, but to this day I will never eat them again! There were other things about food in the Navy programs. You never went hungry. You could eat all you wanted, but you had to eat everything you took on your tray. A guard was stationed at the place where you returned your tray and silverware. If you dumped anything into the trash can, you received demerits.

Bob Smader took me in tow and proceeded to educate me about Rice and Houston. When he found out I had sung in the Glee Club and Chorus in high school, he said, "How would you like to make some extra money?" Fifty dollars a month never went very far so I expressed interest. "I'm singing in the choir of an Episcopal Church. They pay three dollars each Sunday. They need male voices because all of the men have gone off to war. The Choir Director will give you free voice lessons at the Houston Conservatory of Music. Also you get Wednesday evenings off the base for Choir Practice." It sounded like a good deal so I agreed to do it. There also was a Navy Glee Club at Rice so I joined it too. "There's a sorority dance Saturday night on Montrose Boulevard. I signed us up," Bob told me. "I don't know how it will be, but it won't cost anything, and if we don't like it we can leave." I was willing, although I was skeptical about a business woman's sorority. It was March 17th, 1945, St. Patrick's Day, and we were disappointed. The committee issuing the invitations used a formula designed to please the members. There were three men for every girl. There would be no wallflowers at this dance! We arrived early and left the same way after an hour. "We might be able to salvage part of the evening anyway," said Bob. "A friend of my mother lives close to here. I've been intending to stop and visit her ever since I came to Houston. Now is as good a time to do it as any."

We walked several blocks and stopped in front of a white apartment building. It looked like something out of New Orleans. The front porches and balconies were built with distinctive decorative iron work. We went up to the second floor and Bob rang the doorbell. The door was opened by a tall, thin woman with deep, dark eyes. Her hair was combed back into a bun and she was wearing a dress that was plain but expensive. As soon as Bob disclosed his identity, we were invited in and made welcome. I sat in a chair as Bob began to tell the news about their friends and acquaintances in Wisconsin.

A young woman walked into the room. She had a well-tanned complexion and, like her mother, raven, black hair. She walked with her head held high, full of pride. Her name was Mary Louise and she was being punished for staying out later than the time she was told to return home after a dance. She sat down in a chair on the opposite side of the living room. Mrs. Klicpera offered us a glass of wine and continued to talk with Bob. Mary Louise looked at me and I looked at her. We didn't say a word. In a short time Bob and I said our thanks and left.

With problems of getting familiar with the new routine, learning station regulations and the demerit system, finding my way about campus to classrooms, neither of us mentioned one word about Mary Louise. One evening I saw an advertisement in the newspaper. Gene Krupa and his band were going to be playing for a dance at the Houston Coliseum. I went to a telephone booth, looked up the number for the Klicpera's and dialed the number. When Mary Louise answered, I asked the question, "Would you like to go see Gene Krupa Saturday night?"

"I was beginning to think you had forgotten me," she said. "I would love to go, but my school is having a dance I have to go to. Wouldn't you like to go there with me instead?"

"Certainly," I said.

A short time later I mentioned to Bob that I had a date with Mary Louise for Saturday night. A strange look came over his face and he said, "That's funny, so do I!" Saturday we went together to pick up Mary Louise. I never had a "double date" before and this was a strange one. It was an unusual situation, a girl with two escorts. She didn't seem to mind the attention it created. I was beginning to get a better understanding of her. Many of the girls didn't seem to like her and she didn't care. We took turns dancing with her and many of the other girls.

Bob and I agreed we would punish her for asking both of us for the date on the same night. We waited until we were on the way home. After a silent bus ride during which neither of us said a word, Bob and I walked the two blocks together to her apartment with her trailing behind alone. She was close to tears and went straight to her room. Mrs. Klicpera agreed that she received her just reward. She asked me about my home and my family, but most of the conversation centered on Mary Louise. She had an entourage of boyfriends. All had honorable intentions and thought they were the one who would win her hand in marriage. It wasn't long before I was invited to have lunch with the Klicpera family every Sunday and go for a walk afterwards. Holding hands was allowed!

Classes at Rice were intense and the hot and humid weather didn't help. There was no air conditioning and the heat was stiffening. The uniform rules were relaxed during the summer and we were allowed to not wear the khaki shirt and black tie. A white clean t-shirt was satisfactory. Chemistry class was strange. It was taught by Professor Harry Weiser, head of the Chemistry Department. The class was held in the auditorium and everyone was seated alphabetically. The Ks were two thirds up in the hall and I could barely read the blackboard. It really didn't matter because Professor Weiser wrote with his right hand and erased with his left as he wrote on the board. The final exam was just as strange. Nothing looked familiar and when students complained, they learned all questions were from the footnotes in the text book. "I expected you to know everything else," he said. I felt lucky to get out of that class with a "D."

The class in Calculus and Analytical Mechanics was almost as strange as Chemistry. The professor was a refugee from France. There was no doubt he was a brilliant mathematician. The problem was he was not fluent in English. We could not understand most of what he said. Fortunately, Mathematics is a universal language. I couldn't understand what he said, but I could write down what he put on the blackboard. I was forced to start trying to learn on my own. I made a "C" in that five-hour course and was thankful. I was learning how to compete with the best and the brightest!

The Naval Science courses were different. They were taught by Naval Officers. Some knew how to teach and some didn't. When I read the Navy regulations for Rice, I knew what I had to do to. A grade point average of 2.5 constituted a minimum of proficiency. A mark in aptitude for the service was assigned to each NROTC student at the end of each term. The average mark of Naval Science courses and aptitude for service would determine the class standing. These would determine "Officer Like Qualities." I would concentrate on making the best grades in Naval Science since that would decide whether I "washed out" or not. At the end of the first term at Rice I made "Bs" in Seamanship, Piloting and Navigation, and Naval Administration and Law. The transfer to the NROTC Program and Rice were the best things that could have happened to me. Taking twenty semester hours in college is hard. In a school like Rice it's harder.

It is more difficult going to school in the summer in a hot and humid climate without air conditioning. The honor system at Rice was different, too. You never took exams in the regular classroom.

There was an exam schedule and special rooms for exams. You were only allowed to take a pencil and a special pre-printed blue examination book into the exam room. You were seated with an empty chair in front, back, and on each side. Proctors roamed the room watching everyone. You were handed the examination questions, wrote answers in the book, and signed the honor pledge on the front that you had neither given nor received any aid on the exam. Then you returned the questions with your answers to the proctor in charge of the examination. There was no cheating, and if there was, the guilty person went before the Honor Council for a hearing. If you were in NROTC and the Commanding Officer found you did not have officer qualities, you were drummed out of the program and shipped off to Great Lakes as an enlisted man.

I learned self-discipline and confidence at Rice that would allow me to do things I never thought I could do. You don't have to be a straight "A" student to succeed. Those in the middle of the curve learn things that those at the top of the class don't learn, such as how to work hard, how to solve problems, how to overcome difficulties. Everyone has mental and physical abilities they aren't aware of. It is not easy to develop both sides of your brain. The only way these can be developed is to be pushed to the limits of your abilities. Elite programs in the military are designed to do just that. Some individuals learn to do it through intense athletic or academic programs. Very few people have the ability to force themselves to do these things alone. However, when such a vigorous routine has been completed, the sky is the limit as to what you can do!

6

Learning to Cope with Discrimination

I was feeling on top of the world. I gave Mary Louise her first kiss. Her mother was talking about the house they were going to build after the war. It would have an adjacent apartment Mary Louise and I could live in. I could either have a career in the Navy or join in her father's business. We were not officially engaged, but when Mary Louise graduated from high school one of her friends said to me, "I understand you want to give her a ring."

Rice did not have a student center. The closest thing to it was Autry House across Main Street at Palmer Episcopal Church. It was a recreation and religious center, a student meeting ground with ping pong tables, card tables, lounge chairs, a coke bar, and small cafeteria. While singing in the choir at St. John the Devine Episcopal Church in River Oaks, I began to feel comfortable with the service. Wine was served during communion. It was okay to drink in moderation. The prayers were not long and I liked the structure and ritual of the service. I joined the Canterbury Club at Rice. It was coincidental when I learned that Mary Louise and her family were Episcopalians.

When my mother learned I was going to an Episcopal Church, my world started caving in. My grandfather had been a Baptist minister. My mother and all of her family were strict Baptists. I had stopped going to the Baptist Church when I was in high school. The straw that broke the camel's back was when the Sunday School Superintendent made me read in front of all the classes a paper about the "Evils of Tobacco." I smoked cigarettes and everyone at school knew it. I started when I got the job as a bellboy at the Plaza Hotel and started earning some of my own money. There was another important factor. At the hotel I saw a seedy side of life. Men and women would come into the hotel through the basement entrance, get on the elevator with a bottle of whiskey, and go up to a room. It was all prearranged.

Some of these were not married to each other and the next Sunday they would be sitting in the Baptist Church or singing in the choir. It was hypocritical and I was not going to be a hypocrite over smoking! From that time on I had not gone to church. Autry House and the choir at St John the Devine brought me back to church on Sundays. However, my mother was up in the air. In her view the Episcopal Church was the same as the Catholic Church and that was the worst thing I could do.

I received lectures about how Henry the Eighth broke away from the Catholic Church just so he could divorce and remarry. I said, "Mother, for several years I haven't gone to church. Isn't it better that I go to this church than no church?" Her reply was "If it has to be that church, I'd rather you not go to any church." When my mother learned Mary Louise was an Episcopalian, she must have thought it was all her fault. I received a letter that she was coming to Houston for a visit and wanted to meet Mary Louise and her family.

In the meantime I was flourishing. Again, I was taking twenty semester hours. For English Composition & Prose I didn't have to study hard. The course was taught by Instructor Joe Gallegly. Everyone called him "Cowboy Joe" because he liked to reminisce about the early frontier days in Texas. Sociology was taught by Professor John Slaughter. Each week he would give us a research topic and we would come in and write fast and furious what we had learned in our research. I was learning how to learn on my own. Spanish was taught by Professor Oberle. My three years of Latin in high school came in handy. All you had to do was memorize the vocabulary and how to decline the regular and irregular verbs.

Seamanship, Ordnance and Gunnery, Naval Science courses required developing a photographic memory. The exams were all fill in the blanks in sentences taken from the Training Manuals and/or repeating long lists such as the various parts of the fifty caliber machine gun or the twenty millimeter antiaircraft gun. I created a method of using acronyms of the first letters of the things on the lists to help me remember them. We took a fifty caliber machine gun apart, cleaned it, and put it back together again.

Navigation and Nautical astronomy always would be difficult for me. It was football season and Rice was a member of the Southwest Conference. Texans take football seriously, just like basketball is the sport in Indiana. Rice had a special rivalry with Texas A & M, a school which traditionally produced Commissioned Officers for the U.S. Army. The Aggies would descend on Houston for the annual football game and take up a floor of the Rice Hotel. They would try to sneak onto the Rice campus and paint the statue of Mr. Rice red, the A & M colors.

We considered this a desecration since it was his tomb. A week before the game we set up a watch list and maintained a twenty-four-hour guard to protect the founder of the school. The night before the game the Aggies unfolded a huge banner from the windows of the hotel depicting an Asian squatting with the caption "What comes out of a Chinaman's ass? Rice! Rice! Rice!" When this was unfurled at the game at half time, both sides rushed to the center of the playing field. The band had to play the National Anthem to prevent a riot!

The time arrived for my mother's visit. It was a disaster. It was clear she came to break up my relationship with Mary Louise and she was successful. She let everyone know what she thought about the Episcopal Church and anyone who attended it. She announced she had contacted her Missouri Congressman and was going to arrange for me to get an appointment to the Naval Academy and leave Houston. Mary Louise informed me that she knew from the time of my mother's visit that "nothing more could be possible."

My world came crashing down around me. In Houston I had discovered a new way of life where I wasn't judged on the basis of my family or how much money I had. It was a new way of life socio-economically and I was growing into it. I lost my appetite, couldn't hold any food on my stomach, and vomited blood. It was a terrible emotional upset. My grades began to suffer and I realized I had to straighten myself out or I would be on my way to Great Lakes. I broke off with Mary Louise. There wasn't any way we could "just be friends." She was admitted to Rice and I congratulated her. I wrote a poem called "Shadow" about Mary Louise, then threw it away. Bob Smader salvaged it and said I should keep it. In 1950 it was published in an anthology, Modern American Verse.

I broke off with my mother and told her if I ever got married she would not know about it until after it happened. She would never,

ever do that to me again! In order to do better in school I had to improve my test taking ability. I developed a game. "If I were the instructor, what questions would I ask on the material?" In other words, how do you cut through all of the material and filter out what is important? As time passed by I got very good at it. In fact, I got so good I could anticipate eighty percent of the questions on an exam. That was great. I could whiz through the 80 percent and spend almost all of the time remaining to work through the other 20 percent.

I became very pragmatic about the social life at Rice. I was so hurt, no one would get close enough to me to do that to me again. My personal space shield became very hard and strong. However, I still liked girls and to dance. The girls at Rice were smart. If there could be no sororities, they invented what they called "Literary Societies." One was called the "Pallas Athena Literary Society," PALS. Another was called the "Elizabeth Baldwin Literary Society," EBLS. I met a girl who was working in the library and asked her for a date. It turned out she was a member of the EBLS. She said they were having a dance Saturday night and she would be happy for me to be her escort. Her name was Margie Scott and she lived in an apartment at 1108 Bartlett not far from the campus. I picked her up and we went to the dance. We danced the first dance and I didn't see her again until it was time to take her home. It seemed to me like Trenton High School all over again. In my mind I was good enough to be her escort but not good enough to spend the evening dancing. As Frank Sinatra sang in "Luck Be a Lady Tonight," you should dance with the one who brought you!

I met another girl at Autry House who turned out to be the President of the PALS. Her name was Louise Loose. I saw in the school paper where they were having a dance and asked her for a date. She said they were having a dance and would I like to go. She was different from Margie Scott. She lived in a big house at 3132 Rice Boulevard. When I went to pick her up, she wasn't ready yet, so I talked to her mother. Louise loved riding horses and had a trophy case full of ribbons and trophies. Louise didn't disappear when we got to the dance. She liked to dance and we had fun. I later learned Louise's father was the Legal Counsel for Texaco.

She invited me to go riding with her and was very patient with me. It was clear that I was dating girls out of my league. Margie's sister was in the Junior League, and her uncle was on the Board of Trust of Rice. Much to my surprise, when the EBLS had their next dance Margie asked me if I would like to go. Why not? I was beginning to have some fun. The director of the Navy Glee Club decided to have a quartet and asked me to sing bass. The quartet started singing at the school dances, "Tea for Two," "Embraceable You," "Night and Day," "Summer time," "Manhattan Serenade," and "I'll be Seeing You."

Before I realized it two semesters had whizzed by. I made a "B" for the year in English Composition and in Sociology, "Cs" in Spanish and Modern History and Political Geography, "Bs" in Seamanship, Damage Control and Ordnance and Gunnery. However, I failed the final exam in Celestial Navigation. Fortunately I was not alone. Over one half of the class failed. The Commanding Officer said, "Something is wrong when half of a class fails." He ordered a re-examination and we passed. I received a "D+" instead of an "F." Things really began to change.

The war was over. The Navy didn't need Officers any more. It was questionable how much longer the NROTC program would continue. The administration began to look harder for reasons to kick people out of the program. A friend who lived across the hall was crying when I came in one afternoon. He was a straight "A" student. "What's the matter?" I asked.

Through tear-filled eyes he said, "They're shipping me out."

"Why?" I asked.

"I forgot and took my math book into the exam room where I was scheduled to take an English exam. I was turned in for an honor code violation. The Honor Council said there was no way I could have cheated, but the CO said I didn't have officer-like qualities and I'm on my way to Great Lakes." Life is not fair!

Margie's sister, Ruth, was named a debutante for 1946. Her photo and those of Margie and her other sister, Betty, appeared in the society page of the Houston Press on February eighth issue. It was the beginning of a social whirlwind. Margie arranged for me to get an invitation to a dance at the River Oaks Country Club given for Nina Neal. The club was decorated like a circus with monkeys to popcorn and peanut vendors. There was a hot dog stand with sideshows and two bars serving imported French champagne. A society orchestra was flown in from New York to provide the music. When I ran into Beverly Jean Taylor, she expressed surprise to see me there. I guess I had a reputation of being a square that didn't drink. They didn't know I had been there and done that in Kansas. I was surprised to learn when I first arrived in Texas that the law said you could not buy liquor by the drink. You could buy a bottle in a liquor store but not a single cocktail. Navy regulations forbid liquor on campus. I could not drink a whole bottle when on liberty so I didn't drink at parties.

The party lasted all night and we wound up at someone's home for a champagne breakfast. At six a.m. Sunday morning I told Margie I was going back to Rice to get some sleep. Her uncle, who must have been very influential, loaned her family a new 1946 red Pontiac convertible. It wasn't long before Margie and I were using it to go on dates and they let me drive it to campus alone to save walking. One Saturday we went to Galveston to go swimming at the beach. Margie was a lot of fun but I never tried to kiss either she or Louise. I assumed if they were interested in furthering our relationship they would let me know.

One Saturday Louise invited me to her house for dinner for fried shrimp and I was surprised to find we were alone without her parents being home. Another time we had use of her family Buick car to go dancing at one of the nightclubs. Louise liked classical music and I spent several Saturday afternoons at her house listening to music with her. I read where the Rice architectural students were going to hold their Archi-Arts Ball, the "Schauspielermaske," and at Autry House I asked Beverly Taylor for a date. She said okay and I was her escort. The ball was held at the State Guard Armory and I was surprised to learn Beverly was one of the honorees. There was a lot of liquor flowing and I was embarrassed that my date had to ask others for a drink. I hope she understood that my fifty dollars a month didn't go very far and that there wasn't much in the budget for alcohol.

I alternated dates between Margie and Louise, but as time passed by I seemed to be spending more time with Louise. She was an Episcopalian. I saw her more at Autry house and we played a lot of bridge. Both Margie and Louise were nearing graduation and I was surprised when Louise asked me to be her guest at the Senior Banquet and Dance at the River Oaks Country Club on February 28, 1946. I know it was an expensive evening. I guess everyone understood the Navy guys did not make much money.

Graduation exercises took place on March 3rd, 1946. I had been in Houston and at Rice for a year! Margie and Louise went off on a trip to Washington D.C. as a graduation present. My nose was still on the grindstone of study and academics. I had another heavy load of twenty-one semester hours; History of English Literature taught by Professor Alan Mckillop, Introduction to Philosophy by Professor Radoslav Tsanoff, Second year Spanish and Ordnance and Gunnery. Except for the Naval Science Course, the summer classes were accelerated. We took a whole year's course in one semester.

I missed Margie and Louise not being at school. I was content to build my record collection. I found a shop that sold used records from juke boxes at low prices and spent my extra money building my collection of big band music: Tommy Dorsey, Glenn Miller, Benny Goodman, Harry James and Artie Shaw. I had all of the classics: "Marie," "Song of India," "In the Mood," "Chattanooga Choo Choo," "I've Got a Girl in Kalamazoo," "You Made Me Love You." The Navy held a "Farewell Spring Formal Dance" on May 15th at the Crystal Ballroom of the Rice Hotel. Louise was my date. The Navy Quartet sang "I'll Be Seeing You," and the girls cried.

An end was coming to the lives of everyone in the class of 1946. It was the end of an era for the NROTC Unit at Rice. We didn't realize at the time how special it was. My time at Rice was coming to an end. I made "Cs" in Philosophy, Spanish, and Ordnance and Gunnery. I was surprised at the D+ in History of English Literature. However, I could look back with pride. I had been able to hold my own with the best and the brightest. I completed 130 semester hours (the equivalent of four years of college) in twenty-eight months.

I achieved my goal. I was going to become a commissioned officer in the United State Navy. I was able to overcome adversity and succeed in my areas of weakness, Math and Science. I was one of the fifty percent who made it through the V-12 program. I now could look forward to the future. New doors were starting to open for me and I was ready to meet any challenge. It was June 1946. Margie Scott was back in town after working as a counselor at a girl's camp.

The night before I was to leave Houston we were on a date and she asked me, "Are you married?" I thought it a strange question.

"No," I said. "Why do you ask?"

"Because you don't paw around like the other boys do." I asked her if I could kiss her goodbye. She put her arms around me and gave me a kiss. It was the last time I saw her. I read in the Rice Alumni magazine in 2008 she had passed away. What would have been her reaction if I had tried to "paw around like the other boys?" I never tried and I'll never know. I hope Margie didn't think I was gay.

The next day I got on a train for St. Louis and the Navy Separation Center. I was being released to inactive duty and ready for a new turning point. My Navy class commission exercises were held on June 29, 1946 at St. Paul's Methodist Church in Houston. I was not there for the ceremony. My Ensign commission was mailed to me with a date of rank of June 5th, 1946. I waited until it was close to the time to leave Houston before I decided to join the Episcopal Church. I wanted to wait until all of the dust settled after my mother's visit and all of the emotional upset. I wanted my decision to be rational about what was best for me, not a knee jerk reaction against my mother and my family. After thinking it over seriously, I decided this was the church I wanted to attend. I was confirmed at Palmer Memorial Church in Houston. My sponsors were two Rice coeds, Beverly Jean Taylor and Sara Lu Johnson. After that I've always referred to Beverly as my "godmother." I said at the time I had two of the most beautiful godmothers anyone could have! I remained an Episcopalian the rest of my life.

My mother never changed her opinion. On a visit to Indiana she refused to attend the Christening of our daughter, Sheryl. I loved and respected my mother, but she was prejudicial and discriminatory. In Europe wars have been fought over religion and that was wrong. People, including my father, have been discriminated against in employment because of their religious faith. That was and is wrong. My mother was wrong. Because of my experience, I have become very tolerant. Most religions provide a set of boundaries for human behavior, which allow people to live together in a civilized manner. There are many roads that can take you to your destination. It's your choice as to which road you take. We are blessed to live in a country where we have the freedom to make those choices!

7

You've Gone As Far As You Can Go

It was June 1946 and after thirty-one months I was reaching my goal. I was one of the fifty percent who made it through the V-12 program. There had been many disappointments. There were mental and physical trials each day. I learned how to overcome adversity. I never lost focus on my goals. I never considered quitting. I completed the equivalent of four years of college in twenty-eight months. I gained self-discipline and confidence. I developed both sides of my brain. If I could succeed in my areas of weakness, how could I fail? I survived in one of the Navy's elite training programs. I survived not because I was the smartest, I survived because I refused to quit. I believed there was no assignment, regardless of how difficult, that I could not complete.

I was at a turning point. Did I want to become a career Navy Officer or do something else? In the back of my mind was the repressed desire to go to the University of Missouri and study Journalism. However, after twenty-eight months of intense college courses in Math, Physics, Chemistry, Engineering and Naval Science, I decided it would be good to get a job, earn and save some money before I went back to school. My dad had been working on natural gas conversion jobs periodically during the war and informed me that his friend "Hoot" Adams had a contract in Illinois and if I was interested would give me a job. It was not a difficult decision. A short time later I found myself in Rockford, Illinois living at the Hotel Faust. I was issued a tool kit comprised of electric drill, screwdrivers, pipe wrenches, pliers, and other small tools. I would receive one dollar an hour, but would work sixty hours a week. I was assigned to work with a man I'll call "Joe." Joe wasn't interested in being a teacher.

The work wasn't complicated. We went into customer's homes, removed the cast iron burners from the gas ranges, and drilled larger holes in the burner ports with the electric drill. The gas passed into the burner through a brass fitting that screwed onto a pipe manifold the gas flowed through. We made the orifice smaller with what was called a gauging drill because the natural gas contained about twice the calorific value as the manufactured gas. However, when something different came up, Joe would say, "Oh I forgot my widget, it's in my car, go get it." When I returned, he had taken care of the problem.

After the second day I told the Crew Foremen I was ready to go out on my own. "Are you sure you're ready?" he asked.

"Joe has taught me all he is ever going to teach me," I responded. I learned quickly that the tools issued to everyone were very basic. I went to Sears and bought my own ratchet wrenches. Sometimes the threads on the orifice caps would get stripped. I found I could get a set of taps and dies to correct these problems. "Easy Offs" helped remove broken parts from the manifold. We finished in Rockford and moved on to Freeport, Illinois. The work wasn't that hard and with the overtime I was earning almost one hundred dollars a week.We were told the next job was in Nashville, Tennessee. Since I didn't have a car, I hitched a ride to Nashville with one of the Crew Foremen. "Hoot" Adams arranged for us to stay in the Tulane Hotel at a special weekly rate.

Nashville was different. Everyone burned coal for everything. Today, the EPA would go bananas at the air pollution. A large portion of the city population was black. I found it strange that Negro people were not allowed in the restaurants or movie theatres and they had to move to the rear of the streetcars. No black people lived in Trenton. It was my first experience to see Negroes and encounter racial discrimination. My work took me into the homes of everyone in Nashville, both blacks and whites. This was my first visit to a Southern state. I didn't consider Texas the South. I had never seen as many beautiful women as I saw in Nashville. This was before the days of Shopping Malls. The only place to shop was in downtown Nashville. There were Harvey's, Cain Sloan's & Caster Knott Department stores.

Shopping was an all-day event. The housewives of Nashville would put on their best clothes, hats and gloves, and ride the streetcars to town. They were well-groomed southern ladies. They would enjoy a lunch or take in a movie in the afternoon before returning home. On Sundays the girls from Ward Belmont Finishing School would don their hats and gloves and in their Sunday best attend church and have lunch downtown. Today, when we go to a Mall shopping I comment to my wife, Grace, "Where have all the ladies gone?"

I learned the best place to eat dinner in Nashville was a nice restaurant called "Cross Keys." The food was on the expensive side but delicious. I found I liked southern cooking. I didn't realize it but I was approaching the second most important turning point in my life. I became aware of a beautiful, blue-eyed blond waitress and soon started asking to be seated at one of her tables. Her name was "Grace." The dictionary defines the word Grace as *"beauty or charm, a pleasing quality or manner, a sense of what is right and proper."* She was all of these and more.

She had a natural beauty and didn't need makeup. She had a lovely smile and manner that reflected her name. Her older sister also worked there and was going out with one of my friends, an older conversion man. She arranged a date for me with Grace. Grace was different. A blue-eyed blonde in a family of brunettes and brown eyes, she was the youngest girl of a family of seven girls and six boys. At age thirteen she went to work at "Candyland Soda Shop" in Nashville. She asked the owner, not for a job, but if they needed "a worker." She was a worker behind the counter. Boys from Montgomery Bell Academy and Harpeth Hall School for Girls went there after school for fun, to drink Cokes and eat ice cream. She loved people and later went to work at the finest restaurant in Nashville, "Cross Keys."

It was there I saw her and fell in love with her. On October 15th I received my weekly paycheck for working 102 hours grossing $109.47. The job for the Nashville Gas Company was coming to an end. "Hoot" told me the next job was going to be in Washington, D.C. I knew I couldn't leave without her. I received a gift from God when she said "Yes." Grace and I were married at the Church of the Advent on 16th Avenue South, October 20th 1946, and moved to Washington D.C. We lived in a small hotel for almost three months. It was a working honeymoon. We ate our meals in the hotel dining room and we still remember listening to the juke box with Hoagy Carmichael singing "Old Buttermilk Skies."

Housing was very short because of the backlog built up during the war. Finally in desperation we placed an ad in the newspaper. An elderly lady called saying that she had a house and was willing to rent us a bedroom with kitchen privileges. It was at 1906 Naylor Road, across the John Philip Sousa Bridge in Anacostia. We were happy to move out of the hotel. My work was progressing and educational. I was working in the homes of people at every level of the socio-economic scale. I converted appliances in the ghetto and in Bethesda, Maryland. The people with money were demanding but not truthful. They claimed their gas ranges worked perfectly until the natural gas arrived. When I took them apart, the burners were so plugged up with grease they could not have worked properly on manufactured gas.

My job was not to question. I fixed everything, but observed. People in the poorer sections of town were courteous and thankful to have a stove that made biscuits and cornbread again. One black woman offered to pay me a quarter when I fixed her oven door so it would stay closed. Naturally, I declined. How much does a stove bolt cost? Probably two cents! I found it interesting that behind the façade of the beautiful lawns and homes of the politicians and wealthy class in Chevy Chase, Maryland were many rooms without furniture. The image from the street said one thing; a look at the interior told another story. I was getting an education in people they don't teach in college.

There was another side. There were parts of town where I didn't feel safe. I never took more than a dollar with me to work in case someone tried to rob me. There were places where my presence didn't interrupt their lovemaking. Most of the time in these places the first thing I did was take a pipe wrench out of my toolbox and put it within easy reach in the event of trouble. After we moved out of the hotel, Grace went to work at "Ted Lewis Restaurant and Cocktail Lounge" on Connecticut Avenue. Like "Cross Keys" in Nashville, it was one of the finest in the District of Columbia. "Ted Lewis" was frequented by senators, congressmen, and well-known sports figures.

The owner was demanding. Each morning before opening for lunch there was a memory skull session on the new day's menu. Waitresses weren't allowed to look at the menu. They were expected to know it and be able to answer any and all questions without hesitation. It wasn't long before Grace was earning more money in tips than I did and I was working sixty to eighty hours a week.

I didn't cash my checks and we lived nicely on what she earned. I learned the American Gas Association published appliance manuals that gave information on most of the major appliances; how to adjust the oven controls, how the safety bi-metal shut off valves on water heaters worked, etc. I bought them and learned how to deal with problems of most of the stoves and water heaters I came in contact with. Before long I was working on floor furnaces and gas logs. During the winter I was lucky enough to continue with Charlie Shinamon of the Washington Gas Light Company reworking apartment gas ranges, floor furnaces, and gas logs.

One day Bill Woods, the job superintendent, told me he wanted me to be a crew foreman. I knew in order to be a foreman I would have to get a car. Grace and I shopped around looking for a car. New cars were at a premium and we found a used 1941 Plymouth we thought we could afford. We had saved enough for the down payment, but had to apply for a loan from the Commercial Credit Corporation. The manager of the car lot had to go to bat for us because we never had any credit before. He told the finance company, "When you've never had any credit, you have to start sometime."

Our loan was approved and I found myself in charge of a crew of ten appliance adjusters. They were a motley group made up of young guys just back from the army. Their main interest was drinking beer and chasing women. I had lived with their types in the Navy in Topeka, Kansas. I told them, "If you see an appliance you've never worked on before, don't touch it. Come and get me. Don't take anything apart that you have never worked on before." I would come back to my car and find three guys waiting for me. It took a while, but eventually I got them trained.

Conversion of appliances to operate on natural gas had become a big business. "Hoot" Adams turned it over to a company called "Conversions and Surveys." We had to join a union and I became a "Journeyman Gas Conversion," a member of the AFL Pipe fitters on May 10, 1947. The company started printing a report showing the crews and the number of appliances converted to natural gas with the number of customer complaints. There were thirty-three crews and my crew ranked third, having converted the most appliances with the fewest complaints. Mr. Woods called me in, said they had been watching my progress and they were making me a Complaint Specialist. I would be going out and fixing the jobs other people had botched up.

In the back of my mind was the nagging question, "If I had gone to flight training, could I have learned to fly?" I was now free on weekends and learned there was a small airport in Maryland and a school called the "Congressional School of Aeronautics." I could take flight lessons on the GI Bill. Before long on weekends I was in a Piper Club learning how to pull out of a stall, fly pylons, take off, and land. I received my student Pilots Certificate on June 18, 1947. The instructor wrote in my flight log book, "Good landings." Maybe I could have landed on an aircraft carrier after all. It wasn't long before I was allowed to solo. What a great day to be at the controls alone! Next, I did my cross-country requirement and was only three hours away from enough flight time to get my Private Pilots License.

My new job as "Complaint Specialist" became routine and easy. After one week the Union Steward pulled me aside and said, "You are doing too much work. The standard is one appliance per hour." He made it very clear what the consequences would be in the way of bodily harm if I did not comply. Many days I had my appliance quota done by lunchtime. I would drive to Rock Creek Park, eat my lunch, read a book, and listen to the birds sing. It didn't feel right but I didn't want to have a broken leg or arm. This was my first experience, but not my last, of having to work with a union.

It was at this time that Bill Woods took me aside one morning and said, "You've gone as far as you can go. You will be in this job the rest of your life unless you get a college degree." In past conversations he had learned about my background at Rice. He told me that "Conversions and Surveys" was a subsidiary of a much larger company called "Stone & Webster." He said, "If you go back to school and get a degree, we will have a job as an engineer waiting for you. Because of your experience with us, it won't have to be an engineering degree but it must be some kind of science degree." I had reached what is now called the "glass ceiling." That degree in Naval Science would have taken me through it. Now, I was going to have to go back to school. The dream of going to Journalism School was no longer in the picture.

I was at another turning point. I was married to a wonderful wife and needed to think about our future. A science degree would require a lot of hard work. A new door had opened for me with a challenge. The Private Pilots License was no longer important. I satisfied myself I could fly an airplane. We packed up our things in our new 1947 Chevrolet and headed to Nashville. After visiting Grace's family, we would go to Houston and see how long it would take for me to get back into Rice.

In life there are times when you have gone as far as you can go in a job. You can do the same thing over and over again the rest of your life, or you can take a leap into the unknown and try to do something different and better. As I told my students at Belmont, in any career there comes a time when you have gone as far as you can go. You must either move up or move out! The time had come for me to move out!

8

You're Not Getting an Education

Grace and I packed our belongings from Washington, D.C. in our 1947 Chevrolet and started driving to Houston. The plan was to stop in Nashville, visit Grace's family, and go on to Houston to see how long it might take for me to go back to school at Rice. It was still winter and snow was on the ground. This was before Interstate Highways and the roads were two lanes, narrow and winding. Our route took us through West Virginia and over the Smoky Mountains to Tennessee. When we arrived at Wheeling, we decided to keep going.

This was before Holiday Inns and motels. "Trailer Courts," as they were called back then, were few and far between. We almost didn't get out of Wheeling. There was a steep hill that took us three runs before we made it to the top. We drove all night and thought it strange we didn't see any other cars on the road, not even a truck! When you are young, you do foolish things. Many years later we took the same trip in the daylight. It was scary going over those mountain roads in good weather! We had an angel looking over us that night.

We arrived in Nashville safely the next day and after resting up, Grace's sister said, "Why go all the way to Texas to go to school? We have a good school here—Vanderbilt. Why don't you see if you could go there?" I decided to go to see what Vanderbilt would say. I met with Philip Davidson, Dean of the School of Arts and Science. When I gave him my Rice transcript, he looked at it and said, "I don't see any reason you can't enroll here."

"What could I major in to get the job waiting for me?" I asked.

"Major in math and minor in physics," he said.

"When could I start?" I asked.

"Tomorrow at the latest," he said. "The quarter started last week." Vanderbilt was not on a semester system like Rice. The school year was divided into four quarters. I was in school and we hadn't started to look for a place to stay.

The Dean got me registered and I made a big mistake. I let him select my subjects. He enrolled me in six hours of advanced Math courses, three hours of Physics, three hours of Philosophy, and three hours of English. It totaled fifteen hours. That didn't sound bad after the load I had carried at Rice, but I had been out of school for two years. I discovered I had forgotten what calculus I knew. I was jumping off another cliff! The first weekend we found a small furnished house, Grace went back to work at Cross Keys, and we were on our way. I found the academic environment the same as at Rice. I was in class with students who hadn't taken time off. Many were returned GIs who were in school on GI Bill and serious students. They had fought a war and now they were going to make their mark in civilian life.

Soon I was fighting for my life. It didn't matter how much I studied I wasn't making it. I started vomiting blood. It was sink or swim, and I was sinking. Finally I went to a doctor and told him my problem. "If you dropped one course, do you think you could make it?" he asked. "It would help," I replied. He wrote a letter to the Dean and I was allowed to drop four hours of Differential Equations. I was going to school on the GI Bill and was supposed to be receiving a monthly living allowance. Somehow the Veterans' Administration screwed up my papers and I didn't receive anything for three months. We had to sell our car to make it. That meant moving out of the house and into an apartment at 2035 Elliott Avenue closer to the campus where Grace and I could take the streetcar to work and school.

That first quarter I learned a survival lesson. I made an "A" in English, a "B" in Math, and "Ds" in Philosophy and Physics. I found I had enough credit hours in Physics for my minor. From that time on I took only English and Math courses. During one summer break we decided to take a vacation. We went to the American Express office in Castner Knott and signed up for a week trip to Havana Cuba. I don't know why we chose Cuba. It probably was the only thing we could afford. We had a wonderful trip. We danced under the stars to "Moon over Miami" at the former home of Doris Duke, which had been converted into a night club. We learned to like fried bananas and pineapple. We treasured the bottle of Banana Liqueur we brought home with us.

I found I could make "As" in English without studying. I could write a term paper in a weekend. I spent all of my time studying Math and I was able to make "Bs." After the second semester, Dean Davidson called me in. "I've been watching your progress," he said, "but you are not getting an education taking just Math and English courses." The second quarter I made two "As" in English, a "B" and a "C" in Math. The Math was Differential Equations, which I took across the street at Peabody College. I was the only undergraduate student in the class. Most of the other students were teachers working on their Master's Degree. "You should take Philosophy, Psychology, and Sociology as well," said Dean Davidson.

"Yes, sir," I said and went to the Registrar and signed up for more Math and English courses. I have to thank Grace for helping me to make it through those four quarters. Her earnings as a waitress put me through Vanderbilt. It was one of the most difficult times in my life. I thought the Navy program was rough. I didn't quit at Rice, but if I had "washed out" it would not have been the end of the world. I was single and after the war I could have gone to the University of Missouri and studied Journalism.

At Vanderbilt everything was riding on my making it. I was married with responsibilities. I had a job and career waiting for me, but I had to get that piece of paper that had eluded me at Rice. I'm sure I wasn't easy to live with during those twelve months. All I did was study. I learned Professor Donald Davidson taught a course in creative writing. Admission was only with his permission after submitting samples of your writing. He was one of the "Fugitive Poets" at Vanderbilt and I thought I would like to write poetry. I was admitted to his class and felt honored. A lot of English majors were rejected. My first assignment of poetry changed my lesson plan. I had become interested in Fitzgerald's translation of the Rubaiyat of Omar Khayyam. As an exercise to use words with a Middle East flavor, I wrote a short poem I called "Phantom Caravan." His comments were scathing: "Your rhyme scheme is monotonous, and your meter ticks like a metronome. You should write about things within your experience!" After that I started writing short stories, which he liked very much.

Before I left Vanderbilt I read where manuscripts were beings accepted for the 1948 Anthology of College Poetry. As a lark I submitted my poem. Much to my surprise my poem was accepted and published in November 1948. The introduction stated that the selections were made from over twenty-five thousand submitted manuscripts. The only enjoyment I had at Vanderbilt was in the English courses. I found I liked the English Romantic poets Shelley, Keats, and Wordsworth better than Scales of Notation. I liked Shakespeare's plays better than Homogeneous Equations. Professor Davidson taught a course in the English Novel. I found the "flashback" technique used by Joseph Conrad in "Lord Jim" more interesting than solving quadratic equations with a matrix. I enjoyed Emily Dickinson's poetry more than Probability and Statistics.

I'm sure all of the English majors thought I was strange. A math major was in their classes breezing through their English Courses making "As." I sat next to a guy still wearing his Army Air Corps uniform. He seemed strange to me because he was enthralled by the poetry of William Butler Yeats and carried around a book of poetry by T.S. Eliot. I found "The Love Song of J. Alfred Prufrock" weird. Stream of consciousness technique by James Joyce didn't grab me, nor did blank verse. Many years later, he wrote a book that was made into a movie Deliverance, starring Jon Voight, Burt Reynolds, Ronnie Cox, and Billy McKinney. His name was James Dickey.

Once in a while I took time for a little fun. I joined the Canterbury Club and sometimes they would have a social get together which Grace and I would attend. One of the highlights was a group of students who called themselves the "Tennessee Dewdrops." They played hillbilly music and dressed like Grand Ole Opry stars. We never cared much for Country Music, but the little band made it fun. One of the group was Nelson Andrews who later became a millionaire in real estate converting Army married men's housing into homes and selling them to returning GIs. He also became the owner of McClure's Department Stores in Nashville. I didn't have much time to participate in the normal college life.

They did play football at Vanderbilt like at Rice. Vanderbilt was an original member of the South Eastern Conference. Other members like Alabama, Georgia, and Tennessee were national football powerhouses. There was a Vanderbilt/Rice connection. The former Vandy football coach Jess Neeley was at Rice when I was in Houston. Both Rice and Vandy emphasized academics. The coach at Vanderbilt in 1948–49 was "Red" Sanders. The memorable thing about football that year was when Vanderbilt beat arch-rival Tennessee. At the football banquet, the Chancellor was asked to say a few words. He stood at the podium and said, "I'm glad we won a few football games this year, but the purpose of Vanderbilt University is to produce scholars, not winning football teams." That was "Red" Sanders last year as coach at Vanderbilt. He moved on to UCLA where he built a football dynasty.

Between the next two quarters I signed up to take a two-week Navy cruise on a Destroyer out of New Orleans. I would receive two weeks pay as an officer and we could use it. The ship made ports of call at Key West, Florida, San Juan, Puerto Rico, Port of Spain, Trinidad, and Vera Cruz, Mexico. I slept in the forward officer's quarters in the bow of the ship. When we hit bad weather, I had to strap myself in the bunk to keep from being thrown out. Looking back I had a lot to learn about sea duty. They tried to teach me the duties of the underway watch officer and I'm afraid I wasn't a very good student. I was there for the wrong reason. I needed the money. I found going ashore in the Caribbean interesting but I was appalled at the poverty and squalor.

My last two quarters at Vanderbilt I took thirty-two hours with a "B" average. I made "As" in most of my English courses and had enough hours for a double major in English if Vanderbilt had allowed double majors. I made "Bs" in all my Math courses except one, "Advanced Theory of Equations" in which I made a "D." Near the end of the quarter the head of the Math Department, Dr. Hyden, called me in and said; "We've been watching you and think you ought to stay on for your Master's Degree. I felt highly complimented. Once again I had succeeded in my area of weakness. I thanked him for his kind offer, but told him I had other plans. I graduated from Vanderbilt in March of 1949. There was no graduation ceremony and they mailed my diploma to me the same as when I finished NROTC at Rice.

I called the Personnel Manager, Luke Storrs, at Stone & Webster. He told me they had arranged a job for me at Blackstone Valley Gas & Electric Company in Pawtucket, Rhode Island. We packed up our things and had them shipped Railway Express to Rhode Island. We double-checked just before they were picked up and found to our dismay we had packed up our American Express Traveler's Checks. We retrieved them just in time to save ourselves a huge embarrassment. Grace and I took the train to New York and stopped for a visit at Stone & Webster before going on to Rhode Island. A room was reserved for us at the Grand Central Station Hotel. After meeting Bill Woods and others at 90 Broad Street, a VP from the Public Relation

Department took us for dinner at the Rainbow Room at Radio City Music Hall.

The next morning we caught the train to Providence, Rhode Island. When Dean Davidson told me I was not getting an education, he was speaking as an academic. It may be true that I did not learn a lot about Psychology and Philosophy, but I learned a lot more Psychology from my wife, Grace, than I would have from a PhD. In her work with the public, she learned what they don't teach in books. When someone walked into the restaurant she could judge what kind of a tip they were going to leave. She could distinguish the "phonies" from the genuine people. She could advise me on the people I should not trust and she was always right!

There are many different ways to get an education and the best is not always from a book. There is no substitute for personal experience. Sometimes you learn a hard lesson that way, but you never forget it. I also learned that it doesn't matter what school you go to for your education. I attended classes in five different schools: Washburn, Peru State, Rice, Vanderbilt, and Indiana University Night Law School. I learned just as much at the small, lesser known schools as at those with a national reputation. The truth is you only get out of it what you put in.

The resumes of the faculty of the big schools may look impressive, but many of the classes are taught by assistants. The professors are more interested in doing research and writing papers and books for publication than in teaching. I was fortunate to have the opportunity to have Donald Davison as one of my English instructors. He was an anomaly because he did not have a PhD. He only had a Master's Degree. He would not be allowed to teach at Vanderbilt today without a terminal degree.

I received the kind of education I needed from Vanderbilt. I broke through that glass ceiling with the BA degree. The interesting thing is I never used any of that high-powered math I took for twelve months at Vanderbilt. I did hone my writing skills, which helped me immensely as a consultant and as an engineer. I later became a full member of the American Society of Engineers, a Fellow of the Institution of Gas Engineers and the Institute of Energy, and a Chartered Engineer (Registered Professional Engineer) in Britain.

There are many ways to get an education and they are not limited to sitting in a classroom listening to someone lecture. There are many things wrong with the educational system today. Most of the educators are content trying to teach the same way they always have taught and have little interest in preparing students to survive in the real world. That's a sure sign there is a better way of doing it. All it is going to take is someone willing to take some risk and rocking the boat!

9

What Nationality Are You?

Pawtucket, Rhode Island in 1949 was a different world. It had been a center for the Textile Industry because of the water falls on the river. Many of the buildings that held the looms were still around the town. Everything looked old; the railroad station and all of the "tenement houses." This was where Stone & Webster arranged for me to report to Blackstone Valley Gas & Electric Company to start work as a "Cadet Engineer" in their management training program. Mr. Arthur Ring, the manager, met us with his wife at the station and gave us a tour of the area. It was mind-boggling. Central Falls, Rhode Island was only one square mile in area. "Now we're leaving Central Falls and we are in Pawtucket." A short time later we were in Providence. You couldn't tell where one town started and the next one began. All were merged together. Where we came from there was no question. When you left the city limits, you were out in the countryside.

There was no hotel in Pawtucket so we were put up in a hotel in Providence until we could find an apartment. It was clear the company expected that to happen soon. I caught the bus the next morning to Central Falls and walked to the operations office. Quickly I was introduced to the staff; Sadie and Jessie, middle-aged ladies who took the complaint calls and kept customer records; Charlie Schivino, an elderly man of Italian descent, who did the drafting and maintained the map records; Roy Moosett, who was in charge of the meter shop; and John Nave, who was in charge of construction and maintenance crews. It was an exciting time. I managed to tough it through those advanced math courses at Vanderbilt, and was wearing my gold "class of 1949" ring. I was in my best suit, white shirt, and tie and was ready to start my management training. "Do you have any work clothes?" John Nave asked.

"What kind?" I said with surprise.

"Khakis, denims, you know; work clothes. Tomorrow you start with the construction crew. It will be digging ditches."

This is what it had come to. I took a cut in pay to become a "Cadet Engineer" and was going to start a management-training course digging ditches! Some management training! Rhode Island was a different world, a microcosm of the global world. All of the men on the construction crew were Portuguese. They spoke Portuguese, lived in the Portuguese section of town, read the Portuguese language newspaper, and socialized at the Portuguese-American Club. The Crew Foreman was Italian. He lived in the Italian section of town, read the Italian language newspaper, and socialized in the Italian-American Club.

I quickly learned there is a real technique to digging ditches. If you don't want an aching back when you get off work, you learn to lift the weight with your legs and go at a steady pace. The crew tolerated me at first, but when I started to ask for help, we quickly became friends. Looking back, the Blackstone management-training course was the best thing that could have happened to me. I worked at every job in the company operations.

The next week I learned how to install the cast iron gas mains in the street, and worked with the crew that ran the smaller steel service line to the house. I worked with the men of French nationality, like Al Rouseau, who installed the meters. He spoke French, lived in the French section of town, read the French language newspaper, and socialized at the French-American Club. I worked with the English pipe fitters that ran the pipes inside the house and installed the gas stoves and water heaters. They read the English Newspapers, lived in the English section of town, and socialized at the English-American Club.

Al Rousseau came to me and said, "There is a furnished apartment in Central Falls that the owner has been renovating. I think it is almost finished. If you go talk to the owner maybe you can get it before she advertises it for rent." The next Saturday Grace and I went to 76 Olive Street in Central Falls and knocked on the door. A small, dark-haired, beady-eyed woman came to the door. We introduced ourselves and told her we understood she might have an apartment for rent, we were moving and needed a place to stay. The apartment was furnished with one bedroom, a living room, bathroom, and kitchen. It was more than we could afford, but we were desperate to get out of the hotel in Providence. This was furnished, and within walking distance of my work. "We would like very much to have it," we told her.

"Just a minute," she said "What nationality are you?"

In my twenty-three years this was the first time anyone had asked me "What nationality are you?" I grew up in the Middle West, Grace had grown up in the South East, and this woman was questioning our nationality. My first reaction was to say, "American, what else?" but something told me that was not the right answer. "My father's people were German," I said.

"Well, that's all right" she said. "I'm Polish, but I don't rent to French, Italians, Portuguese or Jews!"

I heard comments about discrimination in the South. It didn't mean much to me because there were no Negroes in my hometown. Grace grew up on her Father's tobacco farm in Tennessee with farm hands who were white and black. At meal time all came into the house, sat down at the table with her family, and ate their meal. This was a new experience for us. It was unpleasant and we found it hard to understand. We got the apartment because my father's family was of German descent. If they had been French, Italian, Portuguese, or Jewish, we would have been out of luck. Strangely, at work I had no problem. The French did not talk to the Italians or Portuguese, but they all talked to me and I made friends with each group.

Later I worked in the meter shop with Roy Moosett. I'm not sure what nationality Roy was and I didn't care. The company didn't buy new meters. Every five years the meters were changed, old meters came in the shop; we tested them, stripped them down, replaced the lamb-skin diaphragms, installed new index boxes, soldered the tin case back together, and painted them.

The company was installing a new propane-air peak shaving plant so Roy set up a laboratory for me with gravity meter, calorimeter, and a series of burners representing most of the appliances in customer's homes. The problem was to determine how much propane-air could be mixed with the manufactured gas without interfering with the burner operations. When I finished my report, I was pleased to learn it had been sent through the ranks to vice president Burt Jenkins and eventually to the president Mr. David Daly. Mr. Daly later commended me for a good job and commented his surprise that it was written in the third person.

One job I really enjoyed was working in the office with Charlie Schivino. Charlie was born in Italy and immigrated to the U.S. as a young man. He had no formal education but was one of the most intelligent people I have ever met. He was a voracious reader and could converse on any subject you might choose. I'll never forget one of his favorite quotes: *"The cries of starving children and of dying men cannot penetrate the halls of government buildings and the thick heads within."*

Probably the most difficult experiences I had at Blackstone Valley Gas were the Inhalator calls. These would come in by telephone to Sadie or Jessie, and Jerry Schey would start pulling equipment from a locker. It was my job to check and make sure it was all there: the inhalator, two spare bottles of oxygen, blankets, and the First Aid Kit. We would run to the black sedan parked by the office door. I loaded everything into the trunk, jumped in, and we were on our way. "It's 35 Southside Lane," said Jerry. "Better turn the siren on."

"Why would someone in Southside Acres want to take their life?" I asked Jerry. I knew desperate people tried to commit suicide using the manufactured gas we distributed. It contained carbon monoxide and if you breathed enough of it you were gone. That was the reason the company took any gas leak call seriously. The gas could get you two ways, by poisoning your lungs or by an explosion. When we arrived, an elderly man was kneeling in the kitchen in front of the gas stove with his head in the oven. Jerry turned off the gas burner, threw open all of the windows, and took the man's pulse. "He's gone. I wish we got the call sooner," said Jerry.

I looked around. The man was the only one in the house. Everything was neat. The man had washed the dishes from breakfast and stacked them neatly to dry. "I don't understand it," I said. "If he was going to take his life, why did he bother to wash the dishes? What difference did it make?" Jerry looked at me with those old, wise eyes. "Carroll, there are questions in life for which there are no answers." The police arrived soon after we did and took over. I never forgot those calls. It gave me a greater respect for the danger of manufactured gas and for the frailty of human life. Later I was happy to work with natural gas which did not contain carbon monoxide. It still was dangerous because it could explode, but people could not use it to commit suicide.

My next job was to prepare the plans for the company to change from manufactured gas to natural gas. This was to be supplied by a new company, "Northeastern Pipeline." Blackstone had only one map showing the location and size of all the gas mains in the streets. It was old and color-coded. We needed a new map which could be duplicated and which we could mark up for the location of new valves to be installed. It fell on me to work at the drafting table and draw a new map in black India ink on vellum with all of the streets and distribution system on it.

Fortunately this was no problem because of the engineering drafting course I had at Washburn University. I got to know Charlie very well and we became good friends. About this time Frank Orelup from Stone & Webster appeared. He was soft spoken, and proceeded to check my plans, making sure that the valves were all where they should be and that the flow of manufactured gas was not impeded as the reverse flow of natural gas came in from the new pipeline city gate location.

Frank produced two plastic flow calculators and suggested it would be wise for me to get them. I immediately contacted the American Gas Journal and ordered one for low-pressure work and the second for high-pressure flow calculations. These traveled with me and proved to be reliable tools over the next thirty years. Frank was from Waco, Texas and disappeared as quickly as he came. Grace and I had been married for over three years. My career seemed to be secure and we decided it was time to start a family.

When the landlady learned Grace was pregnant we were told we could stay until the baby came but then we would have to move. We had to start house hunting all over again. We had no car so every weekend we would get a copy of the local newspaper, look in the "for rent" section and go on the bus to look at apartments. It was not an easy task. Following the war with all of the servicemen returning, there was a pent up demand for places to live. Most of what we saw was not suitable or out of our price range. One Saturday we went to the end of the bus line near the North Providence line only to discover there was no apartment but a small new home development in the Italian section. We were about to go back to the bus when the builder came up and insisted on showing us the houses. It was a two-bedroom house with living room, bathroom, and large eat-in kitchen with a full basement. There were no sidewalks and a dirt street. It was nice, but we couldn't buy a house; we were looking for an apartment. "Wait," he said. "Were you in the service? You can get a loan with the GI Bill."

"Yes, but we have no money for a down payment."

"It's only three hundred dollars."

"That takes care of that," I said. "We don't have three hundred dollars." We were living from paycheck to paycheck.

He must have needed to sell his houses for he said, "I like you and your wife. You seem like nice people. If you like this house, I'll loan you the three hundred dollars."

Grace was approaching full-term and the landlady was getting testy. So we agreed to buy the house. I went to the Veteran's Administration and filled out an application for a VA loan. 67 Oneida Street became our first house at the unheard of price of five thousand seven hundred dollars. The company agreed to pay for the shipping of our furniture, which was stored at her sister's house in Nashville. We had a bedroom set, a couch, matching chair, coffee table, and kitchen table with four chairs. We would have to get a stove for the kitchen and a crib for the baby's room. Our neighbors were mostly Italian, although one young Portuguese woman became one of Grace's good friends. I rode to work with Charlie and Tony Martino who lived close by. It was a friendly neighborhood.

The builder never pressed us for the down payment. It was several years before we could pay him. Everyone made wine in their basement and were willing to share. Our son, Carroll Vincent, was born after Grace was driven to the hospital by our next-door neighbor. Nobody asked us what nationality we were. Every Sunday we took the bus to the Episcopal Church in Pawtucket. The baby carriage served as our shopping cart for the small grocery store three blocks from our house. The baby arrival created new problems. I took the two o'clock feeding so Grace could get a full night's rest. We bought the gas stove from the company on credit and made monthly payments. Dirty diapers created the need for a washing machine. In those days there were no disposable diapers. You had to wash them and reuse them.

Since we had no money for a washing machine, I joined the Organized Navy Reserve Unit in Pawtucket. I got a full day's pay for a three-hour drill meeting one night a week. This allowed us to buy our first washing machine. We couldn't afford a clothes dryer. Posts made from company used pipe held up the clothesline for drying the clothes in the back yard. We never were asked our nationality again, but the memory never went away. To this day my stomach turns over when I think back to those words.

Discrimination takes many forms and has many subtleties. Sometimes it's called the glass ceiling. I ran into that when I was told, "You've gone as far as you can go without a college degree." I believe I met it when Rice Institute told me I wasn't eligible for a degree in Naval Science because I hadn't gone to school a full four years although I had fulfilled all of the requirements in seven semesters instead of eight. The Navy gave me my Ensign commission. Those in my graduating class who completed the exact same courses in eight semesters received a BS in Naval Science as well as their Navy commission.

It can take different forms, as when Grace was criticized in Seattle because she was from the South. Friends could not understand when we accepted an invitation for dinner at the home of a company engineer of Chinese background, Charlie Tang. It turned out his wife was the daughter of the Ambassador from Taiwan. We had a pleasant evening meeting the Ambassador and his wife and enjoyed the Asian-style meal. At that time in the late 1950s, people with Asian backgrounds were redlined as to where they could live and work in Seattle.

It was discrimination when, in the 1930s, even though he had seniority, my father had to work the night shift because he was a Protestant and the railroad officials were Catholic. We found it strange in New Zealand when we were criticized for U.S. treatment of blacks, but a native Maori could not get a room in the King George Hotel in Wellington. Was I discriminated against after I enlisted in the Navy Air Corps in 1943, and the FBI checked with all of my parents' neighbors because I had a German name?

The landlady of Polish descent was wrong in 1949. Discrimination in any form is wrong. The United States in unique. We are all Americans, not Polish-Americans, not Italian-Americans, not Portuguese-Americans, not French-Americans, not English-Americans, not German-Americans, or African-Americans. We never should have to answer the question "What nationality are you?" Fortunately, most of this has changed. That's the wonderful thing about this country. We now recognize discrimination is wrong and have fixed it. We all are either immigrants or descended from immigrants. You can move to France and live there for fifty years, but you will never be a Frenchman. You can move to Italy and live there for fifty years, but you will never be an Italian. But anyone can move to the United States and after a short time they will be an American!

10

What You Get for Being in the Reserve

Things were going well. It was November 1950. It would be the first Christmas for our six-month-old son, and we were living in our own house. We did not have a lot of money living from paycheck to paycheck, but our house was full of love. We had nice neighbors and in my job things were going great. I was learning all about the public utility business. Everyone at work was very helpful. I was making the plans for the change of the company business from manufactured gas operations to natural gas operations. I was meeting with Vice President Burt Jenkins and David Daly, the president, a couple of times a week.

I had control of my destiny, was on a fast track, and there was nothing that could stop me! One day the telephone rang and it was Grace. I could hardly understand her she was crying so hard. I couldn't imagine what was wrong. Had something happened to our son? Finally I got her calmed down enough to hear her say, "Come home." It was almost time for me to get off work so I got Tony and Charlie to leave a little early. Grace met me at the door. Her eyes were red and full of tears. "Is the baby all right?" I asked. She nodded affirmatively, then handed me a big brown envelope that had come in the mail. The return address on the envelope read "Bureau of Navy Personnel, Washington, D.C." Inside were orders. They said "Carroll V. Kroeger,

Lt. junior grade, USNR 488418. You will proceed and report for active duty in thirty days to the USS Capricornus, AKA-57 at the Naval Operating Base in Norfolk, Virginia."

I knew that a "Police Action" had erupted in Korea, but I didn't think it had anything to do with me. Suddenly I wasn't in control of my future. It was a huge turning point! Those thirty days flew by. I had to report to the Medical Hospital at the Newport Naval Station for a physical examination. They were running through anyone that could walk and breathe. The last stop was to see the psychologist. He looked at me and said, "I see you bite your fingernails."

"I started when I received my orders."

"Nothing wrong with you," he said. I was physically and mentally fit for duty. When Grace recovered her composure, she said, "I'm going with you. I know I can't be on the ship with you, but I'll be at your home port and with you whenever I can." The company took the news without comment. Some neighbors said "So long, Sucker, That's what you get for being in the reserve."

I had to grin and bear it. After the initial shock I realized there was a reason for having organized reserve units. It was for such a national emergency. On reflection the Navy had been good to me the first time around. I had an angel on my shoulder. I was in college classes while others my age and younger were out there getting shot at. Or, as in the case of my older high school friend, Bill Reynolds, shot down over the Sea of Japan as a gunner in a Navy dive-bomber. We packed up, arranged for the builder to look after our house, and prepared to go. On my last day at the company Burt Jenkins called me up to his office and apologized that the company could not give me the Christmas bonus of twenty-five dollars because I had not worked the full year. I missed it by twenty-eight days! Instead he handed me a carton of cigarettes and wished me good luck.

The train ride to Virginia was uneventful. My Navy buddy from Rice, Bob MacDougal, was working for the National Advisory Council for Aeronautics and lived in Newport News. He arranged a temporary place for us to stay until we could get permanently settled in Norfolk. I rode the ferry across Chesapeake Bay each morning. My first two weeks were at Amphibious Warfare School at Little Creek, Virginia. We learned all about Attack Cargo and Attack Personnel Ships, Amphibious Landings and Landing Craft. We were told our ships and equipment was obsolete. In the next war our LCVPs and LCM boats would be replaced by helicopters. The invasions would be in third dimension.

When I reported for duty, the Capricornus was swinging on the hook out in Hampton Roads. I got a boat to take me out and had to climb up a Jacobs's ladder to get on board. It was obvious they weren't expecting anyone. I found my way to the Ward Room where the Executive Officer, Commander Alvin Robinson and the Engineering Officer Lt. Commander Grader were drinking coffee. "What did you do in civilian life?" the XO asked.

"I was an engineer," I replied.

Lt. Commander Grader perked up. "You promised me I could have the first engineer that reported on board," he exclaimed.

"Okay, but he stands deck watches," said the exec. I was assigned to a room shared with three other officers. Then Grader took me to an office and said, "You're the 'R' Division officer and Damage Control Assistant. You are responsible for the operation and maintenance of all the equipment on the ship except main propulsion plant."

My desk was stacked high with work orders. It seemed nothing on the ship worked properly other than the main propulsion plant. I was given the roster of men assigned to the "R" Division. I was in charge of over one hundred of the three hundred-man crew. The first thing I did was call a meeting of the Chief Petty Officers and Warrant Officers. Warrant Electrician Tansey, Warrant Carpenter Hayes, and Warrant Motor Mechanic Babine were on the front row. "Gentlemen, we have a problem," I said. "This is the first time I've been on a ship. I didn't ask for this job but here we are. You are the professional sailors. You know what needs to be done and how to do it. You tell me what you need to get your job done and I'll bust my butt to see you get what you need. I'll take care of you and I expect you to look out for me."

Looking back I'm reminded of a scene in one of my favorite John Wayne World War Two movies "They Were Expendable." The senior officer explains that it is the job of the professional military to fight with whatever outdated equipment is available, hold the enemy until the country can rebuild, and eventually come back and win. That looked like our job. Our ship had just come out of the Mothball Fleet. None of the equipment worked properly. It had been fine in 1944 and 1945, but it was six years later. The carpenter mates, pipe fitters, electricians, machinists, and enginemen all pitched in. I approved all kinds of requests for replacement parts and equipment. In spite of all the hard work, it became clear we could not get the job done alone. We received orders to go to the private Sun Shipyard at Chester, Pennsylvania for refitting.

I was surprised when the XO called me in and said while the ship was in Chester I was being sent to the Army Chemical Center at Edgewood Maryland for ABC (Atomic, Biological, and Chemical) Warfare School. Grace packed her bag and said, "If you can come home at night I'm going to be close by." We were lucky to find a place to stay that had been housing for workers in a Coop-Shoe Factory that closed. Army personnel and their families who were stationed at the base lived there. I was the only Navy man and was lucky to be able to ride to the base with one of the enlisted men. ABC warfare was scary. We learned how to detect chemical and biological agents. We learned how to don protective clothing, go through decontamination, wear dosimeters, and operate Geiger Counters. We were exposed to mild doses of chemical agents so we would recognize them by odor and change of color on special treated testing gear. We were herded with gas masks into a tent full of tear gas and had to take off our masks, count to ten, and then get out.

It wasn't fun and made us realize what a serious job and business we were in. The Corporal I rode with to and from the base went back to school after the war and earned a Masters Degree in Physics. I was the only officer living at the housing unit and I said to him, "What's your job at the Chemical Center?"

"I run the overhead projector." he said.

"That doesn't make sense," I said.

"I'm lucky," he said. "When I was recalled, it was on the same basis as when I was released to inactive duty seven years ago. They put a rifle in my hand and we were loading on a troop transport headed for Korea. At the last minute I was pulled off when they found out I had the degrees. But for the grace of God I would be in Korea in the front lines fighting for my life."

My class graduated and Grace packed up and we moved to Chester, Pennsylvania. We found a small apartment and made do with what we had. Our son slept in a drawer from a chest of drawers. A pillow worked as mattress for his small bed. Grace was a real trooper, a camp follower wherever we went. It made me realize how much she loved me. The wife of my good friend and fellow officer in the Organized Reserve Unit in Pawtucket, Eddie Ross, said, "I'm staying put. I'll be here waiting whenever you can get leave and come home." I don't say this to criticize Natalie Ross. She and Eddie remained our best friends over forty years until they passed away a few years ago.

We thought so much of Natalie that she was named Godmother for our daughter Sheryl. I mention this only to show my appreciation for how lucky I was to have such a wonderful wife. She calculated that we moved more than fifty-three times and lived throughout the United Sates and in five foreign countries. After a couple of months our ship was deemed seaworthy. Grace took a train with our son back to Norfolk and the Capricornus started down Chesapeake Bay toward the Atlantic. It was a memorable journey.

Our captain was B.S. Hansen and this was his first command. The only other time he had been on a ship was years before as a turret officer on a Cruiser. He was the nicest gentleman you would want to meet, but he lacked confidence and didn't trust anyone. He was a disaster waiting to happen and it almost did. He was in command when we were going to pass an oncoming merchant ship. He ordered a change in course, barely missed hitting the merchant ship, made a 360-degree turn, and almost hit them a second time.

They were frantically sending a signal light message. "What did they say?" he asked.

"Learn the Rules of the Road," said Lt. junior grade Rotollo. Looking back it is a shame that Captain Hansen didn't trust our Executive Officer Commander Robinson. "Robbie" had gone through the academy and would have been senior to Captain Hansen except for leaving the Navy and becoming a lawyer in civilian life. He was called back to active duty when the war started and after the war decided to stay in and make it his career.

All that the Captain needed to do was confide in the exec, as I had with Warrants, and ask for help. He needed a year's command at sea to be eligible for promotion to Rear Admiral. Instead he tried to tough it out alone and ended up with a nervous breakdown on our shakedown cruise. When we pulled alongside the pier in Norfolk, an ambulance and medics were waiting for him. We never saw or heard from him again. Never think you are in full control of your life or career. There are forces that can create a turning point, which you cannot fathom or understand. However, if you roll with the punches, the time can come when you may say it was one of the most memorable things that could happen to you.

I went on to become one of only five out of thirty-five officers to become a qualified underway watch officer. The Officer of Deck when the ship was underway had awesome responsibilities as set out in Navy Regulations;

> The officer of the deck is the officer on watch in charge of the ship. He shall be responsible for the safety of the ship. ...Every per-

> son on board who is subject to the orders of the commanding officer, except the executive officer and those specified in article 1009 shall be subordinate to the officer of the deck.

At the age of twenty-five with only the rank of Lieutenant, junior grade, I was given the responsibility for the safety of a multi-million dollar ship and the crew of over three hundred human lives. The Capricornus sailed the Caribbean, picked up Marines at Moorhead City, North Carolina, and participated in LANTFLEX war game exercises at Viegas Island, Puerto Rico. We joined the Sixth Fleet in the Mediterranean with ports of call at Gibraltar; Cannes, France; Naples, Italy; Piraeus, Greece; and Oran, Algeria. We made practice amphibious landings at Suda Bay, Crete and on the island of Sardinia. We were prepared to go into battle if ordered. The Capricornus carried out its mission successfully.

The Executive Officer, Commander Robinson, asked me to take over the ship's office and assume the duties of Administrative and Personnel Officer. As collateral duties I conducted Devine Services when the ship was at sea. I became the unofficial chaplain for all hands on board. I was promoted to Lieutenant and at age twenty-five. I assumed greater responsibilities than I ever could have in civilian life. In the summer of 1952 I received orders to inactive duty and was able to become a civilian once again.

Today there are young men and women in the military assuming responsibilities beyond their ages of eighteen to twenty years old. The average age of sailors on modern aircraft carriers is about twenty. Their families are having the same experiences as Grace in trying to raise young children while their father is away at war. They need all the thanks and support our nation can give them.

11

Korean War—Man Overboard!

There is nothing comparable to life aboard a navy ship, unless it's a prison. In both instances you are confined, and live in close proximity to others not necessarily of your own choosing. There is nothing in civilian life that compares. When you are confined, little things can grow out of proportion to reality. In civilian life if there is a personality that irritates you, you can avoid that person. On a ship you may not only have to work with the person, you may have to almost sleep with them and eat with them.

Such was the case on the Capricornus. In the beginning I had three roommates. Two of them were okay, but the third became insufferable. He was the kind of personality that irritated everyone. He was one of those who knew everything. If you said it was a nice day, he would give you a lecture on meteorology and why it was a nice day. If you commented on the ice cream being good at lunch, he would tell you how to make ice cream. The thing that made it difficult was he not only was one of my roommates (officers were seated for meals in the Wardroom by rank), I had to sit opposite him at breakfast, lunch, and dinner! It got so bad I had to decide whether I would rather not eat or listen to his idiotic banter. The thing that made it even worse was he was always right! He was a walking, talking encyclopedia.

I used some influence to get moved out of the room and in with the ship's doctor. The doctor and I could tolerate each other. I found him interesting. The first thing he did when he moved in was take all of the confidential publications out of the safe in his desk and filled it with bottles of gin. When I asked about his disregard for Navy regulations, he responded if it wasn't for gin he wouldn't have made it through medical school. Now that he was on the ship it would get him through whatever he had to put up with. He taught me a lot about the medical profession of those days. He said, "What color pills should I give them today, red, blue, or green?" When I looked shocked, he said, "It doesn't matter, they are the same sugar pills, just a different color."

It was evident he found life aboard ship boring. Most of the men who showed up at sick call were looking for an excuse to get off the work detail. One day he came in laughing. "I sure had a cure for the 'miseries' today," he said. (Miseries was the term some members of the crew used for not feeling well.) "I got out the biggest hypodermic needle I could find and filled it with water. When the men lined up at sick call, I said to the first in line, 'Drop your pants and bare your ass.' Then I gave him a jab with the needle and said 'Okay, next.'" He smiled. "The next man in line said 'I'm feeling a lot better, Doc, I think I'll be okay,' and left along with all the others." For those who really had a malady the normal approach was to give them an "APC" pill (mostly aspirin) and say, "Come back tomorrow."

The doctor was a surgeon and felt badly he didn't get enough practice. He went through the medical records and sorted out those men who had not had a circumcision. He called them in and told them they had to have one whether they wanted it or not. One night he told me, "I wish I had a pair of pinking shears. I could give someone a beautiful job!" When we were in the Med he got a call. An enlisted man on a destroyer developed appendicitis. They had no doctor on board so they came alongside and our doctor was hoisted over in a Boatswains Chair. He performed the operation and was in a good mood for several days. I found having Gerry as a roommate had some benefits.

On every cruise he would lose a case of medical brandy, which somehow found its way into our room. When I had a difficult day, he would give me a "feel better" treatment. Shortly after we returned to Norfolk from our tour of duty with the sixth fleet in the Med we were ordered to participate in what was called a "Lantflex Exercise." This was conducted every year as a training exercise for members of the Atlantic Fleet. We steamed south down the coast to Moorhead City, North Carolina. This was the closest port to Camp Lejeune, the Marine Base. We loaded our holds full of "Baker Rations" from the Camp. These were the same as the cases of non-perishable canned goods you find in the Super Market. Someone must have felt that the "Baker Rations" were valuable because two Marine guards were stationed at the entrance of the holds with loaded guns.

We proceeded along the coast in convoy until we reached Viegas Island. This is a small island off the eastern tip of Puerto Rico. The amphibious forces made landings, the APAs unloaded their troops, and we unloaded our cargo. The Norfolk Ledger Dispatch carried a story with the headline "'Black Nation' Force is being forced back from the Beaches by Marine Invaders." The Marines went through their war games on the island for a week and we were told the exercise was over and to proceed to San Juan for liberty. Our Captain said, "We can't go until we load all that cargo back on the ship." So we worked around the clock until we received an order to "cease and desist" and to rejoin the convoy. As we departed, we saw Marine bulldozers burying the remainder of the "Baker Rations" in the sand on the beach.

Officers were called into the Wardroom and the Captain briefed us on the plan for the coming night. "This is to be a darkened ship exercise," he said, "and I don't want to hear that anyone has shown the smallest light, even a cigarette that the opposing force can see." He made it clear that if he got a report of any light on our ship severe penalties would result. Our station in the convoy was astern of the Guide Ship bearing thirty degrees. I was scheduled for the mid-watch and checked the weather report. It didn't look good. A weather front was coming in from the west and the predicted time of arrival was around midnight. Night approached and the hatches were battened down in preparation for the approaching weather. The crew was instructed about the darkened ship exercise. The sun in the Caribbean is intense and our ship did not have air conditioning. It was not unusual for members of the crew to sleep on deck at night because the steel hull had a tendency to retain heat for a long period of time. I went up to the wheelhouse early to read the Captain's Night Order Book and check on the ship's position before I relieved Lt. Tinker as Officer of the Deck.

Everything was in order and I took over responsibility for the watch. About an hour passed and we ran into a series of rain squalls. It was hard to take visual bearings to maintain station and I had to rely on radar. When the squall hit, I could hear men on deck cursing because they were getting wet from the rain. The Boatswain's Mate of the watch, Ernest Clemmons, came in from the port wing of the bridge and said, "Mr. Kroeger, I think I heard someone out in water calling for help." I ran out to the wing of the bridge, looked, and listened. I couldn't see or hear anything. I was thinking about what the Captain said in the Wardroom. If things didn't go right on this darkened ship exercise, someone's ass would be in a sling.

I turned to the Boatswains Mate. "Are you sure you heard someone in the water?" I asked.

"Yes, sir, I'm sure," he said. I went inside, called the Radioman, and chose my words carefully. "Call the Task Force Commander and tell them we believe we have a man overboard on the port side." Then, I instructed the Messenger to wake up the Captain and tell him the same thing. Lt. junior grade Rotollo, the JOD who was familiar with Navy procedure, turned on the ship's running lights. The Captain appeared and called for a muster of the ship's crew. It seemed to take forever but one by one the Divisions reported, "All hands on board and accounted for." My heart sank. There was no one from the Capricornus in the water.

Meanwhile the ships in the screen, the USS Tumult, USS Hobson, and USS Shea, were ordered to go back and search. They were instructed they could use searchlights. Almost an hour later a message crackled over the intercom. "We have found the man floating in the water. He has been recovered and his condition is satisfactory." I heaved a sigh of relief and I'm sure the Captain did too.

The next day, the seventh of November 1951, the following dispatch was received from the commander of the Task Force aboard the USS Taconic:

> A marine sergeant was rescued from the choppy Atlantic Ocean North of Mona Passage in the Caribbean early this morning forty-five minutes after he tumbled without a life jacket from the deck of the transport USS Deuel. After being plucked from the water, the sergeant told the rescuers of the minelayer USS Tumult that he was sleeping on the weather deck when he was awakened by a sudden squall. 'I must have taken a wrong turn and fell overboard,' he said."

The next morning our ship received a message from the USS Duel, APA 160:

> The Commanding Officer wishes to express his thanks and admiration for the alertness and prompted action which resulted in the rescue of the man overboard from the Duel last night.

Another message came from ComPhibLant:

> A Marine SGT probably owes his life to your alert watch spotting him passing your ship. Well done.

When our ship arrived back at Moorhead City the Marines refused to take back the "Baker Rations" in our hold with the comment "The exercise is over." We proceeded to Norfolk and nobody there wanted them. Finally after a day or two of haggling the Marine contingent agreed to take them. Two LCIs offloaded them and went out to sea. When they returned, they were empty! The Navy has a term for this: "Deep Sixing."

I would not have thought too much about this but for a story I read in the Norfolk newspaper about a week later. A Navy enlisted man was arrested for stealing government property going out of the gate of the Navy Operating Base. He was apprehended by the guards who discovered he had taken some food from the garbage cans at the Mess Hall. The food that was being thrown away was called "Government Property" and the man was given a Captain's Mast and punished. The news story concluded with the comment "It was an unfortunate incident, but 'justice must be done.'" The irony was that it was okay to "deep six" a ship full of perfectly good food (the Baker Rations) but illegal for an enlisted man to take home some perfectly good food from a garbage can.

Another event occurred on the Capricornus that reinforced my views of waste in government. In the summer of 1952 the Capricornus was ordered to go to the Boston Navy Shipyard. The ship was to go into dry dock, have the barnacles sandblasted off the hull, and the hull repainted. The First Lieutenant of the ship was responsible for ordering the special paint for the undercoat. It was a very expensive special anti-corrosive paint. He delegated the job to one of the former merchant marine officers in his division. The area of the hull was calculated and the quantity of paint required for the job.

The First Lieutenant, who was not too swift in the opinion of several of the officers, doubled the quantity. He did not want to have to explain if it turned out there was not enough paint to do the job. The hull was sandblasted and painted. There was a problem: what to do with all those five-gallon cans of paint that were left over? Of course there was a typical Navy solution to the problem. As the ship sailed out to sea at sunset all the paint cans were sitting on the deck. The next morning all of the cans had disappeared.

These incidents probably are typical of what goes on all of the time in government at all levels. The problem is that there is no incentive in any level of government to save anything, especially taxpayers' money. Nobody wants to have to explain a mistake. It is much easier to just sweep everything under the carpet and go on. This is especially true in the budgeting process. Each year everyone contends for more money. You ask for more than you spent last year. You better spend it all before the end of the year or you won't get more the next year. If a private business operated this way, it would be bankrupt.

On January 17th, 1952 I was relieved of all duties in the Engineering Department and designated Administrative Officer with collateral duties of Personnel Officer, Ship's Secretary, Confidential Mail and Publications Officer, Legal Officer and Member of the Service Record Verification Board. When the Executive Officer asked if I would like the job and I agreed, he smiled and said, "Of course you understand it will be your job to conduct Devine Services when the ship is at sea." I didn't really understand that I would become the unofficial Chaplain for the ship.

Our ship was a "floating funny farm." The crew was ninety-five percent recalled reserves who would rather have been home with their families. They were not like regular Navy personnel who volunteered and expected to make a career in the Navy. To make matters worse they were recalled on the basis of what their rates were at the end of World War II. Many had gone back to college or started a new business. They had severe financial problems and their wives were left to try to cope with raising the children and find a way to pay all the bills. Many ended up in divorce. A man came to me with his problem. He and his wife had five children and she was having a difficult time. Both the Red Cross and the Minister of their church wrote letters supporting his request for a "Hardship Discharge." The Bureau of Navy Personnel turned down his request. When he informed his wife, she said, "Don't worry, I'll take care of it." Her solution was to get in their station wagon and drive it off a cliff. When the Bureau was made aware of the man's new situation, he was granted a "Hardship Discharge."

My time on active duty was a learning experience. I have tried to retain the positive aspects and repress the negative. I was placed at the age of twenty-five in positions of responsibility I never could have imagined in civilian life. It was a maturing experience. The positive thing for anyone in the military is that you have to grow up fast. You learn how valuable and fragile life can be. You become mature at an early age. This is happening to young men and women today. It's not a coincidence that many elect to go into law enforcement when they become civilians. They certainly learn to be more responsible citizens. We need to help them and their families cope with the problems we civilians are fortunate enough to not have.

12

Engineers—We Hire Them, We Fire Them!

Central Indiana Gas Company was headquartered in Muncie, known in an early sociological study as "Midtown America." We arrived in Muncie the end of June 1952 shortly after I was released from active duty aboard the USS Capricornus, AKA-57. I had been recalled to active duty as a result of the Korean "Police Action" and now was ready to resume my civilian career. A job was still available at Blackstone Valley Gas & Electric in Rhode Island, but the opportunity that took me there was gone. The company's plans for change-over to natural gas operations took place in my absence. No one is indispensable. It took three people to replace me. Under the law they had to give me my job back, but it would be a different job.

Now I was going to work for a company that had been distributing natural gas for several years. The service area included the towns of Anderson, Elwood, Marion, and Muncie. My dad had worked on the conversion of these towns to natural gas in 1942 and 1943. We lived in Marion in 1942 and I had been with my parents in Anderson when I finally received my Navy orders to active duty in November 1943. My boss was the Chief Engineer, Ted Spencer. The engineering and operations office was in an old former manufacturing building. It was a brick building with corrugated tin roof, concrete floors and plywood office dividers. The building was cold in the winter and stifling hot in the summer.

The physical amenities didn't bother me. My office was between Mr. Spencer's office and the office of Don McCafferty, the Operations and Maintenance Manager. I thought this would be great because although I worked for Ted I would have the opportunity to learn operations from Don. My job was interesting and not stressful. Public utility operation generally is pretty routine eight-to-five type work. After twenty-four-hours-a-day duty aboard a Navy ship, this change of pace was appealing. We bought a little three-bedroom house, moved our furniture from Norfolk, and settled into suburban 1950s living. At first my work was interesting. Some might wonder how anyone without an engineering degree could succeed as an engineer.

Looking back, I was very lucky when the Navy required me to take all those Math, Physics, Chemistry, Engineering and Naval Science courses. I learned the basic fundamentals for any assignment. I knew how to research on my own and find out how others solved problems. When I was able to succeed in my area of weakness, I developed the self-confidence that there wasn't anything I couldn't do. Natural gas was in demand by all of the people in the service area for heating their homes. My job was to help process the applications, and check to see if gas was available where they lived. If there wasn't a gas main in the street, I had to figure out what it would take to supply the request, determine the size and length of pipe and work with the draftsmen to prepare the maps and construction orders.

This work became routine. The only problem was we could not get enough gas from Panhandle Eastern Pipeline to supply the demand. As a result we had a list of more than ten thousand people on a waiting list who wanted to heat their homes with gas. I always have been a very inquisitive person. I also was a young man in a company of middle-aged men who were accustomed to doing things the same way. Whenever I asked why something was done the way they did it, the answer usually was "That's the way we have always done it." I put a little sticker on my desk that said, "If anything has been done the same way for fifteen years, it's a sure sign there is a better way of doing it." When I became aware that the major problem was not enough gas I began to wonder "Why?"

One of the major industries in Muncie was "Ball Brothers Glass Company." The local college was named Ball State University. I learned in some historical research at the library that the reason Ball Brothers was located in Muncie was because in the early nineteen hundreds Muncie was sitting on top of what had been a huge natural gas field. In fact, when you drove through the countryside you would see many old six-inch diameter steel pipes sticking up out of the ground. These I was told were old gas wells that had been abandoned when the field became depleted. I became very curious and decided to educate myself further.

I learned Pennsylvania State University had a correspondence course on "Natural Gas Engineering." I signed up and immersed myself in learning all about geology, petroleum, and gas exploration and production. About a year later I received my diploma in "Natural Gas Engineering." On weekends I spent time in the library learning the history of the old gas field. I had been reading trade journals and learned that in other locations people had revived old depleted fields and were using them as underground storage fields.

When I found out that under the company contract there was plenty of gas available in the summer months and only a shortage in the winter because of the demand for heating, the logical question followed: "Why not buy gas in the summer, store it, and resell it in the winter?" When I asked Ted about this, the reply was "We looked at that and it can't be done." This was all I needed to hear. Throughout my life the thing that gets me going is to hear "That's impossible, it can't be done."

It was time to get some help, so I wrote a letter to John Patton, the Principal Geologist for the State of Indiana and requested information on the geologic strata of the area. He was very helpful, and provided me with enough information to write a request for permission to do some fieldwork on company time. Over the next year I was able to collect information on hundreds of abandoned wells and get a map of the underground strata plotted with some prospective locations worthy of investigation.

In the meantime I had been picking the brains of my next-door neighbor, Don McCafferty, the Operations Manager. It turned out there was a personality conflict between Don and my boss. He would stick his head through my door and say, "What you working on?" When I would tell him, his response would be "That's not the way to do it." Then we would go to a nearby restaurant, have a cup of coffee, and he would tell me the difference between the theoretical solution to a problem and the practical solution. It seemed that any job Ted sent them they had to redo to make it work. In talking with the men in the field they said, "It don't do no good to talk to Mister Spencer about a problem because all he will do is draw you a graph showing you what you say is happening can't happen."

I also was saturating my learning from William Reynolds, who worked for Don, the practical aspects of how large volume gas pressure regulator and orifice meter stations work. I was on a learning curve from Don on how to find and repair gas leaks, and the unofficial ways to circumvent management and get a job done. At home I was reading The Oil & Gas Journal about magnetic, gravity and seismic survey methods, and different types of oil and gas drilling rigs.

While engaged in all of this activity there was a nagging thought in the back of my mind. I didn't want to be an engineer all of my life. I discovered that Indiana University had a night School of Law at Indianapolis only sixty miles away. I was eligible under the GI Bill to enroll. Three nights a week I commuted to Indianapolis to classes to learn about torts, contracts, domestic relations, constitutional and criminal law. I managed to carry eight semester hours each term and was able to convince the Dean to allow me to take courses out of order without the prerequisites in order to not go more than three nights a week.

When I began to have an idea to improve something and was met with "No," I started writing articles and sending them off to Industry Trade Journals. Much to my surprise, the American Gas Journal accepted one, then Gas Magazine and more. In one instance an article on "Cavern Storage for Liquefied Petroleum Gas" created interest from as far away as Australia and a company was formed in Cincinnati, Ohio to actually go into the business. An article providing a quick rule of thumb for estimating when a gas main was reaching capacity found its way into the Gas Engineer's Handbook. I was finding an outlet for my long submerged desire to be a writer and establishing a reputation in the industry.

We were getting stretched to the limit economically. I was earning three hundred seventy-five dollars a month. I had been keeping in touch with my boss and every six months would ask, "How am I doing?" His response was, "Fine, actually more than we expected." It eventually became necessary to meet and say, "If my work is more than satisfactory, how about some financial recognition?" His response rocked me back on my heels. "I don't have the authority to give you a raise." He said he had not had an increase in pay in five years. The only people who had gotten raises were those that belonged to the union. It was hard for me to understand that my boss couldn't give me a raise in pay if I had been doing such a good job.

Being young and brash, I said, "Okay, if you can't give me a raise, do I have permission to make an appointment with Mr. Cullison, the President?"

"Sure," he said with a knowing smile. "Be my guest." I had only met Mr. Cullison at company functions like the Christmas Party. All I knew about him was he had an accounting background. Engineers and accountants usually are at odds philosophically. Accountants are regarded by engineers as "bean counters" who give everyone a hard time about their expense accounts. I did know that several of my requests for small expenditures to further the underground storage project had not received any support. "God was in his heaven and all was right with the world." How much better could it be than having ten thousand prospective customers waiting for gas service?

I called and got my appointment and went to the main office. He was sitting behind his desk smiling. After the social amenities of "How's the family?" I made my little presentation of why I thought I was deserving of an increase in my salary. He looked at me, shifted his weight in his chair, and said, "I don't have the authority to give you a raise."

"But you're the president of the company," I replied.

"You don't understand," he said. "This company is owned by a holding company. The only one who can give you a raise sits in New York. His name is Chris Coughlin."

"He doesn't know I exist," I said "He doesn't know if I'm doing a super job or a lousy job."

Mr. Cullison leaned back. "Engineers, accountants, we hire them, we fire them," he said callously. He wasn't smiling anymore and I knew the meeting was over.

I didn't sleep much that night and it wasn't because of the hot weather and no air conditioning. The next morning I said to myself, "You fool, you're not an engineer, you are a salesman. All you are worth is what you can sell yourself for in the job market." Looking back, Mr. Cullison did me a huge favor. It was a painful lesson. Many years later when teaching Personnel Management at Belmont I learned the theoretical side of salary structures. In any organization a job is only worth a certain price range of dollars. When you hit the top of the range, the only raises will come from cost of living. If you want to earn more money, and you don't want to wait for someone to retire or die, you have to either get a promotion in a growing company or move out.

"This is the rest of the story," as Paul Harvey would say. In 1956 I moved on to another company in Seattle, Washington. A short time later an underground storage field was developed by Central Indiana Gas Company with the help of a consultant. There was no longer a waiting list of ten thousand people who wanted to heat their homes with gas. For many years my son and daughter could not understand why I said the word "can't" wasn't in our family dictionary. When someone says, "It can't be done," it means they don't want to do it or they think it's too hard to do. In World War II the Navy Seabees had a motto: "The difficult we do immediately, the impossible takes a little longer!" Our world is full of opportunity. All you have to do is to look and listen. When someone says, "It can't be done," there is an opportunity to solve a problem or to make something happen.

13

You've Never Done That Job Before

I was looking at the job market and especially for someone with my educational background and experience in gas public utilities. In reading the want ads in the American Gas Association Monthly, I discovered that Laclede Gas Company in St. Louis had an opening for a gas engineer. Grace and I planned to take a short vacation and visit my parents in Trenton over the Easter holidays so I gave them a call and made an appointment to interview on the way back from Trenton. The interview went very well, and they offered me a job. They paid more money than Central Indiana so I accepted it. I said I knew they had a contract with Stone and Webster. My change needed to be approved by Luke Storrs, the personnel manager of S & W. They agreed to take care of it. Upon my return to Muncie I was surprised to receive a call from Bill Woods telling me I should give a call to a man called Jim Gary in Seattle Washington. Stone & Webster was in charge of a merger between the old Seattle Gas Company and the Washington Gas Light Company in Tacoma.

A new natural gas pipeline "Pacific Northwest Pipeline" was under construction and would be supplying the new company "Washington Natural Gas Company." I called Jim and he immediately offered me a job at seven thousand five hundred dollars a year. I would be the Assistant Chief Design Engineer responsible for the design and construction of all the control equipment to take gas from the pipeline and supply thirty towns and cities in the Puget Sound Region. I was to move to Seattle immediately. My friends in Muncie presented me with a watch engraved with the words "From CIG Friends." I was touched. I didn't have to wait to retire to receive a gold watch and I knew it came from individual contributions of the folks in the Operations and Engineering Department.

A few days later Grace drove me to the airport at Indianapolis and I was on my way to the Pacific Northwest. I felt badly leaving Grace to sell the house, get packed up, and move again. But there was no choice. It was the middle of March 1956. The company had signed a contract for natural gas supply commencing November first with a take or pay clause. Five City Gate Stations had to be designed and constructed to reduce the pipeline pressure and to meter the gas supply flowing into the Washington Natural Gas system. Thirty new district regulator stations had to be designed and constructed to distribute the gas within the thirty towns and cities from Chehalis on the south near the Oregon line to Everett on the north close to the Canadian border. Metering and regulating stations had to be designed and constructed for seventy new industrial customers.

The Chief Design Engineer had his hands full designing and constructing miles of pipeline to transport the natural gas from "Pacific Northwest" to the thirty towns and cities in the service area. It was a pressure cooker twelve hours a day, seven days a week job. It never entered my mind whether I could do the job! I checked into the hotel, went to the operations office, met Jim Gary, and went to work. It was different. Washington Natural was not a company of old men. The Engineering Department was staffed with a group of young engineers and draftsmen in their twenties from the University of Washington: Paul Hoaglund, Steve Richards, Harry Tang, Paul Leu, and Walter Baychek. I was an anomaly that Stone & Webster parachuted into Seattle, home of the Old Seattle Gas Company. The old Washington Gas Light Company in Tacoma had been the S & W client and was where the managers had S & W affiliations.

I had no time to think about company politics. Washington Natural wasn't a typical public utility of old men. It was refreshing to not be told this is the way we have always done it. Everyone had ideas of how to do it, but no natural gas experience. That was where I came in. I knew from my Navy experience my job was to channel all of that energy into positive directions. I quickly sorted out the people I could trust and didn't try to reinvent the wheel. There was Paul Hoaglund who had been trying to hold down the fort. He had worked with a leasing agent from the pipeline to obtain property adjacent to where the pipeline gate stations were going to be located. No one ever asked me if I had done this job before.

Steve Richards developed a design for the district regulator stations based upon the requirements of the American Society of Mechanical Engineers standards. These were to be installed under the sidewalks with cast iron covers. I had never seen stations installed underground before but they convinced me they were best for the large cities where there was a high flow of traffic. The design contained sufficient redundancy to provide protection in the event of regulator failure and to prevent flooding the low-pressure distribution systems with high pressure gas. Harry Tang and the group had obtained catalogs and information from American Meter Company and Rockwell on metering and regulating equipment to calculate the sizes required for the quantities of gas that would be flowing into our system. Recommendations were on my desk with purchase orders for the necessary equipment.

Frank Orelup from Stone & Webster appeared, checked what we were doing, seemed satisfied, and provided a sketch for the layout of the piping and equipment for the city gate stations. Natural gas does not have any distinguishing odor so odorizing equipment would have to be ordered and installed at each station. An odorant would have to be injected into the natural gas so that in the case of leaks it could be found. A local builder provided bids on the construction of prefabricated steel buildings to house the city gate equipment.

Problems arose when the design for the district regulator stations were reviewed. A provision was made for the installation of filters at the inlet to each station. Literature and experience of other companies that changed to natural gas from manufactured gas said that materials on the inside of the old piping systems would dry out and with the reversal of flow and increased velocity of the moving gas, problems with metering and regulating equipment could occur. The normal method to prevent this had been to install humidifying and oil injection equipment to prevent the drying out. This also would prevent the drying out of the joints of the old cast iron pipes throughout the low-pressure system. If the humidifying equipment were used, there would be no use for filters. In fact, the filters would get clogged up by the moisture.

Jim Gary was pressured by Stone & Webster to have the oil fogging and humidifying equipment installed. Frank Baycheck was one of the most brilliant of the engineers and had recommended the filter installation. He insisted that what had worked in other parts of the country would not work in the Washington Natural systems. "I've researched and read all of the literature on this problem," he said. "I've had the joints of cast iron pipe dug up and tested. Subjecting them to humidity and oil fog will not prevent them from leaking. They have already dried out and if they were going to leak, they would be leaking now. If you want to protect the meters and regulators, the best way is to filter the crap out when it starts to move."

This presented a political problem. Stone & Webster insisted on humidifying and oil fogging. I reviewed all of Baycheck's work and concluded he was correct. The design would include the filters and, to satisfy management, foggers and humidifies would be installed. It was here that I became aware of the management of the company and how it worked. My boss, Jim Gary, was the son-in-law of the President Charley Sturkey. There was another son-in-law who worked in the main office as the Director of Personnel. The two could not have been more different.

I learned more from Jim Gary than from any boss I've ever worked for. Jim was smart, and a hard driver. He was determined to prove he was in his position, not because of marrying the President's daughter, but because of the merit of his work. He, too, had completed the "Natural Gas Engineering" course at Penn State. He read all of the trade journals like I did. We were in the same mindset. However, Jim had to conform to the wishes of the consultants from Stone & Webster. I think he believed me when I told him the foggers and humidifiers weren't necessary, but he had to go along with the recommendations of the New York consultants.

Everything was working well. Grace had sold our house in Indiana, bought us a new 1956 Plymouth, arranged for our furniture to be packed up, and was ready with our children to move to Seattle. I took time off to fly back and drive them to the Pacific Northwest. We rented a house for the summer in a sub-division called "Apple Valley." I took some time off on a few weekends to look for a new house. I liked a new area across Lake Washington in a community called "Bellevue." New homes were under construction in a new area called "Lake Hills." There was a beautiful house plan on one level with a window wall of glass, three bedrooms, a living room, small dining room, kitchen, and two bathrooms. It was ideal for our growing family.

When Grace arrived, I took her around to look at everything under construction. Eventually we got to Lake Hills. When she saw the house, she said, "I like this one best." I had not indicated to her which I liked. We walked back to the crest of a hill, picked out a lot that looked at Cougar Mountain, and signed a contract for the window wall of glass to look out at the mountain. Our house was supposed to be ready before school started. Everything at work was progressing. In order to save time, I arranged for parts of the Gate Station piping to be prefabricated in welding shops in Seattle. I was aware of the strength of unions in Seattle.

This was the home of Dave Beck, the head of the powerful Teamsters Union. Even the department store clerks were members of the union. I made sure the welding for the prefabrication was done by union welders. Everything was on schedule for November first. Then one day I got a call from the construction crews. I went out to site and a union steward said, "You might as well get rid of all this prefabricated stuff because we won't touch it."

"Those were done by union welders," I told him. "Yes, but they are boiler makers. We are pipe fitters. We will only install what has been welded by pipe fitters." This was my first experience with what is called "a jurisdictional dispute."

"What do you expect me to do?" I said. "This has to be ready by November first."

"Order new parts and we will weld them," he said.

"You don't understand," I said. "These had to be special ordered. It took six months to get them. We can't just start over again." We haggled for over a week.

Finally he said, "I like you. You're not like most of the engineering and management types. I'll tell what we will do to help you out. We will cut these fittings apart and then weld them back together again. The welds will be better than the first ones." I had no choice but to agree. A couple of weeks later one of our inspectors told me, "You know what those guys did?"

"No," I said, "all I care about was that they got installed."

"They didn't cut them apart. They sat on their rear ends for several days and then put another bead of welding over the old ones."

Our house was completed the last week of August. Grace got our furniture moved out of storage and into the house. Our son started in the new Lake Hills elementary school, which was within walking distance of our house. All of the control equipment was in place by November first. A news photo shows Charlie Sturkey with the mayor turning the valve to start the flow of natural gas into the system. The conversion of appliances by "Conversions and Surveys" went like clockwork, and before we knew it, we were a natural gas operation.

Jim Gary called me into his office one day and motioned for me to sit down in a chair. A couple of days before, a notice had been distributed announcing he had been promoted to Vice President in Charge of Operations. "We are having a re-organization. The organization chart is going to be turned upside down. You have done an outstanding job and have helped us meet all of our deadlines. Before I start shaking things up, I would like to know what you would like to do in the company from now on. You are the first I have asked and you get first choice. You designed and constructed all of the metering and regulating equipment. Would you like to take over their operations?"

I thought about it for a minute, and said, "No, I think I would like to do what Paul Hoaglund has been doing."

"Paul's the Distribution Engineer. You've never done that job before."

"That's why I want to do it," I said. "But if you don't have the experience, why should we allow you to do something you've never done before?" I didn't tell him I hadn't done the design and construction of the control equipment before. I said, "Jim. You've just been named Vice President of Operations. You've never had that job before, but the management must have enough confidence in you that they think you can do it. I hope you have enough confidence in me that you think I can do this job."

He smiled, thought for a minute, then said, "Okay, if that's what you want, you have the job. I'll put Paul in charge of the metering and regulating operations." I moved into the distribution office and a short time later Jim called. "Stone & Webster wants to know how the foggers and humidifies are working."

"Jim, we never turned them on. The filters are doing great, we have had to empty them several times with all the dried out debris. There has been no increase in the leakage or in unaccounted for gas." There was a pause of silence.

"Do you mean to tell me that you have not turned on the foggers and humidifiers?"

"That's right Jim," I said. "You told us we had to install them. You never told us we had to turn them on."

I don't know what Jim told Stone & Webster about the operation of the foggers and humidifiers. I know that Frank Baycheck was right. Just because something has always been done a certain way is no reason there isn't a better way of doing it. Also, the fact that someone has never had experience of doing something is no reason to believe that they cannot do the job. I had to go back to Vanderbilt and sweat out twelve months of advanced Math and Physics courses in order to get the job of engineer. I never used any of that advanced Math or Physics in any of the work I did in Central Indiana or at Washington Natural Gas.

What was the difference? I had the confidence when I was asked if I could do something to believe I could do it. I had the basic intelligence to know how to learn new things and to solve problems. In my classes at Belmont I told my students, "The most important thing you can take away from here is the ability to learn on your own and how to solve problems." In a fast changing world, managers don't have need for someone who will be content doing the same thing over and over again. That's okay for the worker bees or someone working on an assembly line. The world needs problem solvers. If you can solve problems, you never will have trouble finding a job.

14

What Do You Do About Nepotism?

I completed my first year in Seattle and now was in a new job in charge of the operation, construction, and maintenance of the Northern Division distribution system. I didn't realize it but I was replacing an "old timer," who had been with Seattle Gas for many years. He was one of the older men and had a hard time adjusting to the fast pace of all the changes that came with the conversion to natural gas operations. He was given a desk in an obscure location to wait out retirement.

The distribution office was cluttered. There were four draftsmen who drew sketches from the records of street main locations for the construction crews. The records were in a bookcase of Field Books which had been drawn by the construction crews when the cast iron pipes and steel service lines were installed years ago. The books were frayed and starting to come apart. It was clear they could not last much longer. My impression was that the work of the draftsmen was "busy work."

As soon as the construction crews finished each job, they threw away the sketches. I discovered the 3-M company had developed a copy machine that used a heat transfer method onto an 8 and1/2"x 11" brown thin plastic sheet. I told my Office Manager, Phil Clark, to buy one from petty cash. "There's a daily limit on petty cash," he said. "Then save the max each day until you have enough." I knew that Jim Gary never would approve purchase of the machine because it wasn't in the budget. My learning experience from Don McCafferty was being put to use. Don had built a small warehouse at the Muncie Gas Plant with petty cash!

As soon as the machine arrived, I issued an order that no more sketches were to be made by the draftsmen. Copies of the field book pages would be made on the copy machine and given to the construction crews. "What are the draftsmen going to do?" Phil asked. "They are going to start drawing base maps for a new map record system," I said. When I first arrived in Seattle, Mal. McCallum, the Chief Design Engineer, told me the company needed a new map record system. Each year he put in a budget request and each year it was turned down. I now had the manpower to draw new maps without costing the company any money.

Next, I looked at the office furniture. We were crowded into a small area and four file cabinets were lined up against the wall. "What's in these?" I asked. Phil showed me the contents of the first two. They contained 3" x 5" cards. One set of cards contained the records made by the construction crews of the location of the gas service lines running from the street main to the meter location for each house. The second card was one that was sent to us by the Sales Department, signed by the customer agreeing to gas service. Once the service line was installed I saw no use for retaining it. The Sales Department insisted on keeping them because that's the way it always had been done. I had no wish to engage in a policy battle with the Sales Department, so I agreed to not eliminate it. However, I told Phil to have new cards made with the sales agreement on one side and the service record on the other. That eliminated filing one set of cards.

I learned that although I could not hire any full-time employees, it was possible to hire part-time workers. I contacted the Engineering Department at the University of Washington and offered part time employment to students interested in drafting work. Soon, I had four part-time draftsmen drawing the base maps. They worked at night and on weekends. Very few people knew they were there. The full-time draftsmen began transferring the permanent records onto the new base maps. A new map record system was underway without much added cost to the company.

I said to Phil Clark, the Office Manager, "What's in the other file cabinets?"

"Those are the leak reports," he said. The hair stood up on the back of my neck.

"Do you mean those cabinets are full of reports of leaks which haven't been repaired?"

"That's right," he said. "There are some in there for the same location that people have called in four or five times." It was Friday afternoon. I remembered the course in "Torts" that I took at Indiana University Night Law School. One of the tests for gross negligence was knowledge of a dangerous condition and failure to do anything about it.

Those file cabinets were disasters and law suits waiting to happen! If an explosion occurred at one of those locations, the company would be held liable, and since I was in charge of maintenance, I would be responsible too. "I want you to come in tomorrow morning when no one is working," I told him. "When I come to work Monday morning, I want those file cabinets to be empty and I don't want to know what happened to the contents." He smiled and said, "I understand."

I had a huge problem. The underground piping in Seattle was almost one hundred years old in some places. Immediately I designed a leakage survey form and ordered two men from construction to survey the basements of all of the buildings in the downtown commercial buildings. The first week they discovered three buildings that the explosion meter readings found gas-air mixtures in the explosive range. Gas repair crews were dispatched immediately, the street dug up, and the gas leaks repaired. We surveyed the streets around all public buildings; schools, churches, etc. We started a street survey system whereby every street with a gas main would be checked once a year. If an accident occurred, no lawyer would be able to claim we did not have a preventive system in operation. We would be able to pass the "What an 'Ordinary Man' would have done in that situation" test.

Our procedures were now consistent with industry standards. We might not be able to avoid an accident happening, but we would not be guilty of negligence. The construction crew foremen started calling me after they dug up the street on leak calls. "Why are you calling me?" I asked.

"We always called Mel and he would tell us what to do," they would say.

"I'm in the office and you are there looking at the leak," I said. "Don't just tighten up the bolts on a leaky bell and spigot cast iron pipe joint. That's a temporary fix. Repair the pipe so it doesn't leak and make sure whatever you do, you are not coming back in a few months to dig up the same place again." It wasn't long before they stopped calling.

After a few months things settled into a routine. I joined the Jaycees, ran for President of the Bellevue, Washington Jaycee Club and lost by a small margin. I was appointed State Director in charge of the Americanism Program. The national organization had a project called "True Security." I started traveling about the state promoting the project. A modern day "Paul Revere" was sent by National around the country to promote the program and I accompanied him across the state We were interviewed by radio stations wherever we went. "Paul," Mike Gravel, ten years later was elected Senator from the state of Alaska The Jaycees gave me the opportunity to develop public speaking skills that years later would prove to be invaluable. Grace and I attended church services in Medina at the St. Thomas Episcopal Church. I learned the rector was going to conduct a class for Lay Readers so I applied. Three men completed the class and we read the lessons at the services and later at a mission sponsored by our church.

Lake Hills grew fast and I was elected President of the Lake Hills Community Club. Washington Natural supported my participation in community organizations because they viewed it good public relations. I enjoyed it because I was growing out of my engineer's shell! New homes were springing up like mushrooms and it was clear that before long all of the land would be covered with houses. If some land wasn't set aside for a park and playground in two or three years, no land would be left. We formed a committee to develop plans for a park and playground in our community. Land was found next to the new elementary school and the owner agreed to sell it for a below market value if it was developed as a community park and playground. A local architect volunteered his services to help the committee develop plans for the location.

An appointment was made with the County Park Board and the committee gave a presentation with a request the county purchase the land. The Commissioners looked interested and said they would take it into consideration. We were informed there was no money in the budget and our request was denied. We were not satisfied. We knew parks were being developed in other parts of the county. There was no good reason we should not have one. We had a lawyer in our development and we asked him to help out. He paid a visit to the office of County Parks and presented a written request for a copy of the minutes of the Park Board meetings for the last two years. He was told it would take a long time to meet our request. His response was that they were a matter of public record and if necessary we would get a court order.

A few days later we received a call informing us that the Park Board had reconsidered our request and they were going to approve our request to purchase the land. I learned a lot about politics in King County, Washington and how to get things done! Today there is a park and playground adjacent to the Lake Hills Elementary School! Things were falling into place at my office. I developed job descriptions and an organization chart for my department. There was a constant turnover of the part-time employees and the word got out that if you wanted to add a good employee, go to Kroeger's group.

My philosophy was to hire people who were over-qualified for the job. While they worked for me, I had a really good employee and when an opportunity developed for one of them to advance I was happy and wouldn't stand in their way. Over time this had some unintended consequences. My former employees were spread throughout the company. If something came up that affected me, they were on the telephone alerting me. Along the way I learned the difference between what academics call "unofficial power" and "official power." There are jobs that, because of their job description or title, have official power. Behind the scenes there are people who assume unofficial power.

In the Navy there are three types: Storekeepers, Cooks, and Yeomen. You learn to be friends with them because they control the supplies, the food, personnel records, liberty cards, and leave papers. In civilian life there are people called "Gatekeepers." Their official title is "Executive Secretary." They control access to their boss, the President or Vice President. You better be on their good side if you want your telephone call to get through or you need quick access to see a high official. It's surprising what a box of candy for a birthday or taking someone to lunch once in awhile can do.

When I first arrived in Seattle, I had no secretary and getting my reports out on time was a problem. I would go into my office on Saturday mornings to catch up on my paper work. It was a quiet time with few interruptions. I would write out my letters and reports by hand and turn them over to the secretarial pool on Monday mornings. One day in the lunchroom I mentioned my problem and Jim Gary's secretary, Beth, was getting a cup of coffee. "There are times when I don't have enough to do," she said. "I'd be happy to do your typing if I can do it as I can work it into my schedule. If you get a dictaphone, and dictate you letters on tape, I'll be happy to type them."

From that time on she had my tape on her desk when she came in on Monday morning. Beth was a super secretary, efficient, dependable and a hard worker. About a year later President Charlie Sturkey's secretary got married and moved away. Beth moved up to the main office and became the President's secretary. One day she gave me a call. "I thought you ought to know Mr. Pratt, the Sales Vice President, is in Mr. Sturkey's office and he is blowing his stack about your department. He has a friend whose application for service was turned down. His name is Mr. Sanders and his place of business is 515 Olympia Avenue."

I quickly called Phil and asked him about the application. It wasn't long before Charlie Sturkey was on the phone. "Mr. Sturkey," I said, "company policy says that we can only afford to run a service line from the main in the street to the front of any building." "This man doesn't want a meter at the front of his store." said the President. "I know. He wants it to be at the rear of his commercial building, which is two hundred more feet than our policy allows. If this is a special case and there is some reason company policy should not apply for this prospective customer, you tell me to do it, and I'll do it."

"No, No," said Mr. Sturkey. "I'll tell Fratt his friend must pay for the extra feet of service line." Not long after that Beth received a box of chocolates for her birthday.

I had my job under control and it was becoming routine. In December 1958 I was named "Outstanding Jaycee of the Sixth District," and one of the four finalists for the "Outstanding Citizen of Bellevue Washington" for 1958. There was a Pacific Gas Association Conference in Tucson, Arizona. I requested permission to attend. My request was approved and since I had some vacation coming I asked to add it on to the end of the conference. It would be a great vacation for the family.

We asked for permission to take our son out of school for the two weeks and the teacher said, "Fine, travel is very educational." Seattle had been building new schools because of the rapid growth taking place. They were beautiful, individually designed for each piece of property by an architect, and had a fantastic view of the mountains or lakes. Teachers were the second highest paid in the nation. Our son never had any homework and was not allowed to bring books home. We asked if it wouldn't be a good idea to take his books so he wouldn't fall too far behind. The school reluctantly agreed.

Our family had a fantastic time. On the way we stopped at Disney Land, and we were met by the Vice President of American Meter Company, who gave us free tickets and treated us like royalty. I had a very informative conference and took time to visit Arizona Public

Service Company and pick the brains of their operations people. We visited Tucson and on the way back stopped at Yosemite, the Redwood Forest and Crater Lake. On the way back we discovered our son could not read. He could recite pages from memory but did not recognize any of the words in his books. The class had been divided up into reading groups. He listened to the others and developed a phenomenal memory. He knew how to make applesauce, but could not read!

It became clear to everyone in the company that the president was nearing retirement. Jim was spending more and more time in Charlie's office and bringing work back to his own office. Before long he began to pass more and more of what he had been doing to me. I took over the job of collecting requests from all of the divisions, putting it together into a budget for his review. I saw the opportunity to slip in a request for a company car for myself. After all, I was on the emergency call list and was expected to make periodic visits in the field to make sure everything was going okay.

The budget went sailing through and soon I had a company car for my use. I learned how to use unofficial power to my advantage. Everyone began the guessing game; how long before Charlie Sturkey retires and Jim Gary becomes the new president? It seemed clear to all that I was the likely one to take Jim's place. Hadn't I been doing most of his work? Everyone was stunned when a company memo came out announcing the president's son-in-law had been appointed Jim's assistant and was moving to Operations from Personnel. The son-in-law was being set up before Charlie left. It might not have been so bad except that he wasn't like Jim. He was there only because he married the president's daughter. This was nepotism pure and simple and it was wrong!

I felt betrayed. Obviously management figured that Paul Hoagland and I were competent to keep things going. The son-in-law could sit in the office like he did at Personnel and draw the Vice President's salary. A short time later I received a phone call from Rick Murless, the Rockwell representative. "I'm embarrassed," he said, "and I don't really know how to say this, but I got a call from our Rockwell representative in Arizona and he has been asked to see if you would be interested in going to work for the gas company down there. They were very impressed when you visited and would like to make you an offer." It looked like one door was closing for me and another door might be opening. I had been in Seattle for three years. I really wasn't interested in working in Arizona, so I picked up the phone and called Luke Storrs in New York. I said, "Luke, I haven't been looking for another job but this offer just came out of the blue. I would like to know what other possibilities I might have."

He said, "I'll think about it and get back to you."

About a week later my phone rang and it was Beth. "Mr. Woods from New York is here and he would like to talk to you. He wants to know if you could join him for lunch."

"I'll be there," I said. I went uptown and had lunch with Bill. Over the years I found he had been my mentor. He promoted me in Conversions and Surveys. He arranged my working for Stone and Webster and followed my progress over the years. "There is an opening in our Gas Department for a Consultant of Gas Operations," he said with a smile. "If you are interested in working in New York, it pays ten thousand dollars a year."

"I'm interested," I said without hesitation. If I couldn't move up, it was time for me to move out. "How much time do I have to wind things up here?" I asked.

"We would like for you to be in New York by June first," he said. A short time later there was a company memo announcing my leaving to join Stone & Webster. Apparently Jim Gary was caught off guard and didn't learn about it until the decision had been made. Jim wouldn't talk to me for two weeks. Finally he invited Grace and me to have dinner with he and his wife Helen. When he shook my hand and said goodbye, he said, "Your forward planning is such that we can go a year without replacing you."

Looking back, I made a difference at Washington Natural. The city gate stations and district regulator stations are still operating. The company had a new underground record system when I left and a safety record with no explosions. When I arrived in Seattle, the company served forty thousand customers; the company has grown and serves more than four hundred thousand customers. Lake Hills has a Park and Playground. The Episcopal mission where I conducted services in a school has land and a building and is called the "Church of the Resurrection."

Many years later at the Vanderbilt School of Management, Igor Ansoff talked about training "Change Agents," people who could go into a company and make things happen. I was a change agent without any training or knowing it. Anyone can be a change agent if you are not satisfied with doing things the same way over and over again and are interested in finding a better way of doing it. There are three kinds of people: those who don't know what's happening, those who are content to watch what's happening, and those who make things happen! Anyone can be a “change agent” if they are willing to take some risk and rock the boat once in awhile! Nepotism is wrong and when you encounter it you aren’t powerless. You don’t have to stay and do the work and someone else get the credit for it. You are in the wrong company and the sooner you leave the better off you will be.

15

If You Can't Do This Job, We Don't Need You!

It was June 1, 1959. Once again I had to leave Grace and the children behind to sell the house, pack up, and move. This time it was to New York. I would be working in the Stone & Webster Building at 90 Broad Street in the Wall Street District of Manhattan. Temporarily I was staying in a hotel across the Brooklyn Bridge in Brooklyn. I could ride the subway under the river and be at my office in ten or fifteen minutes. This was the culmination of a career dream. In Rhode Island, Indiana, and Washington State I saw consultants from S & W come when there was a problem, deliver a report, and then go back to New York.

This was Mecca! The great storehouse of knowledge I yearned to tap into, learn all of the things in Marketing and Finance to qualify me to one day be the president of a utility. As soon as I arrived I was escorted to Bill Woods's office. He greeted me and closed the door. "I wanted you to know I'm moving to Seattle to take over Charlie Sturkey's job and probably one of the first things I'm going to have to do is fire Jim Gary!"

I gasped. "That's a fine thing you've done to me," I said. "I just arrived in New York and you're moving to Seattle!" I then went to see Luke Storrs, signed all the necessary papers, and received the company policy manual.

The Manager of the Gas Department was a middle-aged man, Mike Sonney. He was mild-mannered and formerly had served on the Public Service Commission of the State of Montana. The Department consisted of George Carpenter from Oklahoma Natural, Stan Wood from Atlanta Gas Light, Gordon Jerauld from Haverhill Gas via Tacoma Washington, and Bob Willis from Fall River Gas. Most of these had gone through Northeastern University's Coop Program working in the Fall River, Massachusetts Manufactured Gas Plant. All the Northeastern alums were slide rule engineers, Tau Beta Pi National Engineering Honor Society members who loved to collect data and crunch numbers. Their background was making gas from coal or oil, and selling the coke, tar, and other by-products. Sometimes the gas was almost as much a by-product as the real by-products.

The main work seemed to be peak shaving studies for various utilities who were trying to reduce their natural gas contract costs on peak days by mixing propane-air with the natural gas. A lot of the work was repetitive. They didn't mind; I disliked doing the same thing over and over again. The vice-presidents Bill Woods, George Schofield, Frank Sperry, Luke Storrs, and others executives were located on the nineteenth floor. I was assigned an office, a desk with Marchant analog calculator, and spent the first two hours reading trade journals. I wasn't used to doing nothing and it was driving me up the wall. I knocked on the manager's door and walked in. "For God's sake, give me something to do," I said.

He looked up, rummaged through some papers on his desk, and said; "You want something to do? Call Transportation and have them book you a flight to Hartford, Connecticut. The president's name is Jebb. They have some kind of a problem up there. They are going to pay us twenty-five thousand dollars and we must deliver them a report in six weeks." That was the end of the conversation. I now had something to do. Over time I learned, much to my surprise, that Mike had no say on who worked in the department. The big decisions like hiring were made on the nineteenth floor.

I flew up to Hartford, took a taxi to the gas company, and found myself sitting across from the president Mr. Jebb. "I don't know what's going on," he said. "Our revenue has leveled off and we aren't growing like we should be." The more he talked, the more I began to understand the problem was a marketing problem. They needed to sell more gas! My experience was in operations but I couldn't say they had sent the wrong man. When the meeting concluded, I said, "I will have to return to my office and come back and meet with some of your people. I will be back next week."

I rushed back to New York and asked, "Where is our Marketing Expert?"

"He's in California on a long-term assignment and won't be back for two months" was the response.

I went into Mike Sonny's office and said, "Mike, Jebb has a marketing problem."

"You said you wanted something to do, well, do it!" End of conversation. There was no great pool of knowledge. It was sink or swim.

Years later it reminded me of a similar experience my friend at Belmont University, Jay Selleck, had when working for Avco. Jay had become an expert on gas turbines in Nashville. He was promoted and moved to the Connecticut headquarters. The company was going to bid on a Defense Department contract and an engineering handbook on the Avco gas turbine would be required for the presentation at the end of the month. Jay's assignment was to write the handbook.

Jay knew all about gas turbines, but like many engineers, he did not know how to write. A week went by and his boss asked him how he was progressing. He had to admit he was just getting started. "If you can't do this job, we don't need you," his boss said. Jay was shocked. His wife was still unpacking and not settled into their new home. Jay went to the local newspaper and asked for their best technical writer. He hired him to help write the handbook. The job got done and you better believe Jay learned how to write!

I was on my own. I searched the company files for all the reports on marketing. I went to the library and immersed myself in American Marketing Association books. A week later I was the expert that returned to Hartford. I found out from Census data that Hartford was full of houses that used oil for heating the kitchen stove. Other companies in New England were replacing these with gas burners. I estimated the potential number of homes in Hartford with the small oil burners, how much it would cost to replace them with gas burners, and the additional revenue that would come. I liked writing reports. The day came for my presentation. Jebb was happy, S & W was happy. Hartford Gas sent a check for twenty-five thousand dollars (two and a half times my annual salary) and I was ready for my next assignment.

Grace was having a problem selling the house in Lake Hills. Boeing Aircraft, the main employer in Seattle, laid off fifty thousand when the Defense Department stopped buying manned aircraft and started switching over to guided missiles. Fifteen houses between our house and the entrance to Lake Hills went up for sale. Bill Woods advised not waiting for the house to sell but buying a house in New York. S & W would loan me the down payment. I flew back to Seattle, loaded the family into the car, and drove cross-country to New York.

We stopped in Yellowstone National Park long enough to see Old Faithful. It's one way to have a partial vacation. We rented a house for the summer in Manhasset on Long Island and spent the summer teaching our son phonics and how to read. We got him on a Police Athletic Club baseball team to work off some energy. The only position they had open was catcher, so he was the catcher. Later we found a house farther out on the North Shore of Long Island in Huntington. It would be an hour and a half commute each way for me, but we decided the children needed to be where there were good schools and open spaces to play.

We settled on an acre and a half lot with a split-level house formerly owned by a PanAm Airlines pilot. He flew overseas and had a lot of time home. The yard was well landscaped and to us looked like a park. I put in all the new lawns and landscaping in Rhode Island, Indiana, and Seattle and wanted one that was already done. The price was twenty-five thousand dollars but I was on the way up so we would stretch a little bit. Bob Willis was one of those guys who thought outside of the box. There were several utilities in Connecticut that were combination gas and electric. With the arrival of natural gas the two fuels were in competition with each other. In some states the public service commissions were requiring the gas operations to be split off from the electric.

In Rhode Island it was now Blackstone Electric and a separate Valley Gas Company. Bob saw the opportunity to put together one large natural gas company in Connecticut. We spent the rest of the summer doing a series of merger studies with all the permutations and combinations. At the end none seemed to work, but Bob left S & W, went to work with Mr. Jebb, and merged Hartford Gas with the Gas Division of Connecticut Light & Power. A few years later Bob became President of Connecticut Natural Gas.

I learned that S & W was a pyramid of four companies. At the top was S & W Inc. Below were S&W Engineering Corp, S & W Securities Corp, and S & W Service Corp. I worked for Service Corp, the consulting arm which had annual retainer contracts with more than thirty-five public utility firms across the country. There was an Electric Department, a Gas Department, a Tax Department, an Accounting Department, and a Tariff Department. On the nineteenth floor were the vice presidents who were the liaison (sponsors) with the various utility clients.

It wasn't long before I became Assistant Sponsor for Greater Winnipeg Gas Company in Canada. George Schofield was the V.P. Sponsor. George went to Winnipeg in the summer when the fishing was good. I went in the winter when it was thirty below zero! That's the way things worked. The Sponsor's job was to keep the client happy and the retainer money flowing. If the client had problems, it was the responsibility of the Assistant Sponsor to do all the grunt work of solving the problems. So much for the great storehouse of knowledge!

The President of Greater Winnipeg was Arthur Elliott. He was the Sales Manager for Muncie when I was at Central Indiana Gas. Grace and I knew he and his wife Gussie well. They attended the same Episcopal Church we did in Muncie. When I first arrived in Muncie and met Arthur, I learned he was an S & W man. He had an electrical engineering degree and was very likeable. He said, "The best rule in any company is 'Keep your hands out of the cash drawers and out of the female employee's drawers.'" (In those days women's undergarments were called "drawers.")

The company in Winnipeg had almost gone bankrupt. The management had alienated the community and the Province of Manitoba considered convening a Royal Commission to take it over. The shareholders asked Stone & Webster to help. S & W stepped in, changed the management, and saved the shareholder's equity. Winnipeg needed someone to mend relations with the general public. Arthur had been a member of the Muncie Chamber of Commerce, the Rotary Club, etc. He was the ideal man for the job. After I did my first peak shaving study for Haverhill Massachusetts Gas, I had little interest in doing another. It was busy work. I ran into a small problem because I recommended installation of the propane-air plant at the city gate station. Of course all of the old manufactured gas people wanted it at the gas plant. That's how it always had been done. It didn't make sense to me.

At the city gate one hundred percent of the natural gas could be mixed with the propane-air. If the new peak shaving plant was located at the gas plant in the center of the city, only fifty percent of the natural gas could be mixed with the peak shaving gas. I was able to overcome the objections and eventually the new facility was installed at the city gate station. To me doing these studies was boring. Soon, the manager started giving me the unusual jobs.

I became the Assistant Sponsor for Southern California Water Company. (No, I never had worked for a water company before.) I joined the American Water Association, read all of their books, and found the only difference was distribution of water throughout a piping system instead of gas. I did a five-year forecast of operations for Winnipeg that was used to help float a new issue of bonds. I continued to write articles for Industry Trade Journals. On the home front everything was going well. I didn't enjoy commuting in and out of New York, but it was worth it.

Grace would take me to the railroad station where I caught the Long Island Railroad into to Jamaica Station. I changed trains there then onto the subway to the Bowling Green Subway Station. One block walk and I was at 90 Broad Street. If everything went just right it only took one hour and thirty minutes. In the evening it was the same routine but reversed. Grace would be waiting for me at the Huntington Railroad Station. Our son had learned to read and both he and his sister were doing well in school. The schools were not designed by an architect; the teachers were not the highest paid in the nation. The elementary school gym was in a converted barn. But New York State required every student to pass a Regents Standardized Exam before they received a high school diploma. Teachers knew that, parents knew that, and students knew if they didn't pass they didn't get a diploma.

Weekends were spent mowing the lawn and taking our son to baseball games. He was developing into a good baseball player. It wasn't long before he was on an All-Star team as pitcher and third baseman. His team went through the season undefeated. Once again we were close to living paycheck to paycheck. Although I had received a substantial raise in salary, we learned there is a difference in the cost of living in different regions of the country. New York was one of the highest. We went to church every Sunday and, when we could afford it, had lunch at McDonalds. In Seattle we had not been able to visit either of our families. It was just too far away. It was the same in New York. In the winter we shoveled snow. We had a depressed driveway with stone walls leading to the basement garage. In the summer it was beautiful. In the winter it took half a day to shovel the snow out of the driveway.

It was the summer of 1962 and I was on vacation painting the trim of our house. I was up on the ladder when Grace called and said, "It's the office. Mike Sonney wants to talk to you."

"Sorry to bother you on vacation, but I think it would be a good idea for you to get a passport before you come back. We may have to send you out of the country on an assignment." This was to become the start of a great adventure for me and my family. Sometimes when a door opens, fear of the unknown can take hold. If you never have done the job before, speed up the learning curve. When you are standing on the bridge ready for a bungee jump, don't be afraid to leap into the unknown. You may have the most rewarding experiences of your life!

16

You Can't Put That in a Consulting Report

When I got back to my office after vacation, Mike called me in and said, "Did you get your passport? We're going to send you on an assignment to New Zealand. It's for Shell, BP, and Todd Oil Services."

"Yes," I said, "but how long will I be gone?"

"I don't know, but it will not be more than six months." I learned many years ago the one document to study was the book on company policy. It is the bible on important things like the retirement plan, vacations, etc. Mike just told me in those words the company would not pay for my family to go with me on this assignment. The policy manual said that if an employee were given an assignment for more than six months the company would pay for the family to go.

Six months away from your family can be a long time, especially if you are out of the country. I had to do that when I was in the Navy. I wasn't going to do it again. I discussed it with Grace and we decided this was an opportunity to not let go by. We went to the bank and borrowed two thousand dollars to pay for the family's trip. When I told Mike we had decided for the family to go with me, he was upset. He called a meeting of the Gas Department and told everyone that it was my decision and the company had recommended against it and wasn't paying for it. I didn't understand why it mattered.

Looking back, there must have been a lot of jealousy about my getting the assignment. Only two were going; Roy Goddin, Vice President of Conversions & Surveys would also make the trip. When I wrote my family about the news, my mother called and said, "You can't be serious. You're not taking Grace and the children to that God forsaken place. The only reason you are going is it's so dangerous the oil companies can't get any of their own people to go." I couldn't reason with her and had to hang up the telephone.

The decision was made. My family was going with me! Before we knew it, we were on a Qantas 707 jet. We stopped over in Hawaii to catch up with the clock. Talking with a retired Navy Chief, I learned the name of a reasonably priced hotel near the beach and that there was a Navy launch we could take to see the Arizona Memorial at Pearl Harbor without charge. When we got back on the plane, we were pleased to find we had the same crew as from Los Angeles. New Zealand is almost halfway across the world. In 1962 travel by air was a pleasure. The plane was not crowded. There were enough empty seats that the children could stretch out and take a nap if they wanted to.

Our plane had to stop in the middle of the night to refuel at Fiji. When we crossed the International Date Line, we lost a day on our calendar. On our return it gave us an extra day of vacation. We finally arrived at Wellington airport. A Shell driver and car was waiting for us and took us to the King George Hotel. The other members of the team were already there; Roy Goddin from Conversions and Surveys in New York, J. Critchfield and A. H. Lancaster from Shell International in London, Ken Ingles and John Cook from British Petroleum Trading in London. Lancaster and Cook were experts in LPG utilization, Ingles was an Economist, and Critchfield was a Pipeline Engineer. I was to be the Public Distribution expert and Roy Goddin was the expert on appliance changeover.

When we arrived in New Zealand, it was like being transported back in history in a time machine. The culture was more British than the British. If we had seen Queen Victoria in the lobby of the King George Hotel, we would not have been surprised. We learned quickly we could not stay at the hotel because it was too expensive since we were paying for Grace and the children. If we couldn't find something else, Grace and the children would have to return to the United States. We saw an ad in the newspaper for a furnished apartment for rent. We went immediately to talk to the landlord. He was a young man who renovated a house and already had rented the upstairs. The downstairs was available. The only problem was he wanted a six-month or one-year lease. We managed to convince him to let us stay. It was small, one bedroom with two beds, a kitchen, and small living room. There was no central heat. "We have a mild climate here, so heating systems are not considered necessary," we were told. The commode was located outside the back door in a small closet.

We were happy. The family could remain. We would live like New Zealanders. This was one of the best decisions we could have made. It was winter in New Zealand so our children needed to be in school. There was an Anglican church school at St. Marks nearby and they were enrolled immediately. The team started to work. Natural Gas had been discovered halfway up the North Island at Kapuni near New Plymouth. We were to make an energy study for the North Island where nine towns had gas service. The largest two were at Auckland on the North and Wellington in the South. The South Island was separated by enough water it would not be feasible to run a pipeline across the straits. We were to be headquartered at Shell Centre in Wellington.

We made an appointment to meet with representatives of the New Zealand Gas Association. They were very helpful and agreed to make arrangements for us to meet with the officials of the nine gas companies. New Zealand was a country full of scenic beauty. It had an agricultural economy. The mild climate allowed two growing seasons. The main products exported were lamb and dairy products. Outside of the cities the fields were green and full of sheep. The South Island resembled Norway and Sweden with fjords and high mountain ranges. Christchurch was the supply base for all expeditions to the Antarctic. The North Island was completely different. Auckland on the North had a sub-tropical climate and was the base for some of the best deep-sea fishing in the world. Nearby was one of the three thermal areas of the world with bubbling mud pools and geysers. We found the people of New Zealand friendly and very knowledgeable of the rest of the world. They knew about all of the states in the U.S. and were well informed. The team began its work. I was to make five-year forecasts of operations for each of the nine gas companies and then merge them into a summary for the group. My work with Bob Willis on merger of Connecticut companies made this right down my alley.

I gave all of the representatives of the nine companies a list of the information I would require. One of them said, "Is this a takeover bid?" It was clear I knew my business and the right questions to ask.

We made a visit to each firm and viewed their operations. All of the companies manufactured their gas from coal. The first visit was to be with Mathew Kennedy at the Wellington Gas Company. My impression was that everything looked old. At the gas plant I was told their main problem was parking. I looked around and saw an old gas holder that obviously was not in working order. "Why don't you tear down that holder?" I asked. "It could give you room for cars."

"We couldn't do that. It was built by the Chairman when he was a young engineer and he has a great sentimental attachment for it." The Chairman, I was told, was ninety-two years old. I had met my first "It can't be done."

Our next stop was New Plymouth. Grace and the children went on the trip with me. We were met at the airport by members of Shell, BP & Todd, the Chamber of Commerce, and City Council. We were taken immediately to a meeting of the City Council. Roy Goddin and I were asked to address the Council and speak about why they should consider using natural gas. It was here my training with the Jaycees in Seattle stood me in good stead. Next we were transported to the location where Shell was doing the exploration drilling near Kapuni. Every profession has its own language. I was quickly accepted by K. H. Davison, the Technical Manager for Shell & BP, when I started asking questions. "Did you make a gravity and magnetic survey?" "Yes, but we followed with seismic." "Did you do reflection or refraction seismic?" "What kind of structure is the producing zone?" "Does it have high or low porosity and permeability?" I was a member of their club from then on.

My family arrived by train and was taken in by the New Plymouth City Councilman, R. J. Burkitt. He was a businessman with the International Harvester franchise. We were invited to stay at their home for the three days we were in New Plymouth. Sheryl and Carroll Vincent went to school as guests of their children. We were amazed to learn that our son joined the Rugby Team. Before we knew it, our daughter acquired a New Zealand accent. Next, we visited S. J. Ireland at Wanganui, S. McBain at the Hutt Valley, B.D. Russell at Hamilton, and T. Williams at Palmerston North. From there we went and met with Robert Worley in Auckland. The gas company had a few younger men on the staff, but the President was eighty-three years old.

We were surprised to see sheep grazing on the golf course. "I guess they don't have to mow the grass here," our son said. Before we knew it, it was time to go back to Wellington. Then the real work began. All of the material with information I requested began to flow in. I had a lot of number crunching to do. The Shell LPG man gave me the estimated average use of gas per customer; Roy Goddin estimated the cost to convert the appliances. All of this I consolidated and built into the five-year forecasts. For the conclusion I wrote, *"The New Zealand Gas Industry is almost one hundred years old and has been slowly dying. The managements of the gas firms are almost as old as the industry and have been dying with it."* At the time I did not realize the impact of this conclusion.

I had weekends free and Grace and I would rent a car and with the children would travel the North Island as tourists. We learned how to adjust to a different culture and problems of living in a foreign country. All of the things we considered necessities were luxuries in other places in the world. In New Zealand you drove on the left side of the road. You needed to have an International Driving License. The currency was different, too: pounds, schillings, and pence. The IRS follows you wherever you go and you have to pay taxes in both countries. If the language is different, your children have to go to a private school. To live in a foreign country you must be very flexible and adaptable.

The purpose of our team study was to determine the economic feasibility of building a pipeline to supply the seven towns and cities on the North Island. The alternative was to generate electricity at the production field. The use of electricity had been growing in New Zealand and the use of gas had been declining. Much later I drew a life cycle curve for the one hundred years of the New Zealand Gas Industry. A successful change to natural gas requires an aggressive marketing program to amortize the initial investments. A change from a manufacturing mentality to a marketing mindset is necessary. I did not see those elements during my visit.

On our return we unwound at Korlevu Beach in Fiji, the black sand beaches of Tahiti, and Oahu Hawaii. When I returned to my office in New York, two unexpected things happened. A letter arrived from the New Zealand Gas Association requesting Conversions & Surveys open an office in New Zealand. This created quite a stir in the Gas Department and on the nineteenth floor. I didn't understand why until several years later. The second thing that happened was my report was slow in getting approved by the nineteenth floor. Mike Sonney came to me and said, "The part about the gas industry dying and the management dying with it has to be changed. You can't say that in a report."

"Why?" I asked.

"The people on nineteen say you can't."

"Mike," I said, "the people on nineteen didn't go to New Zealand. If they know more about it than I do, why did they bother to send me? If they want to take it out, they can take it out. I'm not changing it." I didn't tell him I had submitted a field report to Shell and BP before I came back. Roy and I were in New Zealand from August 20th to October 12th 1962. It took almost six months for the report to clear the nineteenth floor. The Tariff Department got into the act and wrote a chapter on tariffs, accounting people had to get in their two cents worth, etc. The report finally was mailed on May 3rd, 1963.

The atmosphere changed in the GasDepartment after I returned. I didn't understand what was going on. I learned much later the oil companies decided not to invest in a pipeline. The New Zealand government decided they would build the pipeline. New Zealand was a socialist country. The government owned and operated the Transportation, Communications, and Banking industries. The pipeline was constructed and Conversions and Surveys received the contract to convert the appliances in the nine towns and cities to natural gas operations. A few years later the pipeline went bankrupt and had to be subsidized by the government. In 1966 I was conducting a training course in London for Shell and Esso employees from around the world.

I asked A. E. Vizard, the Shell International Group Director for Natural Gas, to stop by and say a few words of welcome. He smiled, looked at me, and said, "When I see Carroll Kroeger, I think of some words he wrote in a report for us I wanted to frame and hang on my wall." The words were those I was told in New York I couldn't put in a report! There are times in life when you and your principles are tested by your boss or management. It is easy to cave in to the pressure. It's the path of least resistance. "Don't rock the boat."

I'm reminded of what happened to my boss, Ted Spencer, in Indiana. One day he called me into the office and said, "I don't know if I've done the right thing. I've just come back from the main office. Mr. Cullison, the president, called and asked me to come to his office and bring my Professional Engineer's stamp with me. When I got there, he was with the treasurer, John Goodwin. He pointed to some papers on his desk and said, 'We need these to be certified by a professional engineer. Sign and put your stamp at the bottom of this page.'"

"What is this?" asked Ted.

"It's a valuation of our gas plant. The company is floating a new bond issue and it requires a valuation of all the firm's facilities. John has made the valuation. It's just a formality, just sign and put your stamp here."

"What did you do?" I asked.

"I only have three years to go before my retirement plan is vested. My daughter is still in college. I signed and put my stamp on the papers."

"Ted," I said, "you could lose your Professional Engineers License if there's something wrong with that valuation. Even worse, if there is fraud in the bond issue, you could go to prison."

"I know, I was caught off guard and didn't know how I could say no." Fortunately for Ted, the company got the bonds sold and there was no problem. But what he was asked to do was wrong! It was not only a violation of his personal values, it was illegal and against the professional ethics of his engineering profession.

It would have been easy for me to have taken the words out of the report and rewritten it. After all, the boss was telling me to do it. But that is not what the client was paying for. They wanted a truthful, independent assessment of the economic feasibility of building the pipeline and that's what I gave them. It saved them millions of dollars. On reflection I know why I received such cold treatment. The V.P.s on the nineteenth floor were interested in Stone & Webster Engineering Corporation trying to get a contract to build the pipeline. There's even more that went on behind closed doors, but that's another story. There are times when you are asked to do something by your boss or company that you know is wrong. The normal reaction is "I need this job; I have a wife and family. I don't know what will happen if I say 'no.' I could lose my job. What would I do?" The answer is sometimes there are things more important than your job. What about your dignity, your personal reputation?

Former Governor Huckabee of Arkansas wrote a book called *Do the Right Thing*. In it he sets out a value system similar to that of the Navy Seals: "Don't lie. Don't steal. Don't cheat. Have respect for yourself and others." If you are asked to do something against your personal values and principles, no job is worth it! Maybe you are in the wrong job or company. You have to be able to look yourself in the mirror every morning. Once you compromise your principles, it's a slippery slope! I helped establish a course in Business Ethics at Belmont. I taught my students these things come without warning when you least expect them. Everyone should have a value system and have thought through in advance where the line is for them, morally, ethically, and legally. A line they would not be willing to cross.

17

Blazing a Trail for Natural Gas in Germany

After Roy Goddin and I returned from New Zealand, the atmosphere at 90 Broad Street was cool. I didn't understand what was going on. I was only trying to do a good job. It was taking a long time for my report to get out of the nineteenth floor. The New Zealand Gas Association sent a letter suggesting that Conversions and Surveys open an office there. To my way of thinking everyone should have been turning handsprings. I didn't have time to dwell on it. I had other work to do.

I needed to go to Los Angeles, because Southern California Water Company requested a Five-Year Forecast of Operations. Just before I was to leave, George Schofield, the sponsor for Greater Winnipeg, called me and said he had to go out of town but the president, Arthur Elliott, called and said he was going to need a report for the next Board of Directors meeting summarizing the services Stone & Webster had provided in the last year for his company. I thought the quickest way to collect the information would be to write a memo to the various department heads asking them to list the work they had performed and send it to George.

I wrote the memos, sent them off, and got on a plane for California. The water company supplied water to all of the domestic and commercial customers in Orange County south of Los Angeles. California was undergoing a water shortage and the company requested customers limit the watering of lawns, etc. The primary water supply for the southern part of the state came from the Colorado River. Mr. Phillip Walsh was the president of the company. He had the staff brief me and take me to one of the "Poker Palaces" in Gardenia. Gardenia was a municipality one square mile in size, similar to Central Falls, Rhode Island. Size was the only thing the two places had in common. Everything in Rhode Island looked old as Methuselah, but everything in California looked brand spanking new. Gardenia was unique because gambling was legal within its one square mile limit. There were three "Poker Palaces" open twenty-four hours a day where everyone went to play poker. The attraction for us was that the restaurants served luscious food at very reasonable prices.

Mr. Walsh was very forthright. "We like your service," he said, "but New York is too far away. There are competitors with offices on the West Coast that don't require the high cost of air travel to and from New York. You should consider opening a West Coast office." I thanked him for his suggestion, completed the fieldwork for the forecast of operations, and caught a flight back to New York. It hit the fan as soon as I walked into the office. "You better get upstairs and see George Schofield," Mike Sonney said. "He's blowing his stack." I went up to the nineteenth floor and knocked on George's door. "What in the Hell are you trying to do," he yelled, "get me fired?"

"George, what are you talking about?" I asked.

"These memos you sent to everybody. The department heads are mad as Hell!"

"You're a vice president," I said "They can't get you fired."

"You don't understand how things work around here," he said. "They have more influence than I do."

George was right. I didn't understand, just as I didn't understand when Mr. Cullison, the President of Central Indiana, said he didn't have the authority to give me a raise. The department heads told George they were too busy to give him any information. Arthur Elliott called and told George he had scheduled him to come to the board meeting and convince them they were getting worthwhile services for the four hundred thousand dollars a year retainer they were paying Stone and Webster. A couple of months later Greater Winnipeg cancelled their contract. When I told Mike Sonney what Phil Walsh said about opening a West Coast office, he said, "We considered that last year but the nineteenth floor said it wasn't possible."

A few months later Southern California Water cancelled their contract with Stone and Webster. It didn't seem to concern anyone, but it concerned me. After I adjusted to working in New York, I decided I might like to be president of S & W one day. When I first arrived, the firm had annual retainer contracts with thirty-five gas and electric utilities. Within three years the list had dwindled to thirty. It wasn't an encouraging trend. During that time we lost Atlanta Gas Light, Lacleid Gas in St Louis, now Greater Winnipeg and Southern California Water, some of the largest clients. If I wanted to be president of S & W, one day the company would have no business.

I began to wonder about the nature of the business. I sat down and wrote a memo to Luke Storrs expressing my concern. How did the firm get to where it was now? What was the present status of the business? What were the plans for developing business in the future? New Management Consulting firms were springing up with graduates from the Harvard School of Business. How did we intend to meet the competition? I didn't bother to send the letter through Mike Sonney. It went directly to Luke Storrs, the president. I had known Luke for fifteen years, back when he was Personnel Director and considered him a friend.

To my surprise I never received an acknowledgement or reply. I received an assignment that took me to Houston. Rayflex Exploration Company had developed a new method for the rapid detection of gas leaks. The equipment could be mounted in a Jeep and by driving slowly down the street it could detect small quantities of gas that were seeping up through the street surface. Stone & Webster Securities were interested in the company. The management of Rayflex thought they might be on the way to becoming the next Texas Instruments.

I flew to Houston and met with the company officials, and learned all about the equipment and its use. After my meetings, I took a day off, called Louise Loose, and asked her to give me a tour of the Rice campus. A lot had changed in fifteen years. The weather was the same, hot and humid, but the hotels now were air-conditioned. Louise met me with her four children in tow. Our first stop was to see her father, who now was a judge. Judge Loose asked me who I worked for and then said Stone & Webster was a good, respectable company.

Louise showed me around the campus and I was astounded to see more new buildings than there had been on the campus when we went to school there. The new Engineering Building, fully equipped, had been a gift from our classmate, Josephine Abercrombie. I knew she came from a wealthy family, but never realized how much she was worth. Louise seemed bitter about her education. She said, "It would have been better if I had learned how to repair the washing machine when it stopped working."

Later, I called Beverly Taylor, now Beverly Maurice, and she invited me to have dinner with her and her husband. We had a pleasant time reminiscing about the "good old days" at Rice. Bev's husband was an architect and they had a beautiful home. Beverly was the Fashion Editor for the Houston Post and was enjoying her career. I returned to New York and completed my report for Rayflex. The Securities Corporation was disappointed because if Rayflex saturated the market, the maximum number of units they might sell was between fifty and sixty.

Every year the Service Corporation conducted a Management Training Course for the fast track people of their client companies. I heard of the course in Indiana and later at Washington Natural. I dreamed one day I would be selected to attend, but it seemed management's idea was to use the trip as a reward for long and faithful service. Mike called me and said he wanted me to prepare a presentation for the next course. My topic was to be the "Economics of Gas Distribution."

Fine, I thought, I never was able to attend the course, but now I was going to give a half-day's presentation. I researched and worked my tail off getting ready for the presentation. I learned a lot about the energy business; the change from the age of wood to the age of coal to the age of oil and gas. I was disappointed to find that the people attending were not fast track caliber. They were those with some political skills of buttering up the top management. They could have cared less about the course material. They were in New York to have a good time and hitting all of the nightspots. Many had trouble staying awake in class. Welcome to the real world of management training!

Grace and I were invited to join a group of the S & W employees who lived on Long Island and got together once a month to play bridge. It was a fun and social group; Ham Baker from the Electric Department, Ross Parker, the Personnel Director and the rest from the Gas Department; George Carpenter, Gordon Jerauld, Stan Wood, and Fred Sullivan. It was good to meet and get to know the wives of everyone. Grace and I took a special liking to George Carpenter and his wife, Erdine. They were from Oklahoma. We were the only southerners; the rest were Yankees from New England.

I mentioned one evening to the Personnel Director I was thinking about joining the American Management Association. He said, "I wouldn't recommend it. It will just make you frustrated." I didn't understand until much later what he was talking about and went on to become a member. George was the Assistant Sponsor for Consumers Gas in Toronto and said he was going there with a team to conduct a "Paperwork Study." He invited me to go too. I had never been to Toronto and the job sounded interesting. We identified every paper form in use by the company and tried to identify its purpose. Next we followed the flow of each form from its origination through all hands to the final destination. At each step we interviewed the employee and determined if they looked at it and if they found it of any use. At the end of the study we eliminated most of the forms. When we gave our preliminary report, one of the file clerks broke down and started crying. When we asked "Why?" she said if we eliminated the forms she wouldn't have anything to do. The management assured her that she was not losing her job and would be given more productive work to do.

Mike called me one day and said they wanted me to take a trip to Germany for about ten days. I went to the library and tried to bone up on the geography of West Germany. I flew to Frankfurt where I was met by Frank McLain, the manager of the Shell/Esso office "STEGA," the "Study Group for Natural Gas Questions." McLain was an Englishman and the Shell representative in STEGA. He was multi-lingual and had an outgoing personality. I was to catch a train to Hamburg Saturday morning and would be met by the Esso representative, Hans Loblich. I was booked into the Atlantic Hotel.

Hans Loblich could not meet me on Saturday because he had been away from home and needed to spend the weekend with his wife and family. I was on my own for the weekend in Hamburg. Before leaving New York I bought a German/English phrase book to try to begin to learn some German. I checked into the hotel and took a tour of the city. Hamburg was a port city and during the war had been a major base for German Navy Submarines. The submarine pens were heavily bombed and the city was subjected to a terrible firebombing by both the U.S. and British air forces. The weather was nice and warm when I arrived and I enjoyed sitting at a sidewalk café with a glass of wine watching the people walk by.

Loblich met me Monday morning and we drove to Bielefeld in Nordrhein-Westphalia. We met the manager of the local gasworks and discussed their experience in changing from manufactured gas to natural gas. A small natural gas field was nearby. I was surprised to learn that Bielefeld was not far from Bunde, the small village my great-great grandfather immigrated from. We then drove on to Frankfurt where a meeting had been arranged with representatives of the German Gas Association. We were met by Frank McLain from STEGA. I gave a presentation about the experiences in North America in the change to natural gas.

Technical questions were raised about the distribution systems. The members seemed more concerned about the distribution system than the conversion of appliances. The meeting was conducted in German and it wasn't possible for me to get a good reading of how things were going. Loblich and McLain did the translating. "They are dubious that there are enough gas reserves in the Netherlands to serve the German gas market," said Loblich.

"You know the German Coal Cartel has sworn a blood oath to keep Dutch gas out of Germany," said McLain.

The meeting broke up and I was checked into a room at the Savigny Hotel. "We have arranged for you to have the use of a car and driver," said McLain. "He will meet you in the morning at nine a.m. and you can go wherever you want and do whatever you would like. We've booked a flight for you to go to The Hague the next day and meet with the staff of NAM Gas Export." I was on my own again and when I went to my room was surprised to find it did not have a private bathroom. There was a wash basin in the room, but there was one bath and toilet down the hall for the entire floor.

When the driver arrived, I asked him if he could take me to Bunde. I thought it would be interesting to see if I could find some distant relatives there. My uncle Marvin Kroeger did a lot of research about the Kroeger family ancestry and I had the benefit of the address of someone in Bunde. My driver worked for Deutche Shell and was bi-lingual. We drove to Bunde and he found the relatives' house. He went up to the door and knocked. I'm sure they were shocked to have a chauffeur tell them he had an American in the car that claimed to be a relative.

Eventually I was made welcome. They didn't speak English and I didn't speak German. The driver was very helpful in translating. Bunde was located in a farming community. The houses didn't have separate barns. The barns were just another room of the house for the animals. The woman of the house was a widow. Her husband had been killed in World War II on the Russian front. She appeared to be bitter with life. They took us to the cemetery where her husband was buried next to his father who had been killed on the Russian front during World War I. It seemed some things never change. It brought home the tragedy of war.

I flew to The Hague and took a taxi to Smitsvater 23, the NAM Gas Export office. It sat opposite a small canal. The meeting was with the shareholder's representatives for Esso and Shell; Doug Stewart & C. Schepers. They were interested in my impression of the German leaders and if I thought they might be interested in importing Dutch Gas. "Their main concern," I said, "is whether there are enough reserves in Groningen to meet their needs over a reasonable period of time. There will be no serious discussions until they are assured of the supply."

Next I met with the Manager of Stone & Webster Engineering Corp in Amsterdam. He said that he didn't think that the major gas company in West Germany, Ruhrgas, would buy Dutch gas. They were in bed with the Coal Cartel and would never change. I flew back to New York and wrote my report. I said there were very good prospects for S & W in Europe. The prospect for Dutch Gas presented a great opportunity for Conversions and Surveys to convert appliances to natural gas. I gave no further thought to what was going on with Shell and Esso. As far as I was concerned, I did my job. I was ready for my next assignment in North America.

18

The Best Are the First to Leave

It wasn't long after I returned from my trip to Germany that Mike called me into his office and said, "Shell wants you to go to the Netherlands on a six-month assignment. They want Grace and the family to go too and will give you the same overseas allowances as their employees. They would like for you to be there by September first. I wouldn't be surprised if they offered you a job." The last sentence didn't register with me. I was so surprised with the assignment. When I returned from Germany, I didn't have a good feeling about how the trip had gone. I got no response from my report to S & W.

This came to me as a bolt out of the blue. Soon, Grace and I were arranging to move short-term to Holland. It was good news that we would be treated to the same overseas benefits as the oil company's employees. We learned the pitfalls on our two-month assignment in New Zealand. We would be kept neutral on U.S. and Dutch taxes; our children's tuition would be paid at the International School. Since we would have our mortgage to pay in the U.S., we would receive a housing allowance and an overseas allowance of twenty-five percent over my base salary.

We found a temporary home for our dog, and our son said he wasn't going. Although he was going into the eighth grade, the freshman football coach wanted him to try out for the football team. He was informed that he didn't have a choice. We packed up enough clothes and personal possessions to last us for six months and were on our way. Flying into Schipol International airport we got our first taste of Dutch weather. It was dreary and cold! We were met by a Shell car and driver and taken to the Grand Central Hotel in The Hague.

Grace was surprised and pleased at the huge floral arrangement from NAM Gas Export waiting for us in our room. Arrangements were made in advance for our son and daughter to enroll in the International School. Since we left our car behind, we would be dependent upon the public transportation system, the trams (street cars). We ate all of our meals in the hotel restaurant. The staff got to know us well since we were steady customers. Every evening the children would order Peach Melba for desert. We learned to like it when we stayed at Korlevu Beach in Fiji. It was vanilla ice cream with half a peach and a nice sauce poured over it. In Holland it came with slagroom (whipped cream) stacked on top of it.

The children didn't like whipped cream and every night they scraped it off and did not eat it. One night I asked the Head Waiter for a favor. I said, "Would you ask the chef to please leave the slagroom off the Peach Melbas?" He said he would be pleased to do it. When they arrived, they were covered with slagroom. I asked the waiter about it. He said, "I talked with the chef but he said 'It's good for you!'" Every night the children had Peach Melbas. Every night they came loaded with slagroom. Every night the children scraped it off and didn't eat it. In Holland the Dutch know better than you do what's good for you.

We found the same attitude when we went to the doctor. He never answered questions. He was the doctor. He told you what to do and you were supposed to do what he told you! One evening we were bored and decided to try to see a movie. We didn't read Dutch but saw in the newspaper that the movie "PT-109" was being shown at one of the theatres. We took a taxi to the theatre and stood in line for tickets. There was a problem getting the tickets. I said, "It's okay, we'll pay full price for the children." No, that wasn't the problem. Finally someone in the line who spoke English said, "You don't understand. The children must be eighteen years old to see this movie. There's too much violence in it." We took a taxi back to the hotel. It was okay for the children to see movies with sex in them, but not any with violence. Prostitution was legal in Holland. Anyone could go into a bar and buy a drink if they had the money, regardless of their age, but no films with physical violence.

The Shell Office Manager showed me my office on the second floor. "Is everything satisfactory?" he asked. I knew immediately how I fit into the organization chart. My desk was metal, the carpet and drapes were nice, but there was no small table or chairs for visitors. The telephone was plain without any buttons to transfer calls. I was ranked as a technologist, not as a manager. I knew from Shell Centre in Wellington how the amenities worked. The office was Shell standard issue. If I had been a manager, my furniture would have been made of polished wood and my telephone would have had transfer buttons. "There's only one thing I'm interested in," I told the office manager.

"What's that?" he asked.

"The numbers on my paycheck," I replied. He shook his head in disbelief and walked away. "*Crazy American,*" I'm sure he was thinking.

I was introduced to the staff in the office. My immediate boss was Gerry Laufs, Manager of Planning and Analysis from Standard Oil of New Jersey in New York. Jack Windham was Manager of Pipeline Design and Construction from Humble Oil in Houston. My technology counterpart was Tommy Harmsworth from Shell International in London. The office manager immediately started looking to help us find an apartment. After looking at several, we settled on a small one in the Oranje Flats in Scheveningen. It was tiny with one bedroom, a living room, a small room which we converted into a bedroom with bunk beds for the children. The refrigerator was so small that all it would hold was a liter of milk. We found it was possible to rent a larger fridge, which we put in the hall. Scheveningen was a summer North Sea resort. We were on the fifth floor and looked out at the water and the pier, which was lined with small shops.

The summer season was over when we arrived and we wondered why anyone would come there for holiday. The water in the North Sea was cold and the wind was even colder. We soon learned if we listened on the radio to the weather report for Southern England we would have the same in The Hague in a day or two. Soon, we were settled in and trying to adjust to living in a foreign land. The currency was Dutch Guilders. We had to make a mental conversion into dollars in order to get a handle on how prices compared. There were small shops close by for grocery shopping, a bakery for bread, a butcher for meat, a green grocer for vegetables, and a dairy shop for milk, butter, and cheese. You provided your own carry bag to take things home because the shops didn't provide shopping bags.

The first big problem came when we went to the bank to set up a bank account. My work was going to be in Brussels. I would be home only on weekends. Grace would have to pay the bills just like she had been doing in New York. The manager of the bank said that Grace couldn't write checks. In the Netherlands only men wrote the checks. We ended up in the office of the bank president. "The only woman in this country who can write a check is Queen Juliana," he said.

"Well," I said, "if my wife doesn't write the checks, our rent and all of our bills will not get paid because I will not be here to do it."

Finally after a long conversation, he said, "All right, it's highly unusual but because you are Americans we will make an exception to our policy. We will allow your wife to write checks."

From then on any time Grace went into the bank, everything came to a halt. You could almost hear everyone whispering, "There's that woman who is allowed to write checks!" It became clear that the joint venture arrangement between Shell and Esso was still evolving. In the beginning my business card said "NAM Gas Export." But a new plaque went up by the door that read "International Gas Transport." The staffing started to shift and before long my card read IGTM. NAM became the Shell operating company and IGTM became the Esso operation. It was interesting because in North American the oil and gas producers were not allowed to own the pipeline transportation companies. This was Europe and not the United States!

Soon Tommy Harmsworth and I were going to the airport and flying to Brussels. We were with a team of Belgians from our field office negotiating for the export of Dutch gas to Belgium. Tommy and I hit it off immediately. He was a graduate of the Royal College of Technology in England. He had served in the Royal Navy on a Destroyer during World War II. We had much in common. His gas experience was in Liquefied Petroleum Gas utilization in appliance operations. He was a technologist and content knowing he had not attended Oxford or Cambridge, which were the training grounds for managers. We were different in this respect. I believed one day I was going to be in management. The Shell International system was paternalistic. They took care of their employees almost from cradle to grave. They provided recreational facilities for their employees. They provided social activities, medical facilities, and a commissary to buy food and all of the necessities of life. There was no need to worry. You did your job and the company took care of you.

Tommy was a great help to me. He was multilingual in French and German. He advised me on the cultural differences between the different countries. The manager of our Field Office in Brussels was J. DeHousse with Technical and Regional Manager L. Carlier. On September 16, 1963 I made a presentation at a meeting of all the Belgian gas transport and distribution firms arranged by the Federation de l'Industrie du Gaz (FIGAZ), which gave facts about the conversion of public distribution grids and domestic appliances to natural gas.

Later in meetings I sat on the edge of my chair straining to try and recognize a word of French. Because of my three years of Latin, I could read a lot of signs, but the pronunciation in French wasn't phonetic. After a long discussion in a meeting I would say, "What did they say?" and be told, "They said no." It seemed to me the Belgians were more interested in lunch than in negotiating a contract. We would get in their Renault cars and it was like the Grand Prix to see who could get to the restaurant first. Once there, it was a four-course lunch with a different wine with each course. Then it was brandy and cigars. After that it was time to knock off and go back to our offices.

Tommy and I soon learned that portal-to-portal we could get to Brussels better by taking the Trans European Express train. There was no hassle getting to and from the airport. We could eat a meal in the dining car, relax, and read a book along the way. Tommy loved history and said, "You have to understand the Belgians. They have been at the crossroads of almost every war in Europe. They have been over-run and occupied by all kinds of invaders. Because of their history, they are very slow to do anything. You can be assured they are tough in business because they have been through the wringer so many times."

I didn't see much of Brussels. I knew the way from the rail station to the hotel, from the hotel to the office and back. Grace took a trip to Brussels one weekend with a group from the American Women's Club and saw more of Brussels than I did in three months. When we finally began to show dissatisfaction with the progress, we were told, "What's the problem? The last contract took us five years." I learned that time was of less importance than in the United States. In countries where it took centuries to build a cathedral, five years was the bat of an eyelash.

On December 6, 1963 I received a letter from Gird Sottorf, Manager of the STEGA office in Frankfurt saying that they had been approached by the German Gas Industry asking if a paper could be presented on natural gas problems at the annual meeting in Manheim in May 1964. He asked if I could prepare the paper and Hans Loblich would make the presentation in German. I agreed to do it. It was later in December 1963 when I got a call from Mike Sonney in New York. "Your mother is seriously ill and your aunt called and said she thought you should come home. They don't know if your mother is going to make it." Over the years my mother had not been in good health. She had been a diabetic for quite some time and developed a heart condition.

It was mid-winter and snow was on the ground in Holland. The canals were frozen and Dutch children were skating on the ice like Hans Brinker. I caught a Pan American flight to New York and American Airlines to Chicago. I got caught in a snowstorm and finally made it to Kansas City. I took the first train to Trenton and my dad was waiting at the Railroad Station for me. I don't know how he knew when I would arrive, but I guess having worked on the railroad, he knew the train schedules.

After I had time to rest up we went to the hospital to see my mother. She didn't look good but I tried to cheer her up by telling her that as soon as she got better she would be going home. Two days later I woke up in the morning to find dad was not home. My aunt called me and said I needed to get to the hospital as soon as possible. Mom had taken a turn for the worse. I got a taxi and rushed to the hospital only to see her die. I felt bad because I never was able to tell her how much I loved her in spite of our differences over religion. I felt bad for dad, because he was taking it badly. I tried to comfort him as much as I could. It wasn't easy because I never really got to know him. He had worked at night and then had to go away from home on gas jobs to make ends meet.

I stayed for the funeral, but soon had to get back on the train, catch a plane from Kansas City directly to New York and then on to Amsterdam. With the agreement signed with Distrigaz, it was time to turn our thoughts to Germany. Gerry Laufs said, "The Dutch municipalities have made a forecast of operation for a typical gas operation of twenty thousand customers. They call this a 'Public Distribution Study.' Take this, analyze it, and see if it has any possibilities for use in Germany."

It was a lot of number crunching. Finally, Tommy said, "I know a computer programmer in Royal Dutch Shell. If you could write out the step-by-step logic I think I could get it programmed for the IBM 650 computer. (This was before digital computers and operated on punch cards.) It could save us a lot of time." We did it and before long we were getting a one-day turn around at the Shell Computer Center for our studies. We replicated the work done by manual calculations and discovered three minor arithmetical errors in the Dutch study. Soon, Tommy and I started going to Germany to work. He took me to Frankfurt and I met all of the STEGA staff. Hans Loblich was the new manager, with Economist Dr. Dobmeir, Esso A.G. Engineer, Herbert Wittorff, and Otto Baeder, an engineer from Deutche Shell.

Thyssengas, a German Gas Company near the Dutch border at Duisborg-Hamborn, looked like a good place to start exporting gas to Germany. There was the possibility they might agree to do a joint Public Distribution Study for their gas operations. The problem was getting the necessary information for the capital costs of converting their distribution system and appliances to operate on natural gas. On May 6th 1964 a memo was sent to the Staff of NAM/IGTM congratulating everyone on their work leading to the signing of a letter of intent with Distrigaz for the supply of Dutch gas to Belgium. It was about this time I learned the S & W Assistant Manager of the Gas Department was moving to Amsterdam. Engineering Corporation was providing him with a small office and he was starting to talk to Distrigaz about contracts for Conversions and Surveys to convert appliances to operate on natural gas.

It's just like Seattle, I thought. *I've blazed the trail at New Zealand, and here in Europe. Now that it looks good someone else is coming to take charge.* Gerry Laufs called me in and said, "Before long your six-month assignment will be up. Would you consider coming to work for us? You could go on Esso's payroll since we are the U.S. based company."

"I don't know," I said. "I would have to think about it." The Engineering Corporation Manager in Amsterdam called me and said that Luke Storrs was on a world tour and would be staying at the Rotterdam Hilton. I called and made an appointment to see him after dinner.

We met in the cocktail lounge. After exchanging pleasantries, I said, "Luke, I have a problem. Esso has offered me a job."

"I'm not getting into a bidding war with the oil companies," he said.

"No, Luke you don't understand. I have a long-standing relationship with you and Stone & Webster I only want to know what my future is with the company."

"I can't make you any promises," he said. "I can't be sure what *my* future is going to be. Whitney Stone could tell me tomorrow that I'm no longer president."

"Can you tell me if I will be going back to New York, or will I be staying here in Europe?"

"You will be staying here in Europe," he said.

"Luke, the thing that bothers me is that I have seen people come and go at Stone & Webster. In my judgment, it's the best that have left."

He looked at me and said, "Carroll, it's been going on as long as I can remember and it's not ever going to change." He said he had to catch an early morning flight so we said goodbye.

I think he knew when I left what my decision would be. It was clear to me what my future was going to be. I would be doing all of the work and someone else would be getting the credit. I didn't like giving up my nineteen years of affiliation with S & W, but I had to think about my family responsibilities. Before long my children would be ready to go to college. We had not been able to save anything to pay their tuition and expenses. I was making more money now with Standard Oil of New Jersey than I had ever made. I would be jumping off a cliff again, but I was confident I could do the job.

The next morning I went into Gerry Lauf's office and told him I had decided to stay on. He shook my hand and congratulated me. "You will never regret your decision," he said "Welcome to the Jersey family!" I was committed to work overseas for a long time, maybe until I retired. I had come a long way from Trenton, Missouri! When the best people in a company leave, over time the company is bound to go downhill. That leaves only the "caretakers" who do not want to change and are content to do what they always have done. It may take some time but eventually the "dead wood" must be removed by a "business surgeon" or a "business mortician" will be required.

19

The Dangers of Doing a Good Job

It was March 1964. I wrote my letter of resignation to Stone & Webster and sent it to Luke Storrs in New York. Earlier I met with Doug Stewart and he gave me good advice of what to ask for in joining Standard Oil. He said the most they could give me in a raise in salary was fifty percent. That would take me to eighteen thousand dollars a year. I would continue to receive all of the benefits I had been getting, but I should ask for four weeks of vacation a year, home leave for me and my family to return to my point of origin in the United State once a year. He said not to feel I had to use New York as my point of origin, to make my hometown where I grew up my point of origin. I didn't want a repeat of the problem we had selling our house in Seattle. The company would have the house appraised, buy it from us, and then resell it.

As soon as I made my change, I learned a lot of what had been going on behind the scenes over the last two years. In 1962 when Roy Goddin and I were sent to New Zealand, a team of two Stone & Webster vice presidents went to the Netherlands at the request of Standard Oil. After two days they were told they might as well go back to New York, because they weren't being helpful. Their attitude was "Just turn everything over to us. We will design and build the pipelines for you and we will convert all of the appliances to operate on natural gas." No wonder I received such a cold reception when I returned from New Zealand. Now it was clear why my report took six months to get out of the nineteenth floor.

To make matters worse, when Shell ask for me to go to the Hague on a six-month assignment, they were told, "Kroeger is busy, but we have other consultants we can send." Shell responded, "If we can't have Kroeger, we don't want anyone else." A short time later we received word that Joe Ferreni, a longtime friend of my dad from conversion days, was in the hospital in Amsterdam. He had appendicitis and had an appendectomy. We went to visit him and he was pleased to see us. "Carroll, you don't know how relieved everyone was when they heard that you were leaving," he said. Now I knew what had been going on behind my back. I had not been concerned with the internal politics. I was just trying to do a good job.

Looking back it reminds me of a lecture I gave my students at Belmont about "The Danger of Doing a Good Job." The first thing that can happen is you may inadvertently make others look bad. It happened at "Conversions and Surveys" when the Union Steward told me I was doing too much work. I wasn't trying to make anyone look bad; I was just trying to do a good job! I wasn't trying to make anyone look bad at Stone and Webster. How was I to know the two vice presidents had been sent home from Europe by Esso in 1962 when I was in New Zealand? The second thing that can happen to you is you can make yourself indispensable. If you do a job too well, there may not be anyone to replace you if another opportunity comes along. If you are indispensable, you may never be told of the opportunity like I was in New York. Fortunately for me, Shell International said, "If we can't have Kroeger, we don't want anyone."

I'm reminded of an event that happened on the Navy ship I served on during the Korean Conflict. As Administrative Officer, I was the first to see every communication that came on the ship. One day we received a dispatch from the Navy Bureau of Personnel. A new unit was being formed at White Sands, New Mexico. (The Navy was starting to develop a guided missile program.) The dispatch requested all ships and stations to review their compliments and if there were any men who were experienced First Class Electronics Mates to send their names to Washington immediately. We had such a man and I prepared a response and took it to the Captain for approval. He handed it back to me and said, "Don't send it."

I said, "But Captain BuPers says it's mandatory."

"I don't care," the Captain said. "He's the only man on the ship who can fix the radar!" The man never knew about the opportunity that was taken away from him. There's only one way to keep from becoming indispensable. Always bring along and train someone who can replace you. That takes a lot of self-confidence. Most people are afraid of someone taking their place. Things on the home front were progressing. Our son and daughter went through a rough time when they started school. Our son, Carroll, going into the eighth grade, was thrown into French, Dutch, and Latin classes. We were told our daughter, Sheryl, who was going into the fifth grade, was behind two years in German and three years in French. In Europe you start foreign language at an early age. But that's the easiest time to learn a language

We needed to find a house before our furniture arrived and Grace was resourceful. At an American Woman's Club meeting she was told someone had a card table for sale. She went to look at it in Wassanar (an exclusive suburb of The Hague). When she arrived, she learned it was the home of the Air Attaché at the American Embassy. She bought the table and chairs, and said to the woman, "Are you moving?" She could tell from the expression she had stumbled on to something. "Yes," the woman said, "but we are sub-leasing it to a new person being transferred in."

Grace immediately told the real estate agent we were working with and the agent said, "She can't sub-lease that house. I have the agreement with the owner." We got the house. It was called a "Semi-Villa." The interior was painted a terrible "Kelly Green" throughout. We got permission to paint it white to lighten it up. The problem came with the Dutch painters. They said, "It's summer, we only paint the outside of houses in the summer. We paint the inside of houses in the winter." Our house was next door to the Ambassador from Venezuela. We surprised everyone in the neighborhood with our ingenuity. We bought paint and in American fashion did it ourselves. We flew back to the States, packed up all of our household effects, and prepared to begin a prolonged life abroad. The major problem came with finding a home for our dog. He was like a member of the family but we couldn't see subjecting him to six months in quarantine. Finally we found a nice family that would love him.

We said "goodbye" to our friends and neighbors and flew back to Europe. Our furniture and car arrived safely and we began to settle in. When I was finishing the paperwork to go to work with Jersey, Doug called me in his office. "There is a non-denominational English-speaking church here that you and Grace should attend. You can make a lot of good business contacts there." I thanked him but ignored his suggestion. I've always considered religion a personal matter, not to use to find good business contacts.

Grace and I were married in the Episcopal Church and attended it in Rhode Island, Indiana, Washington State, and on Long Island. It was the one stable thing we could count on wherever we went. The service was the same. We felt right at home in St. Mark's Anglican Church in Wellington, New Zealand and weren't about to change now. We found the St. John's & St. Phillip's Anglican Church in the Hague. It had an interesting congregation. Most of the diplomats from all of the Commonwealth Countries attended services there. We quickly made friends with a couple from South Africa whose husband worked in the Refinery for Royal Dutch Shell.

There was one American Family from Houston—the Jefferys. I was surprised to learn that Jean had graduated from Rice in 1945 and was a friend of Louise Loose. Her husband Jeff was a University of Texas graduate and worked for "Pipeline Technologists." At a coffee hour following the service one Sunday I mentioned that our son was having problems with his French class. A man overheard the conversation and introduced himself. "I'm Nick. I work for Hercules Powder Company, a subsidiary of DuPont. I used to teach at the Air Force Foreign Language School in Colorado Springs," he said. "I'd be happy to tutor your son in French on Sunday afternoons if you would like." That was the beginning of an interesting friendship.

On most Sunday afternoons we would drop our son off and Nick would tutor him. Nick sang in the choir, so he was there almost every Sunday. Our son said, "It's interesting. They have a German Shepherd dog who only takes commands from Nick in Russian!" Later Nick told me he had grown up in Latvia. His family had immigrated to Paris. He was multilingual. He also said he had to be careful when he traveled never to get near the Eastern Sector of Germany because he would be in trouble if his plane was diverted into any of the Eastern Bloc Countries.

At the time I didn't think about what Nick told me. Years later we learned what it meant. When the Rector, Reverend Wyneburn, found out I had been a Lay Reader, it wasn't long before he had me licensed and I became his Lay Assistant. Life in Holland was different. We went with the best of intentions. We were not going to be "ugly Americans." We would learn to speak Dutch and try to fit in and live like the Dutch just as we had tried to live like New Zealanders. However, the Dutch had other ideas. They either answered us in English or laughed at us when we tried to speak Dutch. It is a very guttural sounding language. My German colleague, Otto Baeder, once told me, "Dutch isn't a language, it's a throat disease!"

There were many other adjustments. Most of the housing was owned by the government and leased as apartments. You had to obtain a "Living Permit" from a Government Bureau in order to rent a house or apartment. The size of what you were allowed to live in depended upon the number of people in your family. In order to buy a radio you had to obtain a permit and pay a government tax on it once a year. The government owned and operated all of the radio stations. We were surprised to learn that there was a "pirate" radio station on a ship in the North Sea that operated as a commercial station and played American and English pop songs.

There were other things to get used to. The culture was completely different. In commercial transactions you had better know how to count your change. Everyone was fair game, even the children. The general attitude of the Dutch was that all Americans were wealthy. We told everyone, "We're not tourists, we live here!" It was an adjustment to move from a culture where you assumed that everyone was trustworthy until they proved otherwise, to one where you had to assume everyone was going to try to cheat you. The attitude was "If I can cheat you, I'm more clever than you are. Therefore, I'm a better person."

It was a game; if you caught someone in a lie, they smiled and moved on. They didn't play football in the International School, so our son tried out for the Basketball team. He lettered as a freshman on the varsity team, which won the European tournament at Leon, France. When school was out, he was invited to go back and play baseball with the "Eagles" team on Long Island, which he played on before. The coach said he could stay with him for the summer. We insisted on paying for his room and board. The team was undefeated, not losing a single game during the season. Carroll was a pitcher and played third base. Sheryl also was taking French at school. One evening at dinner I asked how it was going. She pointed to a book. "It's stupid! The Little Black Cat. What good is that if I'm in Paris and need to find the bathroom?"

She was right. I gave up trying to learn Dutch. When I started to work in Germany, Tommy Harmsworth went with me the first six months. After that I was on my own. I tried taking Berlitz lessons. Like Sheryl I was frustrated. The lessons were full of idiot words like blackboard, pencil, chalk, and teacher. I needed to know how to tell the taxi driver to take me to the hotel and ask how much the fare was before I got in so I wouldn't be cheated! There was a saving grace. From the beginning, unlike in Belgium, I began to recognize some words. I found my phrase book invaluable and my German colleagues helpful. They would tell me my German was improving and not laugh at me. Age thirty-seven is not the best time to start trying to learn a foreign language.

I did learn some important things. English is an impossible language. We have many words that have more than one meaning. When we use them, we assume others know which meaning we are using. This was brought home to me when I received a telephone call from Otto. "We got your memo about the flowers," he chuckled. I had a wonderful Dutch secretary who was multilingual. I would write a memo to Germany in English and she would translate it into German and I would sign it and send it off. The memo was about the manufactured gas plants in the Ruhr area. What I really meant was the manufactured gas factories. She translated the word "plants" to mean flowers.

One of the first German phrases I learned was "Speak slowly please." From that time on, I tried to use only words that had one meaning and when I spoke in English I spoke slowly and tried to enunciate clearly. Eventually my German friends said, "Carroll, don't worry about speaking German. We can understand you when you speak English." By that time I had learned enough German I could understand them. We held interesting conversation with them speaking to me in German and me answering them back in English. More important we had established a bond of trust!

The secret to getting along in a foreign country is: first realize you are a guest in their country and conduct yourself as a guest should. It doesn't matter what you did back home or what the rules or laws were there. As I was soundly reminded in negotiations one time, "This is Hamburg, not New York!" Second, don't expect everyone to speak English (even if they can). When you are living or working in their country, make an effort to learn the language. They will not expect you to become completely fluent, but they will appreciate you making the effort. Third, learn the customs and traditions. You can save yourself much embarrassment by doing so. Remember, just because you think nobody knows you is no excuse to make a fool of yourself.

20

A Plan for the Change to Natural Gas in Germany

As Yogi Berra said, "It was déjà vu all over again!" It was the same as at Blackstone Valley Gas & Electric and Washington Natural Gas. Esso and Shell were in competition with each other all over the world. In the Netherlands they were strange bedfellows in a joint venture where they were supposed to work together. I was an outsider parachuted into their midst. They did not talk much to each other but they would talk with me. For people with Shell, it was easier. They knew what I had done in New Zealand. In fact, they were responsible for me being here; The Esso people were a little more wary. I hadn't come up through the ranks of training in the Bay Way, New Jersey Refinery.

It was easier in Germany, too. Perhaps it was because I had a German name. At least it didn't hurt. They were closer to the problems and they needed all the help they could get. They knew how to sell petrol and oil to industries but natural gas and dealing with public utilities was a different ball game. They welcomed me because I could answer the questions thrown at them by the engineers in the Gas Works. These engineers weren't interested in changing to natural gas operations. They liked things the way they were. They were experts in making gas from coal and selling the by-products, coke and chemicals. During the war they had made synthetic gasoline from coal. They only asked questions to throw up roadblocks. It was an education for me. I had to rethink my whole career experience because of their questions. Americans are impatient. If we have a problem, we find a solution and move on.

When I started talking about how we solved the problems, the first question was "Why did you do it that way? What were the alternatives? Why was that the best way to do it?" In the United States, engineering schools taught a course called "Engineering Economics." The solution had to be economically feasible in addition to being technically feasible. When I started to talk about cost effectiveness, I was stopped. "You'll have to talk with the economists about that," the engineers said. "We only deal with the technical solutions." Another problem emerged which was difficult for me to understand. The German engineers were mostly concerned with safety. They said all pipes and meters would have to be replaced with new ones. I knew this would make the change prohibitive. They weren't interested that none had been replaced in the United States and Canada.

Once again I was told, "This is Germany, not North America!" It was only when I was discussing this with a Dutch lawyer I began to understand what was going on. "We have a different legal system over here," he said. "It's based upon the 'Napoleonic Code.' We only have Criminal Negligence. If there is an accident, the person in charge of safety goes to prison." The sun broke through; these guys weren't trying to throw up roadblocks. They were trying to protect their rear ends. They didn't want to go to jail! Now that I knew where they were coming from, I could begin to try to find a solution to the problems. My experience was okay, but now I would have to rethink the problems and be innovative.

The German team at STEGA in Frankfurt was fun to work with. They worked hard, but they played hard. We started at eight in the morning, sent out for sandwiches, had a working lunch, and kept going to eight at night. On one of my first visits, at eight o'clock one night, Hans Loblich said, "Have you ever been to a wine cellar?" When I said "No," he insisted we do that before going out for dinner. We descended into a wine cellar, sat down at a table with some bread and cheese, and looked at the place mats. They were maps of the Rhine and Mosel Rivers with all of the vineyards plotted on the maps. "We will start here," said Hans, pointing at a place at the beginning of the Rhine. Having never been to a wine tasting, I assumed we would take a sip of wine from each vineyard. Instead we had a bottle from each vineyard, stopping to clear our palate with some bread and cheese before moving on down the river. We never went for dinner that evening, but we traveled all the way down the Rhine. I learned the game in Germany was to see if they could drink me under the table.

Fortunately I passed the test. I didn't go under the table and I learned something important about German wines. I liked them! Gird Sortoff left STEGA and went back to Deutche Shell about the time I left Stone & Webster. Hans Loblich became the manager of the office. The team found that there might be a possibility of doing a joint study with Thyssengas at Duisborg-Hamborn. This company was located near the Dutch border in the Ruhr valley. As soon as we started working there, I got an understanding of why some Germans thought going to Scheveningen beach and swimming in the North Sea was a great holiday. If environmentalists think the air is polluted here, they should have seen the Ruhr valley! The air was full of contaminants from the burning and steaming of coal and the buildings were blackened by the smoke. The game was we would provide the know-how to do the study and they would provide the cost elements.

The hidden agenda was for us to try to find the maximum price they could afford to pay for Dutch gas. One study was to forecast their operations if they continued on manufactured gas and another to show results if they converted to natural gas. Hopefully the comparison would show the benefits of making the change. It soon became apparent they were bent on making the costs as high as possible. One of my jobs was to check if they were reasonable. When it came to costs of new facilities, it was the job of Dr. Dobmeir and Otto Baeder to check with suppliers as to prices, etc. Every day when we would catch them in lies, they would smile and we would move on to the next item. During this time I was writing the paper to be presented at Manheim. It was an interesting exercise. At Stone and Webster everything was departmentalized. We would determine the quantities of gas used by customer appliances and combine them into daily and monthly quantities; the Tariff Department would develop revenues from our quantities and the Accounting Department would develop a financial statement.

All of a sudden I was doing it all. There was no "Storehouse of Knowledge!" For the first time, I was putting all of the pieces together and seeing the big picture. It was a good thing I learned how to learn on my own in the Navy program. I developed a life cycle for a gas distribution company. After I turned the draft of the paper over to Hans Loblich, the team read it, we made corrections, it was translated into German, and Hans said, "You have written the Bible for the Change to Natural Gas in Germany." The paper was presented at the annual meeting in Manheim on May 14,1964 after I left Stone & Webster.

It probably was a good thing. It would have taken six months to get it approved by the V.P.s on the nineteenth floor and they probably would have said, "You can't say that in the paper." Hans read the paper in German as I stood at his side. All of the objections were answered during the discussion period. At the end, the chairman thanked me profusely and presented me with three bottles of the finest German wines. A short time later the paper was published in the Das Gas-und Wasserfach magazine and I got a letter of thanks from the President of the DVGW saying that the labor leaders of the gas supply concerns were present and found it of great interest. I also received a letter from the General Secretary of the Association Royale des Gaziers Belges (Belgium Gas Industry) saying he was delighted to have met me in Manheim and was going to publish a French translation of my paper in their Revue Generale du Gaz.

It wasn't long after that Conversions & Surveys was in Belgium with a contract with Distrigaz for the conversion of the Belgian gas appliances. Apparently my work helped them get the business I had predicted possible in both New Zealand and Belgium. Looking back, I made the right decision. For the first time we weren't living from paycheck to paycheck. We were able to put aside enough that the college education of our children was assured. The company had an incentive plan for saving. If you put in five percent of your salary into company stock, Esso would match it with another five percent.

For the first time in our married life we were able to take nice vacations. At Christmas 1963 we went skiing at Zell am Zee in Austria and in 1964 to Davos in Switzerland. I found the stress of my job such that I needed time off about every six months to unwind. Since the children always had a spring break at Easter, it was a good time for the family to take a trip somewhere interesting. Our son always elected to take a school trip and go skiing. He became an expert with experience on the slopes of Austria, Switzerland, Norway, and Italy. In 1964 we went to Berlin behind the Iron Curtain. We flew into Templehof Aerodrome, stayed at the Berlin Hilton, saw "The Wall," crossed through "Checkpoint Charlie," and took a tour of East Berlin.

Another time the entire family went on a school tour to Athens, Greece, where we saw the real Parthenon on the Acropolis, visited the ruins of Corinth where St. Paul preached and wrote his epistles to the

Corinthians, and visited Delphi, the site of the Oracle of Pythia. We flew to Crete and walked the streets of Knossos where Minoan men and women lived two thousand years before Christ. We spent a week in Israel. We stayed in Youth Camps and Kibbutz's, toured the Holy Land from the Lebanon border on the north to Tel Aviv, then to Jerusalem. We ate camel burgers in the desert and were fortunate to take a trip through the Negev to Beersheba and had a memorable audience with the first Chancellor of Israel, David Ben Gurion.

My concern for the future of Stone & Webster Service Corporation was verified. The Securities Corporation was the first to go. When I asked how the company arrived at the position of having so many annual retainer clients, someone should have listened. There was a reason the list was shrinking. Stone & Webster was founded in the 1880s as electrical engineering was emerging as a new field. The founders graduated from MIT and formed the company. They started out small doing feasibility studies and gradually moved into the design and construction of electric generating plants. By 1920 the company was managing fifty-nine utility companies in eighteen states and in 1927 merged with an investment company to form the Securities Corporation. In 1930 S & W became a holding company.

When the Federal Holding Company Act was passed, the company was forced to divest itself of public utility ownerships. When the utilities were spun off, a new subsidiary, the Service Corporation, was formed and received retainer contracts for management assistance to the utilities. The same process took place with two other competing firms, Ebasco Services and Commonwealth Services. These three groups controlled the major portion of the gas and electric utilities in the United States. In 1942 the Engineering Corporation became the contractor for the Manhattan Project during World War II, constructing the electromagnetic separation plant and the city of Oak Ridge, Tennessee.

Following the war the big and little inch oil product pipelines from the Southwest to the East coast were transformed into natural gas pipelines, Transcontinental and Tennessee Gas Transmission. Stone & Webster helped finance the change and became the largest shareholder of Tennessee Gas Transmission. Looking back, it's clear what was taking place. S & W had been accustomed to taking engineering contracts during the war on a cost plus basis. After the war they expected to continue doing so. However, competition was developing, such as Bechtel and Brown & Root. These firms, based in Texas, were full of young, aggressive engineers who had no qualms in taking risks and bidding jobs on a firm price basis.

As new managements came to power in the utilities, they became more independent and questioned the value of the services they were receiving for the annual retainer fees they were paying. The utilities were also finding competing stock brokers to assist in the financing of their new stock and bond offerings. When I was at 90 Broad Street, things were starting to come apart at the seams, but the management was not willing to change and look for new business. New business consulting firms were being formed by a new type of consultants coming out of the academic institutions like the Harvard Business School.

It wasn't long before Whitney Stone sold the building at 90 Broad Street in Manhattan. Service Corporation leased office space and the list of annual clients continued to decline. Service Corporation eventually closed its doors and went out of business. As Luke Storrs said, the best people were always leaving and he saw no reason things were going to change. The Engineering Corporation filed for bankruptcy in 2000.

The staff of the Gas Department slowly moved out into the operating companies; George Carpenter became President of Consumer's Gas in Toronto, Jim Thorpe replaced Bill Woods as President at Washington Natural when he retired, Gordon Jerauld became Vice President of the Gas Company in West Palm Beach, Florida and Fred Sullivan joined Long Island Lighting as a Vice President. It does not give me pleasure to look back at what happened. I may have been a prophet whose predictions were ignored. Prophets are not well received because their predictions do not tell people in positions of responsibility what they want to hear. Usually they fall on deaf ears because nobody wants to change. It's too easy to take the path of least resistance. As Mr. Cullison, president of Central Indiana Gas, once told me, "I've found most problems solve themselves if you wait long enough." Being young and brash, I responded, "Yes, and you can find yourself out of business."

21

An Explosion Takes Four Lives in Austria

Things were changing in The Hague. Personnel began turning over. Doug Stewart left and was replaced by Dick Marriner. They were completely different personalities. Whereas Doug had been a boisterous Texan, Dick was a mild-mannered mid-westerner. Dick was one of the new breed starting to infiltrate the Esso ranks. He wasn't a Chemical Engineer but a Harvard Business School MBA. Things were happening in Shell as well. Tommy Harmsworth was transferred back to Shell Centre in London and was replaced by Otto Baeder from STEGA. I began to learn more about the Esso organization. The shareholder's representative, and a Director of Esso Nederlands, was Don Cox, an American. John Chalsty was his assistant. John was a Mining Engineer from South Africa but also was a Harvard MBA. Cox was not married and had no family. The rumor mill said he was married to Standard Oil of New Jersey. He lived in the Des Indies Hotel and worked seven days a week. He made life miserable for Gerry Laufs calling him at all hours of the day or night, asking questions regardless of whether it was Saturday or Sunday.

Gerry apparently thought this was the business model for success and began to follow the Cox model, calling me at night and on Sundays. Cox was a workaholic so Jerry became a workaholic. As soon as we would get a job done, Gerry would think up a lot of other things that had to be done ASAP. It wasn't long before we were staying longer at night. Soon it was necessary to go into the office on Saturdays. Gerry always had more and more for us to do. One Saturday Schepers happened by the office. "What the hell is going on?" he asked. When told, he said, "Either we don't have enough people to do the work, or we're doing things that aren't necessary. Everybody go home and I don't want to see anyone in here again on the weekend!" Apparently there was a different philosophy about work in Shell than in Esso. We never worked on Saturday again and somehow the necessary work got done. Don Cox said he would hire only those he thought had the potential to one day sit on the Jersey Board of Directors. Several years later he made it to the board. For Gerry Laufs, who was married with two daughters, it was another story.

The negotiations with the staff of Thyssengas were grueling. We spent each day haggling over the costs of new gas meters, gas regulators, installation of pipe in the street, from the street to the building, the cost of installation and testing pipe in the houses, and the cost of replacing the burners on each type of gas appliance: stove, water heater, etc. Because natural gas did not contain the illuminants of manufactured gas, all gas streetlights would have to be replaced with electric. This was Germany, not the United States!

A break came for Esso and Shell. The major shareholder of Thyssengas developed a money problem. He met a young woman while skiing in Switzerland at St. Moritz and fell in love. The only problem was that he was already married! His wife sued for divorce and he needed money for the settlement. When Esso and Shell learned of his problem, they began to discuss buying his shareholding. It was one way to break the hold of the German Coal Cartel. By this time our joint study was almost completed and NAM and IGTM knew what the assets of Thyssengas were worth.

At the same time, as the work was going on with Thyssengas, STEGA started talking with the Stadtwerke Dusseldorf. The municipality agreed to do a joint study and the work began. Dusseldorf was different than Duisborg-Hamborn. Dusseldorf was called the Paris of Germany. Its main boulevard Koenigsalle was known as the fashionable shopping center of the country with sidewalk cafes. But more importantly, it was the location of the headquarters of all the major German industrial coal, steel, and chemical companies. The first morning we met in the board room of the Stadtwerke. It was impressive with magnificent wood paneling and a huge long table. We met the Director of Public Works, Dr. Paul Schenk, and his staff. The

Director of the Gasworks was out of the movies, with a typical Prussian appearance, crew cut hair, and even a dueling scar on his cheek. We agreed on the procedure. We would make a ten-year forecast of operations from 1965 to 1975. The municipality would provide operating data for the past five years 1960 to 1964 as a basis for the forecast.

The first study would be for a continuation of their operations on coal gas. The second study would be for operations with imported Dutch natural gas. It required the collection of a mass of data, verification, and number crunching. We had just started discussion when the director looked at me and said in German, "Would you like to have something to drink?" Thinking a cup of coffee or cola would be nice, I replied, "Ja, bitte." "Yes, Thanks."

Everything came to a halt. A cabinet was opened, revealing a large, well-stocked bar. "You must try one of our favorite regional drinks," I was told. "It's called 'Iron and Steel.'" I thought, *Here we go, the game begins!* It turned out that "Iron and Steel" was a mixture of German champagne and orange juice. I could see it had dangerous complications. It went down smoothly, but had a high alcohol content. The game started, but they had it down to science. The custom was for the host to look you in the eye and say "Prosit." You looked back and said "Prosit" and quaffed down the contents of your glass. The only problem was every time I emptied my glass, another person was looking at me, saying, "Prosit." It was clear what was going on. They were double teaming me.

They weren't matching me individually drink for drink. They were taking turns to see if they could drink me under the table. When we had gone through their entire team and I was still standing, they were ready to proceed. I had passed their test, but from then on I only drank a glass of blackberry juice when the bar was opened. I found the Germans interesting to work with and against. They were tough negotiators looking for any advantage they could find. A major problem for the Director of Public Works was that the gas works had been losing money for a long time. Customers were declining and the future looked glum. When he saw that natural gas could reverse this trend, he got very interested. My goal was to get them to agree to a reasonable return on their investment.

When he said they would be happy to accept a breakeven, I didn't smile, but I wanted to turn handsprings. When I reported back to the Hague, Gerry Laufs didn't believe me. I saved NAM Gas Export millions of dollars. We completed the study for Dusseldorf, Umstellung der Stadt Dusseldorf auf Erdgas, before Christmas on December 23, 1964. The report included a copy of my paper, Planung und Vorbereitung fur die Umstellung einer Stadtgasversorgung auf Erdgas. We were invited to a special dinner to celebrate, with our wives included. Grace was treated to a visit to Dusseldorf. The Chief Economist who had been very tough in the negotiations looked at me and said, "I never could tell what you were thinking. You must have done this many times."

I smiled, nodded, and thanked him. I couldn't say, "I've never done this job before." The real shocker came at dinner when I was struggling to talk to the Director of the Gas Works. He turned, smiled, and said in perfect English, "It's okay. We can speak English now." I would have sworn in a court of law he couldn't speak a word of English. We had gone through weeks of negotiations and meetings and he always spoke German and waited for an interpreter to translate back to him. "I was a prisoner for two years in one of your POW camps in Wyoming," he told me. On January 29th, 1965 a contract was signed with Thyssengas to import Dutch Natural Gas. The German Coal Cartel was broken and several months later a contract was finalized with Dusseldorf. When you are working in a foreign country, never assume that everyone can't speak your language or understand what you are saying. Language can be a very powerful weapon in business negotiations.

It can be normal, in everyday life. John Chalsty and his wife were from South Africa. One evening in London they were standing in queue (that's British for line) waiting to go into a theatre. A rude young couple pushed in front of them. The young woman said to her husband in Afrikaans, "Don't you think we should have gone to the end of the line?" He answered her briskly, "These stupid people don't know the difference." John said to him in Afrikaans, "These people aren't as stupid as you think, go back to the end of the line!"

I was sitting at my desk one morning when my phone rang. A guttural voice said, "This is Dr. Rechberger, Technical Director of Shell Austria in Vienna. We've had an explosion with four people killed and need your assistance. Shell in London said I should call and make arrangements for you to come as soon as possible. How soon can you catch a plane to Vienna?"

"I'll have to clear this with my management here in the Hague," I said.

"I understand, but London said they are making your travel arrangements and will be in touch with you."

I went immediately to see Dick Marriner. "I just had a call, too," he said. "They have a serious problem and it looks like you are the only one with the expertise to help them. They've booked you on a flight to Vienna tomorrow morning. When you get back, let me know the results." The next morning I was on a Lufthansa plane on my way to Vienna. I busied myself preparing for arrival in a new country. In addition to my phrase book I always carried the Institute of Directors' Guide to Europe. It was chock full of information about each country, customs, holidays, and all of the information needed to get acquainted with the business customs of each European Country. In addition I had a German Guide Book, which would tell me more than I needed to know. The plane set down on time in Vienna. I checked through Customs and Immigration and walked into the terminal.

A portly man was holding a sign that said "Kroeger." I walked over to him and he said, "Herr Kroeger?"

I replied, "Yes."

"Good," he said, looking at my large briefcase. "Where is your luggage?"

"This is it," I said. "I travel light. If I can't carry it on the plane, I don't take it. I never have a problem with an airline losing my luggage."

"Fine," he said, "we better be on our way because it's a long drive to Lintz."

"I thought the explosion was here in Vienna," I said. "No, it was in Salzburg at one of our Petrol Stations, but we must go to Lintz first."

Strange, I thought, *Why didn't we just meet in Salzburg?*

"You will be our surprise witness," he said. The City Council in Salzburg was in an uproar. They had called a meeting for the next afternoon to determine who was responsible for the accident. Dr. Rectberger was responsible for safety at Shell and was on the hot seat. If they found Shell Austria responsible for the explosion and deaths, he would go to prison. "We think that Towns Gas leaking from a pipe in the street was the cause," he said, "but we need an expert witness to prove it. You are the expert witness."

We were going to Lintz because Shell had arranged with the Gas Works in Lintz to do a leakage survey around the station. Officials in Salzburg did not know about it. We were to meet with the people in Lintz and learn the results of the survey. We went immediately to Dr. Rechberger's Mercedes. "I hope you won't mind riding in the 'Dead Man's Seat,'" he said, pointing to the front passenger's side. He went on to explain that when there were automobile accidents in Austria the person most likely to be killed was the passenger in the front seat. (This was in the days before seat belts.) On the way to Lintz he told me the details of the accident in Salzburg. Two cars had stopped and were filling up with petrol. An explosion blew a huge crater in the ground lifting the concrete pad over a four-story apartment building and dropping the fragments in the parking lot. The attendant and three people were killed. The newspapers were full of stories about the accident and trying to place the blame on Shell Austria. I understood what was going on. Nobody wanted to be the person going to prison!

We arrived in Lintz in the late afternoon and checked into the hotel. Lintz was called "the prettiest little city in Europe." It was situated between the dramatic dolomites and the Tauren peaks. The man who conducted the leakage survey did a thorough job, consisting of driving a steel rod into the ground and testing the hole for gas vapors with an explosion meter. He found traces of Towns Gas in two locations, but not in sufficient quantities to have caused the explosion. Dr. Rectberger wasn't pleased with the results. A dark cloud was starting to hang over his head. I tried to cheer him up. "I've done some calculations and I don't see how petrol could have been the combustible that caused the explosion," I said. "That was one hell of a force to lift all that concrete so high and over the apartment building."

"I know," he said.

The next morning we got an early start and arrived in Salzburg. We inspected the location of the accident. "I think we ought to dig in the crater to see if we can find anything," I said. He ordered some men to start digging. It wasn't long before there was a shout. A workman was holding up a piece of metal. We took a look at it. "It's part of a bomb casing," Rectberger said. It wasn't long before several more pieces were found. Dr. Rectberger was starting to have a look of relief on his face. A man came running from the direction of the parking lot with something. Printed on it was *"Fuse Bomb Tall, M 124, 12 hours, Lot 49–4A-44."* "It's a time delay fuse from an American bomb." I said.

"We're near the railway station. It was heavily bombed during the war," the Technical Director said. "It was an act of God. This bomb laid dormant for over twenty years. It took that long for the acid to eat through the wire and for it to explode." At the meeting of the City Council there was a look of relief on the face of everyone. The cause of the explosion was evident. Several pieces of the bomb casing were on the table. Anyone could see the fresh breaks on the edges of the casing. No one could be held responsible for the accident. Nobody was going to prison. "It was a miracle," said the Technical Director for the Gas Works. "We found some leakage in our pipes in the street. I was afraid I would be held responsible."

"I know," I said, "you have some stray current in the ground because of the proximity of the electric trams passing by. You ought to look at putting in a cathodic protection system to prevent the corrosion."

After the meeting the Technical Director said he must be getting back to Vienna. He asked if I wanted to ride back with him and get a flight back to Amsterdam the next morning. I asked if I could get a plane back to Amsterdam from Salzburg. The Salzburg Manager for Shell said it was possible but not until the next morning. I decided to stay in Salzburg. The manager got me a hotel room and said he would make my travel arrangements for the next morning. It was late in August of 1965. He said, "You are in luck. This is the birthplace of Mozart. Each year we have in Salzburg a Music Festival. People come from all over the world to hear the beautiful music. You are invited to have dinner with me and my wife and go to hear the music this evening."

I agreed that would be nice. They picked me up, we enjoyed a nice dinner and attended the festival. We had coffee at the Glockenspiel afterwards. He thanked me profusely for my help in the resolution of the accident and bid me farewell. The next morning I caught my flight back to the Netherlands.

Looking back it seems almost like the plot of a movie film. It happened within a period of three days. When I returned to my office, I wrote a report and submitted it to Gerry Laufs. There are things that happen in life for which there is no explanation. Dr. Rectberger called it an "Act of God." In English Common Law it's called "force majeure." It doesn't matter what you call it; it's an intervening force that cannot be explained. Some people might call it "a coincidence." Whatever you call it, for some reason that bomb stayed dormant for about twenty years, then exploded, killing four people. We will never know why.

22

Natural Gas for Fourteen Million Customers in Britain

Things were changing at NAM and IGTM. I didn't pay much attention because I was so busy. Looking back, it was inevitable. NAM had signed contracts for export of Dutch gas to Belgium with transit rights to France. IGTM had negotiated for part ownership in the Belgium pipeline system. I made a few trips to France but it wasn't necessary. The French knew about natural gas operations because of experience with the use from their Lacq field of natural gas. They had solved the technical problems of distribution in their own way and were interested only in an additional supply of Dutch gas. With the signing of the contract for export to Thyssengas and the Stadtwerke of Dusseldorf, the German Coal Cartel had been broken. IGTM negotiated partnerships in pipelines to Hamburg on the North and to Munich on the South with transit rights to Italy. IGTM had looked at the possibility of an undersea pipeline to Britain, but it was not feasible. Shell and Esso discovered natural gas in the North Sea off the coast of Britain. Change was in the air!

On April 8th, 1964 I made a presentation on natural gas distribution at the Shell International "Natural Gas Course" at Shell Centre in London. The following year I made another presentation at the Shell "Natural Gas Technical Course" at the Richmond Hills Hotel. Shell people from their world-wide operations attended these courses.

While working in the Hague, I made a few visits to England to meet with Gordon Usmar, Manager of the U.K. Field Office. Grace and the children were invited to go to London as his guests for the weekend.

When Grace arrived at the Rotterdam airport on Friday evening, she was told there were only two seats left on the plane. She couldn't leave one of the children behind and she couldn't send them on alone without her. She insisted she had confirmed reservations and the plane wasn't leaving without her and the children on board. Grace is a very nice person, but you don't push her around. She can be tough as nails when she has to be. Finally, after conferring with the pilot, she was told the children could take the two passenger seats. There was an extra seat in the cockpit with the pilot and she could sit in it. She not only was one of two women in Holland that could write checks, but she also became the first female passenger to fly from Rotterdam to London with the pilot in the cockpit of the plane!

We spent a pleasant weekend as guests of the Usmars at their home at Cherry Orchard farm, Hawks Hill, at Leatherhead in Surrey. Grace and Sheryl had a field day shopping in London. They discovered Marks and Spencer, a department store that had reasonably priced clothing. Grace was insulted by a sales lady in The Hague when she tried to buy a bra. Dutch women were buxomly. Grace had small breasts. The sales woman looked at Grace and said, "You are so small you don't need a bra!" Then the sales woman walked away. End of conversation. The Dutch know better than you do what you need.

When Grace learned I had a trip scheduled for London, she presented me with a shopping list. I was to purchase bras for both she and our daughter Sheryl. It was my first experience in a lingerie department. I walked in among all the displays of women's undergarments. I was not comfortable when a sales lady approached and asked if she could help me. I gave her the size bras Grace had requested, then said, "And I would like these others for our daughter." She gave me a knowing look, smiled, and said, "Sure."

On one visit I was walking down a street in London and it hit me. I stopped in my tracks and listened. Everyone was speaking English! I could understand everything that was said. I was so accustomed to hearing everyone speaking Dutch, French, or German that I didn't realize the difference. It was August of 1966. One morning Dick Marriner called and asked me to come to his office. He closed the door and said, "This is for your ears only. You are being transferred to London. You aren't to tell anyone. Don't go through the normal channels. Buy your own tickets, don't tell anyone at the company where you are going. Take a week off with Grace and find a place to live in London."

Our son was on Long Island playing baseball and our daughter was in the U.S. visiting her godmother in Rhode Island. It was a surprise, but if the boss says you're being transferred, you do what you are told. We went to the local office of British European Airways and booked a flight to London. Arrangements were made for us to stay at the White House Hotel in Regents Park. We were surprised to see John Chalsty there. He had already found a place and recommended we look at Harley House on Marylebone Road.

Harley House was an exclusive block of flats being renovated. They had three bedrooms, two bathrooms, a kitchen, a dining room, and living room. New central heating and electrical were being installed. They were at a stage where we could make any changes we wanted. It would be almost like building a house. From my standpoint it was ideal. My office would be at Hanover Square. The flats were within walking distance of the office. I had enough commuting in New York to last a lifetime. There was only one problem; the lease was for twenty years! We didn't know how long we would be in London, but twenty years was scary. It was the custom in Britain so we jumped off the cliff and signed the lease.

We would move to London, stay at the White House Hotel until the flat was ready, and then move our furniture from the Hague. The estimated time for completion of the work was to be three months; December first. We learned what was going on. Standard Oil was going through reorganization to internationalize its corporate structure. Four new regional organizations were being formed. One "Esso Europe" would be headquartered in London and coordinate activities in Europe. The purpose was to bring the management closer to the scene and bring more effective coordination of operations. We were given a small book, *In London with ESSO Europe*. It was full of information for employees being transferred to London. The thing I found most interesting was a glossary with the difference in British and American terms.

There is a difference between speaking pure English and American. The currency (pounds, shillings, and pence) was not a problem for us because we learned it in New Zealand. When we moved to the Netherlands, we had to adjust to a different measurement system. All of the countries on the continent used the metric system. We had to adjust from inches, feet, yards, and miles to millimeters, centimeters, meters, and kilometers, also from quarts to liters and from pounds to kilos. In gas measurement we had to change from British thermal units to calories, and from cubic feet to cubic meters. Now, we would be back to the systems we used in the United States.

We made a quick, temporary move to the White House and got the children enrolled in the American School in London. We were fortunate the school was adjacent to Regents Park and was within walking distance of our future home at Harley House. Esso arranged "A Ministry of Labour Permit" issued by the Foreign Labour Division. My permit number was 717483 issued on the 17th of August 1966. The family received National Health Service Medical Cards. My card was Number 3994211. Every time we lived in a foreign country we had to have proper permission. In the Netherlands we not only had to have a "Living Permit," I had to have a "Work Permit." My company had to prove that I had special expertise and was not displacing a local worker. Grace could not work because she could not get a "Work Permit" or a "Labour Permit."

My office was located at 5 Hanover Square, at Hanover Court. Don Cox was the vice president in charge of the Natural Gas Organization. John Chalsty was his assistant. Gerry Laufs was transferred to the Esso A.G. office in Hamburg. Bob Sanders came from Gas Coordination in New York as Manager of Planning and Analysis, Martin Orleans was moved from the Hague, to be an Economist in Planning and Analysis. J. L. Byrd came from Houston and was a Pipeline Engineer. I was to be in charge of Gas Engineering and Technology.

As soon as we got settled in the hotel, I was immediately loaned to the British Gas Council for six months. My job was to help the British Gas Industry develop plans for the importation and distribution of gas from the North Sea. The first thing I ran into was resistance to a change to a pure natural gas operation. The British Gas Industry was developed by a group of chemical engineers who became world experts at manufacturing Town's Gas using petroleum or petroleum products as the feedstock. They developed sophisticated catalytic cracking units to break down the feedstock into a low btu gas.

They were unanimous in their view the best way to utilize the natural gas was to reform it into a low btu gas and continue distribution the way they had always done it. The first confrontation came at the Institution of Gas Engineers Annual Meeting at which they invited the Manager of the Philadelphia Gas Company to be the featured speaker. Philadelphia was the only city in the United States that had not converted to pure natural gas, but reformed it to a low-grade manufactured gas. The reason was that the local company that made and sold reforming equipment had a contract to manage and operate the City of Philadelphia gas public utility system.

At the meeting the speaker extolled all of the virtues of his operations and the time arrived for discussion. He stated their operations had proven to be highly satisfactory. I asked the question "Operations satisfactory to whom? Satisfactory to the shareholders of his company that manufactured the gas reforming equipment? What about the cost of service to the customers? What about opportunities for growth for the employees? What about the owners, the City of Philadelphia? How did he justify that Philadelphia was the only gas public utility in North America that hadn't converted to pure natural gas?" I gave statistics to show the growth in the gas sales in Philadelphia were much less than other comparable companies. He had not expected any opposition and was not prepared to answer my questions.

I met with Sir Kenneth Hutchinson, Chair of the British Gas Council, and shortly afterwards Arthur Hetherington from the East Midlands Gas Board was named Deputy Chairman. My contact was to be Mr. Hetherington. We had many discussions about the pros and cons of pure natural gas operations and got to know each other very well. We met each other's families, and his mother, who was an artist, insisted on painting an oil portrait of my wife Grace. Today this hangs on the wall of the entrance hall of our home. The staff of Arthur Hetherington started giving me all kinds of written materials to review. I met with Sir Kenneth Hutchinson and said, "There is a lot of confidential information here that does not concern conversion. Some of it is relevant to the negotiations for the pricing of gas at the wellhead in the North Sea. I shouldn't be seeing this as an employee of one of the oil companies." Sir Kenneth looked at me and said, "We know we can trust you."

I said, "That's not the point. This contains sensitive information. If the British Press learned about it, they wouldn't care about trust. They would have a field day with embarrassing publicity for the British Gas Council and Esso and Shell. Take it back. I don't want to see any more. Appoint someone on your staff to review all materials before they are given to me." The work on our flat finally was finished just before Christmas. We were on the third floor of Harley House in number sixty-three. To the rear we looked out at Regent's Park, which originally was intended as a pleasure ground for a new royal palace for King George IV. From our living room we looked down Wimpole Street and the former world of Elizabeth Barrett Browning. Among our Harley House neighbors were two movie starlets and Mick Jaeger, the leader of the "Rolling Stones." We were in London at the time it was known as "The Most Swinging City."

The Gas Council formed a "Conversion Committee," which had its first meeting on March 22nd 1967. The meetings were held at Hyde Park House at 4–5 Grosvenor Place in London. It was comprised of members from all of the regional gas boards; Scottish, Northern, North Western, North Eastern, East Midlands, West Midlands, Wales, Eastern, North Thames, South Eastern, Southern, South Western and Watson House. The later was the Technology Laboratory for the Gas Council. W. Desmond Ellis from the Gas Council was named Chairman of the Committee.

I was honored when Desmond Ellis invited me to attend a meeting of his Guild. It was a very formal affair. The required dress was evening dress with tails. We had dinner in the Guild Hall, which went back centuries in time. At the end a huge silver vessel full of wine was passed for everyone to drink from and a toast was given to Elizabeth the Queen. It reminded me of the communion service in the Anglican Church. It was impressive and I was honored to be a guest. On another occasion I was taken to the House of Commons and sat in the gallery to watch a debate that was taking place.

On May 2, 1967 I was elected a member of the Institution of Gas Engineers. Although we had our car in London it proved to be more of a problem in finding a place to park than it was worth. A city like London relies on a huge public transportation system to move people in and out of and around the city. Learning how to get around the Metro Underground takes a learning curve, but once mastered, allows you to move around freely and quickly. We found our car useful only on weekends when we wanted to take a trip out into the country or go on holiday. Our children learned how to move around without difficulty. The only problem was occasionally London Transport workers would go on strike. When that happened, they would almost shut down the city. I did not have that problem because I could walk to work.

Living in London was a most interesting experience. It is a city full of history. You get more interested in history when you grow older. When you are young, history just means memorizing a lot of dates. London is full of historic places: the Houses of Parliament, the Tower of London, Big Ben at Westminster, Eros Fountain at Piccadilly Circus, St Paul's Cathedral, and the Tower Bridge. Of equal interest to me was Shell Centre just across the Thames from the Houses of Parliament.

Shell Centre reminded me of the Pentagon it was so large. It was impressive. The entrance doors were etched with the Shell logo. The Centre contained several restaurants, swimming pools, a rifle range, theatres and commissaries, as well as the offices. Once inside you needed a map to find your way around. The doors had only numbers without any names on them. You had to check in with security and the person you were visiting had to know you were coming. Once in the office, members of the Shell staff were very hospitable. They offered coffee in the morning and tea in the afternoon. It was served by a woman with a cart who brought it around to every office. It was served British fashion, mixed with milk. I felt flattered when they knew me well enough to know I preferred my coffee black.

I told the Director for Natural Gas that they had a better diplomatic service than the government. They were a world-wide operation, but their employees weren't transferred around like Standard Oil. Shell employees for the most part stayed in one place, were married to local citizens who had their ears to the ground and knew what was going to happen before it happened. Shell took care of their people and their people took care of Shell! Living in London was much easier than in The Hague.

However, the government was paternalistic like Shell. Citizens were granted their freedom by the government. They paid high taxes to the point where the incentive to work hard didn't exist. People refrained from making improvements in their homes because it would mean a higher tax rate. It was similar to what my Dutch secretary told me when she was going to get married. She said she could never work for a Dutchman again after working for Americans. They had given her too much freedom and responsibility.

When she got married, she would have to quit work because the tax system for married couples would be so high she would be working to pay taxes and have nothing more for herself. There is no other country like ours in the world. In most places there are two classes of people; the very rich and the very poor. We have a middle class and that makes all the difference. Our Constitution says that freedom comes from our Creator not from the government. If you work hard, you can improve and change your economic status in the United States. In most places you have to be satisfied with the way things are, the status quo.

23

A Natural Gas Assignment in Australia

When the time arrived for me to move out of my office and say goodbye, Dick Marriner presented me with a silver ashtray. It had the Shell and Esso logos on it as well as the NAM/IGTM logos. It was inscribed *"From your friends in the Hague with the most pleasant memories, November 4, 1966."* Dick had tears in his eyes and said he was sorry to see me go "You should have been twins," he said, "one for Germany and one for Britain."

"Yes," I replied with a smile, "but Esso would have wanted to pay me only one salary." Later I learned that his father's health was failing and he had to resign from Esso and return to the States to take over and run the family business.

We met the movers at Klingelaan 13 and packed up all of our household effects. Our plan was to drive our car to Rotterdam and take the ferry across the English Channel then drive to London. Nick and his wife were kind enough to take us in for the night since we weren't leaving until the next morning. We were terribly embarrassed to learn our Dutch neighbors had planned a going away party for us. We, the guests of honor, didn't appear at our own going away party. We were so tired we completely forgot it. We said goodbye to Nick and his family and never saw them again.

Many years later we were living in Nashville and watching the television news. The Cosmonauts from the Soviet Union were making a tour of the United States. One of their stops was Nashville. We were surprised to see Nick with them as a "State Department Interpreter." We tried to contact him to no avail. When we asked our Tennessee Senator to try to find him at the State Department, the answer came back that the State Department had no one by that name working for them. It became clear to us why Nick was different from everyone else in The Hague. He was CIA!

The meetings with the Conversion Committee continued throughout the summer of 1967. The Chemical Engineers were hard to convince they should give up their catalytic cracking units. Unlike the gasholder in Wellington New Zealand, these were in perfect working order and constituted a sizable investment. However, the Conversion Committee work progressed and eventually the decision was made. The manufacturing facilities would be phased out and operations would change to pure natural. Once the decision was made, it then became a question of how to do it.

My recommendation was to change to universal burners. It would mean changing every burner on every appliance, which would be expensive short-term but could be less expensive long-term. These burners would work with any quality of natural gas. No one could say with certainty what changes would take place in the calorific value and specific gravity of future natural gas finds. This had been the decision after much thought in Germany and was the right thing to do in Britain. It meant the manufacturers of gas appliances in the U.K. would have to prepare conversion kits for each one of their appliances.

I'm sure that the nineteenth floor of S & W would have told me I couldn't say that because it would mean Conversions and Surveys would not be necessary to carry out a conversion program. Anyone without much training could switch the burners on a gas appliance. On July 7th 1967 my six-month full-time assignment with the Gas Council was over. A meeting was arranged for me to meet with Arthur Hetherington to finalize the arrangements. He thanked me for the "extraordinarily job I had done and the way I had done it." He was appreciative of my assistance in setting up the planning and organization to change the industry to a pure natural gas operation. Then he said, "We would like for you to join us and take over the job of overseeing the natural gas program."

What a leap for someone who started out carrying a tool box converting appliances in the United States and now was being asked to take charge of a program to change over fourteen million customers for an entire nation! I was surprised by his offer and not sure of the consequences. I didn't know how it would affect my citizenship if I took a job working for a subsidiary of a foreign government. It probably would mean me and my family would spend the rest of our life living and working in England. I also knew that I was earning more money than the Chairman of the Gas Council. It was a supreme compliment, but I declined.

On April 14th James Buckley, Chairman of the East Midlands Gas Board asked me to prepare a presentation, Technical & Economic Parameters of Conversion, for the Short Residential Course on Natural Gas Technology at Pembroke College, Oxford, which I presented on September 8th 1967. Next, I presented a paper, The Challenges and Opportunities of Natural Gas, at the East Midlands Staff Conference on September 29th in Skegness, England. On the 7th of November I was a guest speaker in London along with Sir Henry Jones at "An Open Meeting on Natural Gas World Wide" sponsored by the Women's Gas Federation and Young Homemakers. This was attended by over two hundred representatives from forty women's organizations.

Grace and our son passed their examinations for British Drivers Licenses. Both became experts at driving on the left side of the road. During the summer we visited Canterbury, gazed at the White Cliffs of Dover, strolled among the ancient monuments at Stonehenge, visited Shakespeare's home in Stratford on Avon, stayed overnight at the "Three Mariners Inn" mentioned in Thomas Hardy's Mayor of Casterbridge, and walked the walls which surrounded the mediaeval town of Chester. Our son won the "Most Valuable Player" award for the varsity soccer team at the American School and was Captain of the varsity basketball team.

At Christmas we decided to do something different from ski holidays. I learned that British Overseas Air was starting flights to Kenya in East Africa and had a special offer for tours. We signed up but were disappointed to be too late for the Safari tour. We settled for one that was for two weeks at the Nyali Beach Hotel near Mombasa on the Indian Ocean. We rented a car and made our own safari through the Tsavo and Nairobi National Parks. We wandered through the ancient Arab city of Gedi, sixty-five miles north of Mombasa.

We enjoyed hearing the singing of Christmas carols in Swahili by the staff of the Tsavo Inn and drinking a "tot" of rum in the wardroom of HMS London, a British Destroyer which made a port of call to Mombasa on Christmas day. While we were at the Nylia Beach hotel, the President of Kenya and Mrs. Kenyatta stopped by for tea. We had a memorable time at the Kilaguni Lodge watching elephants, gazelles, zebras, and a baboon at a water hole with Mount Kilimanjaro on the horizon.

In January 1968 Don Cox moved to the Jersey headquarters in New York. I was called in by Mr. R. M. Crockett, his replacement, to tell me that Bob Sanders was leaving to return to Gas Coordination in New York. I knew that Esso transferred their people like clockwork every three years. Shortly after Bob arrived in London, I told him I wanted his job and that I was going to work hard to get him promoted. He slowly gave me more of his work to do such as administration of the Natural Gas Research budget and later the Planning and Analysis Department budget. Crockett was very apologetic in telling me that unfortunately higher management decided to bring Mr. S.A. Rissick, a Dutchman in the Hague, to replace Bob. He wanted me to be the first to know. The top management of Esso Europe wanted to groom Rissick so he could return to Holland and sit on the board of Esso Nederlands. I was given a new boss to train.

In February I was asked to go to Australia on a two-week assignment to assist Esso Standard Oil of Australia. Natural gas had been discovered in the Bass Straits and there were sufficient reserves to supply the requirements of Sydney and Melbourne. I was surprised to learn that Doug Stewart was Manager of the Gas Department of Esso Eastern and had requested my help in making an evaluation of the capital costs for Australian Gas Light in Sydney to change to natural gas operations.

I flew non-stop to Sydney and was met by Alan Castle, an economist I had worked with at NAM on the Belgian negotiations. They had a formidable list of questions and an extensive series of visits in Sydney and Melbourne were arranged for me with industry representatives. S.J. Resso, Manager of the Natural Gas Department of Esso Standard Oil of Australia, wrote in a letter to Doug Stewart,

> Meetings we arranged enabled him to greatly improve our feel for the problems and cost of conversion and distribution; and to pick just one example of the benefits of his visit, he is confident that Australian Gas Light in Sydney are over estimating their conversion cost by some U.S. ten million dollars.

I returned to London and on the 9th of April was elected a member of the British Institute of Fuel. One day I saw in the American Gas Association Monthly a call for papers to be presented at the AGA

Transmission Conference to be held in Cleveland, Ohio. A dream of mine had always been to give a presentation at an AGA conference. As a lark I submitted a proposal and to my delight received an invitation to present my paper on May 27th, 1968. I sent John Chalsty a request for permission to attend the conference and present the paper. A short time later he called me in and said he was sorry but they did not feel that presentation of a paper in the United States would be any benefit to Esso Europe.

I requested the time off as part of my vacation and told him I was willing to pay the expenses myself (echoes of my experiences with Stone & Webster). I flew to Cleveland and presented my paper "Computer Technology in the European Gas Industry." A short time later I received a thank you letter from L.V. Parent, who had served as the Chairman of the Computer Committee. In the letter he wrote, *"It may interest you to know that the attendance for your presentation exceeded that for any previous Computer Committee sponsored program."* I was satisfied. I had achieved a long-desired goal.

In June I was asked to take a trip to Barcelona, Spain. Esso had a Liquefied Natural Gas Project underway with an investment of about three hundred fifty million dollars. New ports were constructed at Marsha el Brega in Libya and in Barcelona. A liquefaction plant was under construction to take associated gas from the oil production, liquefy it at minus four hundred fifty degrees and transport it to Spain in specially constructed tankers. Gas Natural was a new company in Spain to receive the tankers and store the gas for distribution in a new industrial supply system. The Spanish partner was Catalane de Gas y Electricidad, which supplied four hundred thousand domestic and commercial customers in the Barcelona area.

I met with a young bi-lingual Spanish engineer, Pedro Grau Hoyas. From college days I could read all of the signs and restaurant menus, but I had not learned to speak Spanish. I found Barcelona interesting. The warm and sunny climate was a welcome change from the cold, damp, rainy weather of Northern Europe. Unlike the Northern Europeans, I found the Spanish people to be like the climate, warm, friendly, and honest.

In London we decided to take a short holiday and drive down to the Southeastern coast for a weekend. When we stopped to look for a hotel, I experienced such sharp pains in my left side I couldn't move for several minutes. I took it easy for the rest of the weekend and the next Monday went to the Esso Medical Clinic for a complete checkup. They found my heart to be in good condition, but said I was stressed out. The angel was still on my shoulder and was trying to tell me something. They gave me some Valium pills and told me to not work so hard. I didn't take the Valium and set a goal for myself to move toward a stress-free life. Management agreed for me to get an assistant. I selected John Smith, a young engineer from the Gas Department of Stone & Webster. It was just before Christmas and Gerry Laufs stopped by the office to visit. He and his wife, Anita, had divorced and she moved back to the States with their two daughters. She tired of living in Europe and wanted to go home. Gerry was locked in his career with Esso and could not change.

This, we observed, was not an unusual situation. In the Netherlands we knew several American families that ended up in divorce. Adjusting to and living in a foreign land is not easy under the best of circumstances and it is especially hard for wives and children. We invited Gerry to have dinner with us. When I told him about the Valium, he surprised me by saying that he had been taking it for a long time. His condition was complicated by the fact he was diabetic. We wished him well and hoped he had a nice visit and merry Christmas. He said that on his return he was planning to stop in Spain and play some golf.

I found the demands on my time did not allow me to reduce the stress. I would be away from my office and in Germany or the Netherlands all week and home Friday nights if the weather was good and the planes were flying. On Sunday afternoons I would be on my way to the airport. There was one saving grace. When I joined Esso, my expense account changed. Shell employees received a per diem allowance. If they stayed in a low-cost hotel and pocketed some of the money, the company didn't care. Esso was different. I was on an unlimited expense account. I could stay in the best hotels and eat in the finest restaurants. I had a car and driver to take me to and from the airport.

On the staff of the Natural Gas Organization was a young man assigned to the group of economists and said to be a mathematician. I wasn't able to figure out what he did or see any results of his work. He walked around with a big ego and talked all of the time but never really said anything of substance. A year later he announced that he and his wife had returned from New Orleans where they attended the AGA Transmission Conference at company expense. He took glee in blabbing that he and his wife saw her father and mother at the conference. His father-in-law, he told everyone, was the President of Humble Oil Company in Houston, Standard Oil's largest subsidiary in the U.S.

I was shocked and shades of Washington Natural came flooding back. The Natural Gas Organization had refused to give me the time off and expenses to present a paper at the AGA Conference in 1968 but saw fit to foot the bill for this young man and his wife to attend the same conference in New Orleans in 1969 because his father-in-law was the President of Humble Oil! That is what is called "nepotism" and it is wrong! It was wrong in Seattle and it was wrong in London. It would affect my thinking about my future in Esso. It appeared to me to get ahead in the world's largest corporation you either had to have a mentor somewhere or be a relative of someone in an influential position. I had neither.

24

How to Save a $350 Million Project in Spain

I was happy to have John Smith join me at Esso Europe. He had a degree in Gas Engineering from a Texas College and was one of the younger members of the S & W Gas Department staff. At S & W he worked with a member of the accounting department, using Fortran programming language, to mechanize financial statements for five-year forecasts. As soon as he and his family got settled into their new home at Harley House, he started relieving me of some of the detail work I had been doing. I took him to the German field office and introduced him. He immediately hit it off with Herbert Wittorf. They were about the same age and worked well together.

The computer program I developed with Tommy Harmsworth at IGTM was a success but needed to be improved and refined. I wanted it to be adaptable for use in any country, in any tax system, in any currency, and in the metric system as well as the British system of measurement. I also thought it would be great if we could add a financial section with a Profit and Loss Statement and Balance Sheet. About this time a representative from Esso Math and Systems, Bob Dietz, came to London to see if there was any work they could help Esso Europe with. We were able to get Bob assigned to help us. He and John started adapting the old program so that the new ideas could be incorporated.

When I reported aboard the USS Capricornus in 1950, one of the first jobs I was given was to develop a Damage Control Book. This was to contain plans for the crew to meet any kind of event that might happen. Hit by a torpedo—what do we do? Hit by a bomb—what do we do? etc. It was an interesting exercise, scary at first but then it turned into a game. I thought up all of the terrible things that could happen to our ship. With the help of the Chiefs and Warrants we developed plans and training exercises for the crew to meet any problem. This had a lasting impact upon my thinking. Always have a plan "B" for whatever you do! This is the way to minimize surprises. Murphy's Law always is lurking around the corner.

The work I did at S & W was to try to forecast a firm's operations five years into the future. We would take the past five years' data and project it into the next five years, assuming there would be no changes in the factors affecting the company. At IGTM we added the feature of a second forecast assuming all the changes that natural gas conversion would make. Questions by Gerry Laufs taught me about sensitivity analysis. "What if this assumption changed five percent? What if that assumption changed five percent, ten percent?" The answers to these types of questions require a mass of calculations (in effect more forecasts). Gerry would drive us crazy with these questions, but it finally dawned on me that the assumptions were the keys to understanding the background to the study.

With the mathematics computerized, it was easy to test the sensitivity of each assumption. It was a revelation in learning what was really important in making a plan or forecast and studying the results. We asked Bob to add a sensitivity analysis to the program. While Bob and John were working on the computer program, other things were happening. I made several trips to Barcelona and became familiar with the operations of Catalana de Gas. My Spanish vocabulary began to come back and I was struggling to learn to speak the language. I was pleased to find that unlike German, Spanish was almost completely phonetic. Once you learned the rules there was no problem in pronouncing the words when you saw them.

I continued to make trips to Germany. The STEGA Field Office was shut down and Hans Loblich and the Esso people were moved to the main office of Esso A.G in Hamburg. The office manager for gas operations was Dick Tabeling with Gerry Laufs as his assistant. On occasions I would stop off at the NAM and IGTM office in the Hague. I always looked forward to talking with my friend Otto Baeder. On one visit he confided in me a personal problem. He was getting an allowance for the use of his car. He calculated that if he bought a Mercedes with diesel engine he could pay for it with the savings difference in the price of gasoline compared to diesel fuel. "What's the problem?" I asked.

"You don't understand," he said. "The only person in my Shell office in Germany that drives a Mercedes is the manager. It could create a problem if I drive a car as good as the manager."

"Otto," I said, "if you want to have a Mercedes and can afford it, get it. You are in the Hague and he is in Germany. He will not know what you are driving here and it shouldn't matter anyway."

Another time he said to me; "Carroll, don't take life so seriously. You are too soon dead!"

Things were progressing in Germany but occasionally I was called in when a technical-economic problem would arise. I was expected to help make the plans work! At a staff meeting of the Gas Department the Manager R. Crockett and John Chalsty mentioned that the LNG project in Spain was in jeopardy. The cost of the new LNG tankers had cost overruns double the original estimates. The liquefaction plant in Libya was taking a year longer than planned to go online. The return on the three hundred-fifty million dollar investment disappeared.

During lunch John and I put the project on our "Planalyzer" program and tested all of the assumptions. The major problem was the assumption that the re-liquefied gas would be sold for industrial uses. That was the lowest possible price for the gas. If the gas were sold as a premium fuel for domestic and commercial use, the sick project could be made well. I went to Mr. Crockett and gave him the study. "I can make your sick LNG project well," I said.

He took the study and the next morning said, "We want you to go to Barcelona and try to convince them that Catalana should convert their customers to operate on natural gas."

In April of 1968 Stone & Webster made a feasibility study for the conversion to natural gas for Catalana de Gas. I was asked to review it. We put it on our "Planalyzer" program and ran an analysis of the assumptions. Our conclusion was that the S & W study was merely a projection of past years' experience. With a new set of assumptions the project could be made feasible. I made a trip to Barcelona and met with Pedro Duran, the Chairman of the Board of both Catalana and Gas Natural. Mr. Paul Temple, the Esso Shareholder's Representative for Spain, acted as interpreter. I presented the results of our analysis and gave him a one-page listing of the ten things that the management of Catalana would have to do for the conversion to natural gas to be successful.

In London I assumed more duties. A representative from Commonwealth Services came to London and proposed to the oil companies the development of a Natural Gas Training Course. After reviewing their proposal, I said I could do the same thing for them. They agreed and from that time on once a year I was in charge of the weeklong course for oil company employees who came in from all over the world. Bob Sanders gave me the responsibility for coordinating the Natural Gas Research budget. In addition I developed materials with the help from Esso Research Centre in Abingdon for a book titled "Natural Gas Text."

In a letter dated February 10, 1969 Esso International in New York were impressed and requested one hundred copies. *"We feel it will be valuable in our efforts to sell LNG."* Things were progressing on all fronts. I became a member of the DVGW (German Association of Gas Engineers) and became a Chartered Engineer in Britain (the same as "Registered Professional Engineer" in the United States). My memberships in the Institution of Gas Engineers and Institute of Energy were changed to "Fellow." Things began to change in Spain when on one visit Pedro Grau said, "I'm going to take you for lunch to the restaurant my family goes to." I knew this was like making me a member of his family. He said, "Carroll, we want you to know that from now on we are doing business with you, not Esso." They had waited long enough to get to know me and to feel they could trust me. We drove to a restaurant on the waterfront that specialized in seafood. I knew it was a special occasion, because normally the Catalans went home to have lunch with their families.

We were greeted by the proprietor with open arms and I was told, "We know the menu and will order the specialties of the house for you." I knew I was in for a test. Unlike the Germans they were not going to try to drink me under the table; they were going to treat me with their favorite foods. Having grown up in the Middle West I was a "meat and potatoes" person. When we lived in Rhode Island, I thought I made a major breakthrough when I learned to eat fried shrimp. I had problems at Clam Bakes and never was able to pry open and eat raw clams. As soon as we sat down, the waiter brought each of us a platter with twelve raw oysters on the half shell. I looked at the platter and said to myself, "Kroeger, you can either eat these or insult your host."

Fortunately at each place setting was a bottle of wine. I filled my glass, took a swig, and downed an oyster. When in Rome, you do as the Romans do! The first course was just the beginning. We were served barnacles and then the real specialty "pulpitos." These were baby octopus served in their own black juice! They stared back at you with small eyes. I learned on previous visits to become accustomed to how seafood was served in Barcelona. On one visit Grace said, "They must expect you to be a surgeon to eat this food." Fish, shrimp, and lobster came with the head and eyes attached. It was up to you to find the edible parts.

The bottle of red wine was my salvation. I was able to eat the oysters, barnacles, and pulpitos without incident. In fact, I found once I crossed the mental barrier, the food tasted pretty good.

In London the weather was getting to Grace. She developed a bronchial problem that would not go away. Finally the doctor told her, "You need to get in a warm sunny climate." Easter was just around the corner so we arranged to take a holiday in Majorca. We flew to Spain and then took a plane to the island. We were surprised to find the weather had changed. In fact, it rained the entire weekend we were in Palma. The London Times had photos of the unusual sunny weather in London with photos of people sunbathing in Hyde Park. However, we had fun learning how to drink wine from a perone and Grace bought a beautiful leather coat with matching hat and purse.

We found one of the advantages to living in the city of London was the good restaurants. English food is not known as a fine cuisine. Because of the weather and climate, it is hearty, but bland. I enjoyed going to lunch with people from the office. We would go to the pubs, which served "Shepherd's Pie." Of course everyone had to have a pint of beer or ale. For dinner Grace and I preferred "Mirabel's," "Tiberio's," and "Trader Vic's." London theatres were fun and relatively inexpensive. We enjoyed them more than New York because we could stay to see the end of the show. In New York we had to leave early to catch the last train to Long Island.

Dining in Europe was always a pleasure. It is one of the few things I miss. Americans always are in a hurry. Europeans have learned how to slow down and enjoy life. Grace had been a waitress when we met and found it to be educational. She always was comparing the difference in service. Waiters in Europe were professional. It was a career they aspired to from the time they were very young. They went through special training for years. I always was amazed at the art of de-boning a fish, which they made look so easy!

1968 was the year of the appendix for our family. Our son came down with an acute case and was rushed to the London Clinic across the street from Harley House. We were fortunate to live so close to a hospital because his appendix was nearly ruptured when he arrived. Grace had been having chronic pains in her side for quite some time. The doctor, whose office was also nearby on Harley Street, finally concluded it was chronic appendicitis. Two days after her surgery she told me, "I still have the same pain."

Two years later when she was home in Tennessee to attend an older brother's funeral she stopped to see the Bolton family doctor. Upon examination he said, "You are going into the hospital in the morning. You have tumor of the uterus. Your mother and two sisters had the same problem and two of them were malignant!" Grace had a hysterectomy and fortunately there was no cancer. There is no substitute for a family doctor who knows your family's medical history.

Our son, Carroll, graduated from the American School in London in May of 1968. His graduation was marked by typical London weather and there were teardrops mixed with rain drops on the cheeks of both old and young as many touched hands for the last time that day. After much anticipation, trials and tribulations of submitting applications for college, he accepted the offer of Vanderbilt University in Nashville. We were pleased to know he would be in Nashville where we first met and were married.

It was time for me to make another trip to Barcelona. Paul Temple said that Pedro Duran wanted to meet with me. He wanted to know my opinion on how things were progressing at Catalana de Gas. I told him one year before I gave him a one-page listing of the ten things they would have to do in order to make the project work. A year had gone by and none of them had been done. He said, "You are right and no one is going to get them done. It is going to take someone from the outside to make things happen. When can you move to Barcelona?"

I was shocked. I said, "I work for Esso, I can't just move to Barcelona."

He looked at Paul Temple and said, "Get me the President of Esso Europe on the phone; I want to talk to him." When he put down the phone, he said, "It's all arranged for you to leave London and come here. You can work out the details." I found a way to make a sick project well and it was going to be my job to make it work! This turning point came out of the blue!

25

A Business Surgeon for a Sick Company

The calendar had just turned over to 1969. I was shocked to read on the fourth page of the "Esso Europe News" that Gerry Laufs died of a heart attack in Madrid, Spain. We saw him before Christmas in London and he seemed to be in good health. The news article was a one-inch story on a back page saying he would be missed by colleagues and friends. There was no information as to his funeral or where a letter of condolence or flowers could be sent. Gerry gave his all for the company and this was the thanks he got for it. Three months later his boss, Dick Tabeling, the Manager of the Gas Office in Hamburg, had a heart attack and died on a flight from London to Hamburg. In three months Esso lost the two top managers of the Gas Department in Germany.

Several events took place that made me begin to question whether I wanted to stay with Esso. The nepotism I encountered in our office and the fact that advancement was dependent on who you knew in high places was troubling. S. Rissick was leaving to go back to the Netherlands and a new face was coming from Gas Coordination in New York to be Manger of Planning and Analysis. I had neither mentor nor relative in high places to look after me. I made it there on my own because of my special expertise and ability. There was a limit as to how far that could carry me in the largest corporation in the world.

Life is not fair, but that does not mean that you are helpless. Now was the time to do some serious thinking about my future. I had been in Europe for almost six years. Grace needed to be in a warm, sunny climate. There was no question about whether we would be moving to Barcelona. The Spanish made it clear they wanted to work with just me, not with Esso. John said he was going with me and the more we discussed it, the more we thought it would be better to form our own company and do it on our own. In discussions with Pedro Grau and Pedro Duran it became clear it didn't matter to them. If we wanted to do it with a new company it would be okay. Pedro Duran made it clear he wanted to make sure that I would be living and working in Barcelona to do the job. We agreed on how the arrangement would be worked out. I would be in effect the General Manager of the company. Jose Arbos Batista was the General Manager and would retain the title, but I would make the decisions; he would be responsible to see what I wanted to be done got done.

I always thought I would like to be the head of a big public utility. Catalana de Gas had four hundred thousand customers with the potential for many more. Our contract would be for two years to reorganize the company and set up the organization for conversion of all the appliances to operate on natural gas. "Kroeger & Smith, S.A." would receive Five Hundred Thousand Dollars or the equivalent in Swiss francs. John and I made a trip to Zurich, Switzerland and made the arrangements for our company to be chartered in Zug.

Back in London, Rissick's replacement arrived and wanted to talk to me. He said I didn't have to leave Esso to do the Spanish assignment. When I learned what his job was in New York I told him he didn't move to London to be a Department Head. I thought he was there to replace John Chalsty. John's three years were about over and it was time for him to go somewhere else. He told me I was very astute and that was the plan. He promised if I stayed with Esso I would be the Manager of Planning and Analysis when I returned to London.

As far as I was concerned, it was too little and too late. If I stayed with Esso they could tell me how to do the job. If I was going to reorganize the company, I wanted to do it my way not have to report to someone else. It was a challenge I had to face. I had to prove to myself I could do the job. Our son was going to be back in the States going to Vanderbilt. We checked out the schools in Barcelona. The International School was housed in the building with the U.S. Information Office. Rumor said the children drank wine for lunch. That might be the custom in Spain, but we decided it wasn't the lifestyle we wanted for our daughter Sheryl. We enrolled her in the Kensington English School.

Grace and I made a trip to Barcelona to look for a place to live. We told the Spanish Estate Agent we didn't want to live in the International Community, but we wanted to be in a Spanish neighborhood. Since I was going to be working in a Spanish company, we wanted to be totally immersed so we would have to learn Spanish. She found us an apartment on the sixth floor of Balmes 470, an apartment building near the beginning of the funicular going up Mount Tibidabo. We returned and made arrangements for our household effects to be moved to Spain. The moving company said the best way was to move them by lorry across France. We were lucky to find the British Estate Agent had no problem in selling the remainder of our twenty-year lease to a family that worked for another oil company. We were advised by Pedro Grau to sell our car in England and that we would have no need for one in Barcelona. Public transportation was not expensive and parking for a car would be expensive and a problem in Spain.

Grace was happy because this time I did not go ahead of the family. I was there to help out with all of the work in overseeing the packing up of all our household effects. She and Sheryl and I caught a plane and together we flew to Spain. When we arrived, we stayed at the Hotel Derby until our furniture arrived. My office would be in the Catalana building at Puerto del Angel. Jose Arbos said that he was turning his bilingual secretary over to work for me. John Smith and I made a trip to the United States to hire three of the most experienced conversion men, Bud Fahs, Leo Lamont, and J. Saxton to work for us. Conversion & Surveys always hired these people when they needed them but did not keep them on their payroll when there was no contract.

Before I left I was asked to have an exit interview with R. M. Crockett. He asked me several questions. "Why do you want to leave? Would you like more money? Is there something about the benefits?" I told him it wasn't the money. I was making more than I had ever made. The company benefits were as good as anyone could want. It was clear he couldn't understand why anyone would want to leave. I told him it was a personal challenge I had to meet because if I didn't, I would always wonder if I could have done the job. I received a letter from Mr. Crockett, which said,

> During the past five years you have made a major contribution to Esso and indeed to many European companies and nations. Your valuable advice, assistance, and creativity were key factors in helping to bring about a major expansion of the natural gas industry of Western Europe.

When we arrived in Barcelona, it was warm and the sun was shining. Grace was happy to be back in a sunny climate. Catalana arranged for my work permit and the visas for the family. As soon as we arrived, we were called to a meeting with the U.S. Consul. He welcomed us to Barcelona. He said, "There are some rules here you need to know about. It is especially important since you have a teenage daughter. Spanish law states it is illegal to have in your possession any controlled substances regardless of how small it may be. The penalty is six years in a Spanish prison. It doesn't matter what passport you carry, how much money you have, or who you know. You go for six years and Spanish prisons aren't rehabilitation centers!"

We found the Spanish people to be warm and friendly. The Catalans had a strong work ethic and were family-oriented. Personal honor was held in the highest regard. Every man was a gentleman regardless of his economic station. Every Spanish woman was a lady even if she was the cleaning woman.

I resigned from Esso, formed our company in Switzerland, and moved to Spain on a handshake. That was more binding in the Spanish culture than any contract written by the smartest lawyers. I had been working in Barcelona for about three months when Pedro Grau said, "I guess it's time we put our agreement down on paper and make it formal." We began to learn more about the people we were working with. The Catalans were different from the other Spaniards. Historically they had been the business people of the country from the time the Phoenician trading ships started making ports of call at Barcelona. During the Spanish Civil War they had been the last to be conquered by General Franco. He outlawed their language and newspapers, but the people went underground and spoke Catalan at home to keep it alive. Jose Arbos, the General Manager, had been a member of the secret police and I suspected him of still having those kinds of ties.

When we returned to our homeland on home leave, people would say to us, "What's it like living in that Fascist Country?" We found it no problem. We liked walking down the streets, which were kept squeaky clean. There were no beggars or prostitutes soliciting. There were no bank robberies because there were police stationed at the entrance of each bank. If Grace or our daughter decided to take a walk in the middle of the night in the park across the street, it was safe to do so. Unlike the people in Northern Europe the Spanish were honest as the day is long. One time when we got on a bus and I paid the driver for our fares, I was distracted and walked away without waiting for my change. He called me back to get it!

Eventually our furniture arrived and was unloaded to be hoisted up the six floors through a window into our apartment. The elevator was too small for household effects. This was the standard way to move. Grace became accustomed to shopping at the neighborhood stores; the baker, the butcher, the green grocer, etc. It was a treat to go to the "Mercado" to shop for fresh fish and seafood.

We decided to do our shopping at the Spanish Department Store even though there was a Sears Store in Barcelona. We were doing everything we could to force ourselves to learn to speak Spanish. Grace had an interesting experience in having drapes made for our apartment. She was told how long it would take to make them. When she returned and they weren't ready, she asked when she should come back. The reply was "manana," "tomorrow." When she went back the next day and they weren't ready and they told her "manana," she lost it. "No manana," she said. "Hoy!" "Today." They smiled and said in Spanish, "Oh you're German." The drapes were ready the next day!

My experience in the office was similar. Every Friday evening Jose Arbos would call a meeting of all of the Department Heads to discuss progress and lay out the plans for the next week. At least that's what I thought the purpose of the meeting was. However, all that happened was that the Director of Finance thought he knew the solution to the technical problems, The Technical Director thought he knew the solution to the Marketing problems, etc. At the second meeting I slowly put my papers in my briefcase and got up and walked out.

Every Monday morning I would get together with the General Manager to discuss the plans for the coming week. He said to me, "Do you know what you did Friday night? Even the Janitor is talking about your leaving the staff meeting."

"Yes," I said, "and I am not coming back unless there is a written agenda for the meeting. We must stop all of the talking and start reporting on what has been done and outlining the things that must be done." I'm sure that everyone after that said or thought, "Oh, he's German." From that time on we started making some progress. Before I arrived, I thought I had a good idea of the financial condition of the company. I had seen two sets of books. One was for the shareholders, and one was for the government. I was surprised to see a third set setting out the real situation.

The company was near bankruptcy. They had been capitalizing expenses among other things. When I looked at payroll, they were overstaffed by at least thirty-three percent. And the amount going out of the company for retirement was as much as the active payroll. "Doesn't anyone ever die here?" I asked. It turned out in Spain nobody wrote checks. All transactions were in cash. Employees were paid in cash in two ways; first the official amount, which was subject to social security taxes, then another payment under the table for which the company paid no taxes. For the people on retirement the former employee or a member of his family came to pick up the money.

It was easy to see why nobody ever died. It was too easy to keep picking up the money! That changed. Only the employee could pick up their retirement pay. We were amazed to discover that the company storerooms had no locks and anyone could take whatever they might want day or night. This was considered to be a fringe benefit. Stealing from the company seemed to be an accepted practice. Everyone was shocked when locks were installed and the storerooms were locked at night.

We found one of the company Directors had formed a company that bought the old gas meters to junk them, but instead was repairing them, repainting them, and, through another company he owned, selling them back as new meters. Spanish Law said you could not discharge anyone unless you had evidence they had committed a crime. The Director was confronted with the evidence and he was given the choice of resigning or going to prison. He resigned. The word spread quickly throughout the company. If it happened to a director, it could happen to anyone. At one of our staff meetings one of the engineers came forward with a plan for the appliance conversion. He said the company had ordered an IBM computer and he had made a plan for conversion, which he unrolled like a roll of wallpaper.

Bud Fahs, Leo Lamont, and our conversion people were proceeding with the system that had been used in the U.S. and Belgium. It was simple and didn't require the use of a computer. I said there was no assurance the computer would be delivered on time or that it could be programmed and debugged in time to meet our schedule. The engineer insisted. It was showdown at the OK Corral!

You never avoid confrontations. I called Pedro Grau, he talked with Pedro Duran and the man was told he was being transferred to another job. He came to me pleading for another chance. His plea fell on deaf ears. An example was being set for others. I was there to do what others weren't willing to do and I was going to get the job done! I'm sure I didn't make any friends as a result of this, but I wasn't sent there to make friends. I was there to make the necessary changes. This is a postscript to the story. When I left Barcelona two years later, the IBM computer still hadn't arrived. Our conversion plans were underway and working!

26

Behind the Iron Curtain during the Cold War

To round out our conversion team we hired a Dutch Engineer, J. Bolier, to work on sectionalizing the distribution system and an engineer, Norm Armstrong, from Australia who had worked on the change over in Melbourne. The LNG storage tanks of Gas Natural were filling from the tankers and soon we would start doing limited conversion of some customer's appliances. We received a contact from a Greek Shipping owner and builder asking us to come to Athens for a meeting. John and I took pains to not let anyone know where we were going. We agreed we would do a preliminary study of the feasibility for the importation of LNG to Greece. The next Monday the first thing Jose Arbos said to me was "I hope you had a pleasant trip to Greece!" My suspicions of his connections to the Spanish secret police were confirmed.

A problem arose with our agreement with Catalana for management services. Since we were a foreign company, it had to be approved by the Spanish government. They refused to approve the section on marketing, saying there were Spanish firms who could provide this kind of service. The amount was fifty thousand dollars. It would have been easy for Catalana to have said "Sorry." Pedro Grau said they had agreed for us to do this work and they were honor bound. Standard Oil was holding some U.S. dollars for Gas Natural and it was arranged that the fifty thousand would be transferred in the U.S. to our U.S. bank account.

The other problem that arose was that Spanish law said we had to be paid in Spanish Pesetas. We were already living and working in Spain and it was not possible to back out of our side of the contract. Every week John and I would walk to the bank in Barcelona and put fifteen thousand dollars worth of pesetas in a briefcase. These we would use to make our payroll. The problem came when we needed to have money for personal costs in the United States. When we needed money to pay for our son's tuition and expenses at Vanderbilt, I would fill my briefcase with Pesetas and take a trip to Zurich where they would be exchanged for dollars and transferred to our personal U.S. bank account. Fortunately at that time there was little checking of baggage on international flights.

I received a call from Shell International in London. They were recommending our company to the authorities in Turkey for the possibility of doing work there. We were to meet with the Minister of Energy and Minister of Economic Affairs in the Capitol of Ankara and with the Mayor and Director of Public Works for the City of Istanbul. I was forewarned by Shell that business practice in Turkey was for foreign firms to have an important Turkish citizen as their local representative. Grace and I flew to Ankara and I met with the government officials. The capitol city was modern and interesting.

The meetings went very well and we flew on to Istanbul. We were met by representatives of the city and checked into our hotel. It was like something out of a movie film. It was old and must have been there when the British colonials stayed there. I wouldn't have been surprised to see Lawrence of Arabia come walking through the lobby. Our impression of the city was much the same. Everything was old. We thought that the buildings in Rhode Island looked old; these were ancient! The streets were crowded with people of all descriptions.

On October 3, 1970 we met with the Mayor and Director of Public Works and had interesting discussions about problems of changing a Town Gas distribution system and appliances to operate on natural gas. The Mayor's assistant took us on a tour of the city. Istanbul is a city of mosques. We were impressed by the Blue Mosque and the Aya Sofia, which is a thousand years older than St. Peter's in Rome and is considered to be one of the Seven Wonders of the World. Although we were well treated, the culture wasn't one we felt comfortable in. The Mayor presented us with a book on Turkey before we departed. Grace found her element at the Bazaar and had fun negotiating with the vendors. However, being the comparative shopper she was, we ended up buying a brass brazier at the gift shop in the Hilton Hotel. I said to her, "How in the world do you think we are going to get this on a plane and back to Barcelona?"

She said, "Don't worry, we will find a way." I borrowed a screw-driver from a maintenance man at our hotel and proceeded to take the Brazier apart so it would be easier to carry. At the airport she convinced the airline to put it in the baggage compartment. It still is one of the showpieces in our home.

We were getting to know our Spanish friends better. Pedro Grau invited us to their home for a Spanish "cookout." They call the special dish "paella," yellow rice with chicken and a variety of seafood. We found his wife, Merchi, a delightful lady and his two daughter's fun. Paul Temple invited us to have dinner with them one evening. Paul had been stationed in Madrid and had adopted the Castilian Spanish customs. He never started work until mid-day. We stopped by his home for cocktails at nine-thirty p.m. and it was almost midnight when we went to one of the best restaurants for dinner. It was close to four a.m. when we got home. It was a short night for me because I was expected to be in my office at seven-thirty a.m.

We found the Spanish culture different. When I asked Pedro about Spanish taxes, he told me we would not have to pay any. When I asked "Why?" he explained the system. The federal government got its annual revenue from the Industrial Consortiums; Steel, Auto, Glass, etc. Each consortium was told what their share would be for the coming year. On the local level there were tax districts presided over by a collector who received no money from the government. It was his job to find and collect enough to pay his staff and expenses. He used a "Means Test" to determine who should pay. The test was made up of three parts; who owned automobiles, who owned real estate, and who employed servants. Since we didn't own a car or real estate and Grace didn't have a full-time cleaning woman, we would not be called upon to pay any taxes. "Yes," I said, "but we are Americans. Everyone thinks Americans are rich. What do we do if he comes knocking on our door?"

"In that event, you say, 'we will go to the bodega, have a glass of wine, and negotiate.'"

We also were learning how things worked. There was an English speaking non-denominational church in Barcelona. It was meeting on Sundays in a school. I was told they had purchased land and had plans to build a new church. They had the money and were waiting on a building permit. Previously the church had owned property in the port area of the city that had been an Anglican church for sailors off British ships that made ports of call. The property was in a commercial area and had become very valuable. It was sold and the church had enough money to build a new church in the suburbs. I asked how long they had been waiting on the building permit and was told three years. The officials kept losing their application. Knowing what was going on, I asked why they didn't get an "expediter?"

"The Reverend doesn't believe in bribing the officials," I was told.

"The church will never be built," I said.

I had been in Spain long enough to understand the culture. "Propinas" or "tips" were a way of life. We learned the next annual meeting of the International Gas Union was to be held in Moscow. John and I made plans to attend. The Cold War was still going on and the war in Viet Nam was in progress but in Spain we seemed far removed from any of it. We made our reservations. All arrangements had to go through the Soviet Travel Bureau and payments for everything had to be in advance; airline travel, hotel and food, and all touring. We elected to make it a vacation, taking another week tour of Yalta, Sochi and Leningrad. We flew to Moscow from Amsterdam on the Dutch airline KLM arriving in Moscow about ten p.m. It took almost two hours to get through Customs and Immigration. We had to declare anything we had of value, money, jewelry, etc. When we finally arrived at our hotel we were not expected and the busload of people were kept waiting in the lobby. We were at the Roseia Hotel, the Russian tourist hotel in Moscow. It was like four Hilton hotels built in a square. We had paid for a first-class room, but were thankful to get any kind of room after a three-hour wait.

It was nice to meet with all of our German, British, and Dutch friends at the meetings. Grace and I were pleased to see that the President of the Nashville Gas Company and his wife were there and tried to locate them. We found Russia to be an interesting place. It was clear that it was a police state. Everything was strictly controlled. We were surprised to find there were very few cars on the roads. Trams were the primary means of transport. Eating meals was a challenge. We were given "chits" to give to the restaurants to pay for our meals. There were long lines waiting to get in. Once in the restaurant the menu was the size of a telephone directory but the only food available seemed to be "Borch Soup," a soup made from cabbage.

We discovered that in the corner of some floors of the hotel was a small place for the hotel staff to eat. There were two tables and chairs and on display were bread, cheese, hardboiled eggs, and tea. At least we could see what we were going to eat. They were happy to take our "chits" and we were able to eat something other than soup. One evening we were eating and a Russian man motioned, asking if he could join us at our table. We could tell from the metal pin he was wearing that he also was attending the conference. He didn't speak English and we didn't speak Russian, but we soon discovered he spoke some German.

We were able to communicate. He was from Kiev. We offered to buy him a glass of vodka but he deferred because he was on limited expense account and could not return the favor. Finally he agreed to have a glass with us. We found him to be an interesting, jovial person. He had been in the Russian army and a POW of the Germans. That's how he learned to speak some German. He invited us to come visit him in Kiev and promised to take me fishing. When the time came to say goodbye, he had tears in his eyes and gave us both a bear hug. When the first week was up, John and his wife said they were going to spend their second week in Rome. They didn't like Russia. We found it interesting to see how the other half lives. Grace attended a tea given by Russian ladies. All of them were professional women who worked, engineers, lawyers, etc. They were intrigued to learn Grace was a housewife and were surprised to learn she had a car to drive. They asked to see a photo of her family and were amazed at the color picture of Grace and our children. They had tears in their eyes when the time came for Grace to say farewell. They, too, were "huggers."

Our tour group for the second week was interesting. We were the only English-speaking people on the trip. There were Germans, Belgians, Czechoslovakians, etc. The first morning at breakfast we sat with a German couple. I had worked with Hans Kluss at Thyssengas. They said, "Have you figured out which of our group is the KGB?" We were surprised but they knew. Han's wife had grown up in East Germany and spoke Russian. Five in our group of thirty were secret police. After breakfast our guide told us that the tour was going to take us to the Pioneer Youth Camp and then to the hospital that treated Russian miners for Black Lung Disease.

I told her we were not going. Sochi was a resort on the Black Sea and Grace and I were on holiday and wanted to go to the beach. A German standing near said, "Ja, I go to the beach too." Our guide went over to confer with the man who apparently was in charge of the secret police. "Okay," she said, "those who want to go to the beach can go." One of the secret police went with us. From that time on we didn't go with the group all of the time. We always got permission, did exactly what we said we were going to do, and strictly observed all of the rules. Grace is a comparative shopper and wanted to look in some of the shops to see the quality of goods and compare prices. We were surprised to see a crowd at one store and stopped to see what was going on. It turned out the shop was selling wedding rings. Later when we asked our guide she said that until recently it was against the law to wear a wedding ring. The law had changed and now people were buying rings.

We attended a nightclub at the Dollar Shop in Yalta. There was an extra charge for those who wanted to go. It clearly was designed to get more foreign exchange from tourists. There was a band playing for dancing and plenty of liquor flowing. Our group was seated at a table and one from each country would stand and make a toast. Hans Kluss nudged me and said, "Now it's your turn." I stood up and gave a toast. "To world peace and the brotherhood of man." Everyone cheered and quaffed down their drink. The man, who was in charge of the secret police, came over and motioned to me, asking permission to dance with my wife. Grace had the distinction of dancing with the head of the KGB for our tour group.

When we arrived at Leningrad, we took a tour of the Hermitage Museum. Four in our group were from Brazil and one lost his wife in the museum. We obliged and went back to help find her. He was very thankful, gave me his card, and I learned he was an Army General in charge of the Gas Industry in Brazil. When he learned about my business, he invited me to come to Brazil to talk about importation of LNG. That evening we attended what was supposed to be a performance of an English Musical. It was very boring and not well done.

At intermission Grace and I decided to leave and go back to our hotel. We noticed the number on the trams passing by was the same as those that went by our hotel and felt certain we could find our way back alone. Riding on Russian trams was interesting. You could get on either at the front where you could pay the driver or you could get on in the back. If you got on in the back, you gave the money for your fare to the people standing next to you and they passed it up to the driver. Change was passed on the way back to you. Either Russians were very honest or they thought Big Brother was watching! The time came for us to fly back to Moscow and catch our flight back to Amsterdam. Our tour was over when we arrived at the gate at the airport. The members of the secret police said goodbye with tears in their eyes, gave us a big bear hug, and the chief presented Grace with a gift of note cards embossed in gold with the historic buildings of Leningrad. We found the Russian people to be nice and friendly once you got beyond the confines of the political system.

27

Time to Go Home and Settle Down

John Smith and I were convinced that our automated computer program for forecasting and analyzing plans was so revolutionary we could sell it. We formed a company in the United States with the fifty thousand dollars from Gas Natural and opened an office in New Jersey. We called the Company "Kroeger & Smith Management Consultants." We thought we could sell the program to public utilities and to insurance companies. The program was way ahead of its time. We failed to understand the way the financial world worked. No one was interested in finding the best way to do a forecast. They were satisfied with the way they always had done it. The office in New Jersey was costing us almost ten thousand dollars a month.

After a year we had to shut it down without having sold a single program. It was like killing one of your children. Economics is a cruel teacher. When something fails, you have to let it go! Today with the advent of personal computers, everyone does their own forecasting and business plans on a Microsoft program called "Spreadsheet." We were just ahead of our time.

Our conversion program was going well in Barcelona. Then Esso got into a dispute with the Libyan government over the royalty paid for crude oil. Libya shut down the LNG operations and nationalized Esso's holdings. We were going to run out of LNG with no assurance of future supply. We did quick calculations and started up a propane air plant to supply substitute gas while negotiations were made with the British Gas Council to divert LNG from Algeria to Spain instead of it going to Britain. Norm Armstrong said he thought we should go to Australia and bid on doing the conversion for Sydney. He made the contacts and we flew to meet with the management of the Sydney Gas Company. Norm was familiar with the experience in Melbourne and we felt we had a good chance of competing with Conversions and Surveys. The meetings went very well and we thought it would be a good idea to stop off in Brazil on the way home. I contacted the General I met in Leningrad and he was happy to meet with us and set up meetings with the government officials. The most direct way was to get a flight from Sydney to Tahiti, then to Santiago Chile, and then on to Brazil. It would mean we were making a flight around the world in two weeks. There was only one flight a week from Tahiti to Chile so we had to spend a couple of days waiting.

Much to our surprise, our plane stopped at Easter Island on the way to refuel so we had a chance to take a quick tour of the island in the back of a pickup truck to see the stone statues. When we arrived at Santiago, it was Easter weekend so we took a tour to Valparaiso to see the beach. We were awakened in the middle of the night with the screeching of tires and the sound of gunfire. It was clear we were in a country governed by a dictator. Our tour guide told us not to take pictures of anything without permission. We were stopped out in the middle of a country cross roads by two young soldiers with machine guns. The tour guide told us there was no problem but we could tell she was frightened. You could not go anywhere in the country without government permission.

We flew on to Rio and got a room at a hotel on Coca Cabana Beach. We were surprised to read in the morning paper that the Director of the Liquefied Petroleum Gas Organization was gunned down in his driveway as he was leaving to go to his office. When we arrived at the office of the Director of the Rio Gas Company, there were soldiers at the entrance and an atmosphere of high security. Our meeting went well and we flew to Sao Paulo for a meeting with the Gas Company and the Provincial Minister of Energy. We made our presentation on LNG experience and were well received.We flew back to Madrid and then to Barcelona. When I told Grace I was tired, she said, "You've just flown around the world. No wonder you are tired."

It started me thinking. One of the reasons I decided to leave Esso and form my own company was to reduce stress and not become like Gerry Laufs who was only thirty-six years old when he died. I reduced my traveling in Spain, but I inherited many other problems.

Now I had all of the personal problems of my employees to worry about. Things at Catalana were back on track. LNG was now coming from Algeria instead of from Libya. Esso wasn't happy about it, but stood firm in their dispute with the Libyan Government. Five of the things on the one-page memo I had given Pedro Duran had been achieved. The conversion of customer appliances was proceeding on schedule and at the estimated costs.

Our daughter Sheryl flourished at the Kensington English School. I read where Vanderbilt had a "Pre-freshman Summer School Program" for special students in high school between their junior and senior years. Those with the proper grade average and recommendation of their high school principals could attend. Sheryl was accepted into the program. The manager of Pan Am for Spain was a friend of ours and we made arrangements for her to fly back while we were going to Moscow. She took her "O Level" exams at the school and the same afternoon boarded a plane for New York. Pan Am people met her in New York and made certain she got on her flight to Nashville.

There is a big difference between the schools in the United States and those in Europe. There were very few extracurricular activities. The purpose of the English school in Barcelona was the preparation of students to pass the competitive "O" level and "A" level" exams. These were necessary for admission to university. At Vanderbilt in the engineering school Sheryl breezed through the first year Math course with a "B." The dean called her in and said, "I don't see any reason for you to go back for another year of high school. Why don't you stay here and continue on?" She was in Vanderbilt at sixteen years old without a high school diploma. When she called us and asked if she could stay, it was hard to say "No." Looking back, we should have said "No." Not because we didn't think she could do the work, but because she was not prepared for the social and cultural adjustments. She was more European than she was an American.

At sixteen she spent the last half of her life living in three European countries and traveling the world. She saw the real Parthenon in Athens. She went skiing in the finest ski resorts in the world in Austria and Switzerland. She toured the Holy Land and went swimming in the Dead Sea. She went on Safari in Africa and walked the beaches of Hawaii, Tahiti, and Fiji. However, she had not been to a formal dance or a football game. She was not familiar with the pop songs of her American peers. She had not been on a real date and wondered if there was something wrong with the way she looked. She came back to a United States that went through the "Sexual Revolution." A short time after she arrived at Vanderbilt the school opened up to "coed dorms."

Looking back, it's not surprising she had social adjustment problems. Her peers could not relate to her experiences. When she said she lived in London, they thought she was from Kentucky. They thought she was either the biggest snob or the biggest liar they had ever met. Her brother, Carroll, on the other hand, had no problems. He was glad to get back home. He was in the engineering school and majoring in Systems and Information Science. After his first year, he had to make a decision. He was either going to play baseball or he was going to make it in the engineering school. Without consulting us, he elected to drop baseball and study. He knew where he wanted to go and he knew what he had to do to get there.

We received a call from Sheryl's roommate telling us that she was in the hospital. Grace was on the next flight back to Nashville to find out what was wrong. She made the decision for Sheryl to drop out of school and come back to Spain until she was feeling better. It was time for the Christmas holidays so our son, Carroll, flew back with Grace and Sheryl, and we went skiing in Andorra.

In the office we took on the problem of Catalana being overstaffed by one third. Under Spanish Law an employee could not be discharged without having committed a crime. We had to find another way. We discovered the company was contracting out a large amount of work that could be done by their own employees. Jose Arbos said we couldn't just change their jobs, so we developed a new wage structure with new jobs that paid more than the old jobs. The employee could voluntarily elect to change, take the training for the new job, and receive more pay for doing it. It's surprising how motivating a little more money can be!

Although Grace and I didn't have a car in Spain, we decided to get a Spanish driver's license so we could rent a car and take trips on the weekends. It was not easy because the exams were in Spanish. If we wanted a driver's license we had to pass the exam in Spanish. By this time we had learned enough Spanish to get by. We could read the signs and we could understand more Spanish than we could speak. We successfully passed the exams and were pleased when we received our license.

In 2009 when we were living in Franklin, Tennessee, I was shocked when I went shopping at a Publix Market to find I had to "Push 1 for English" when I slid my credit card through the machine. It was set to operate first on Spanish. I called the manager and complained. In a country where English is the predominant language I felt if someone couldn't speak English they could at least "Push 1 for Spanish." It wasn't long and the machines were changed. I do not feel that I'm biased or discriminating. When I was in Germany or Spain or Brazil, I didn't expect to see all the signs in English or everything printed in English.

One weekend Paul Temple and his wife invited Grace and I to visit Madrid with them. We were guests of a Spanish friend of theirs who owned a castle near Seville. We found the Roman aqueduct interesting, and when we went through a museum, Grace stopped me and pointed. "You see that Gothic Style piece of furniture?" she asked. "It's exactly the same as that bedroom set I wanted to buy in Barcelona."

"Okay," I said, "when we go back, if it's still for sale, buy it." In Madrid we also saw a dining room set that was hand-carved and we arranged to have it shipped to our apartment in Barcelona. Both the bedroom set and dining room furniture are show pieces and prized possession in our present home.

On July 16, 1970 a progress report was given to Catalana outlining the work provided under our contract. The following was established: an investment control system, standards and specifications for construction, methods and procedures for purchasing and storing of materials, a system of tariffs, a grid leakage reduction program, marketing goals, and recommendations for sales of appliances meeting natural gas standards. The following reports on the conversion program were submitted; survey of possible conversion methods, proposed organization for domestic and commercial appliance conversion, grid sectionalization for conversion, a meters program and a gas conditioning program.

On June 23, 1970 I presented a paper at a United Nations Symposium on the problems relevant to natural gas markets in Europe, titled Factors in the Introduction of natural gas in Spain. I also authored an article Barcelona LNG Facility Meets Spanish Needs, which was published in the September 1970 issue of Gas Magazine. In July 1971 our contract with Catalana was completed. All ten changes set out in my memo to Pedro Duran had been accomplished. They were achieved over the objections of many of the Catalana employees. It was hard for me to understand how anyone could want to continue operating in a manner that was going to bankrupt the company. Human nature seems to want to always take the path of least resistance. By mid July 1971 the company established an earnings record and was able to sell a new issue of common stock. A letter from Pedro Grau said that "*Kroeger & Smith performed competently and to our complete satisfaction.*" A letter from Jose Arbos dated July 5, 1971 said in Spanish that our company completed the terms of the contract to their satisfaction.

It was time to decide where the next opportunities would lead us. There were possibilities for work in Turkey, Greece, Brazil, and Australia. All would require long-term commitments, which could mean working and living outside of the United States possibly until retirement. I sat down with Grace to do some soul searching. "Since we were married, where have we lived that you have enjoyed the most and been the happiest?" I asked her.

She looked at me and said, "We have been married for more than twenty-five years. We have been in Europe for eight years. The longest time we have ever lived in one place is three years. Both of our children are back in the United States. Don't you think it's time we go back home and settle down?"

There was no way I could disagree with her. I was blessed to have a wife who had followed me all over the world. She wanted to go home and be near our children. It also was time to reduce the stress in my life. The decision was made. We were going home! Postscript: a short time ago I went on the Internet and looked up Gas Natural. It is the largest gas organization in Spain supplying natural gas to over five million customers and with LNG investments in Italy, Greece, and Brazil. It has a secure natural gas supply from Algeria in North Africa from both LNG tankers and an undersea pipeline.

28

Too High Powered for Nashville

It was the summer of 1971. We closed "Kroeger & Smith S.A." in Switzerland. Unfortunately, we had to close our company in New Jersey because it failed to develop new business. Now, any new business in Australia, Turkey, Greece, or Brazil seemed to be wholly dependent upon me remaining overseas. I was not willing to do that, so our working arrangement came to an end. Closing any company is not a pleasant experience. Moving back to the United States involved risk. It was clear that my experience in the energy business would not be transferable to Nashville, Tennessee.

We could have moved anywhere but Nashville was our choice for several reasons. Both of our children were in school at Vanderbilt. We would be close to Sheryl in case she needed our support. There were three other factors; first was climate. We wanted to be where there were four seasons, but I didn't want to shovel any snow. Second, we wanted to be in the south or the mid-west because we were more comfortable with the culture. Third, we didn't want to be in a very small town, or a large city like Atlanta. At the time Nashville was a "Fifteen Minute City." You could go anywhere in fifteen minutes.

Grace scouted around and found a three-bedroom apartment at "Park Road" on West End Avenue. It was within walking distance of Vanderbilt so it would be easy for our children to visit if they wanted or were in need of a home cooked meal. It had large rooms with high ceilings, which would accommodate the furniture we acquired in

Europe. My problem was the career change. After the death of Gerry Laufs, I was certain that stress was a killer. It creates both mental and physical problems. I was looking for a stress-free life. So, what was I going to do?

I made an appointment with Sam Fleming, the President of the Third National Bank, gave him my resume, and told him I was looking for something to do. He read my resume and asked me what my salary requirements were. I told him twenty-five thousand dollars a year, which was scaled down from what I had been making abroad. Looking back, I was ahead of the curve again. People in the United States didn't have a clue about business in the rest of the world. He asked me what was the work of a "Senior Advisor" at Esso. Then, he put down my resume and said, "You are too high-powered for Nashville. You should go to Houston or New York." I told him I had lived in Houston and New York and that was why I wanted to live in Nashville. It was clear he thought I was "a fish out of water."

Later, Bill Dickson, a professor at Vanderbilt, told me how things worked in Nashville. There were three different communities: Business, Academic, and Music. They were independent and did not work with each other. The business community was controlled by five "Old Money" families. They controlled every aspect of business and social life in the city. They set the salary structure down to the wages even janitors were paid. It was clear my experience wasn't transferable. I needed to develop different credentials. We had saved some money so I didn't have to worry about paying the bills for a while.

I learned Vanderbilt was starting up a new school of management. The new dean was Igor Ansoff, a nationally recognized expert on Corporate Strategy and Strategic Management. He had a different philosophy about business schools. He thought the product should have a combination of skills, Behavioral Science in addition to the traditional "hard skills" of Accounting, Economics, and Finance. I competed with the Harvard Business Graduates, but in the back of my mind I always thought they must know something I didn't. Also, I was confused by the human problems I encountered in my work. The solutions to technical problems were not difficult. It was the people problems I didn't understand. If a business firm was sinking, why didn't the crew want to save the ship? It's the same today. People riot in bankrupt countries and they expect to keep on receiving government benefits. I made an appointment with Dean Ansoff and we immediately were on the same page. He said they were starting a doctorial program and I was the ideal kind of candidate they were looking for.

I signed up and started classes. The students were an interesting group. The average age was about twenty-seven or twenty-eight. Many of them had returned to the States after working in the Peace Corps. One third of the student body was foreign students from Brazil, France, India, and other countries. The faculty was a strange group as well; a mixture of traditional teachers of business subjects but another group who developed courses like "Individual Behavior," "Small Group Behavior," "Learning to Learn," "Organization Theory and Design," "Influence Processes," "Organization Change," and "Strategic Management." Ansoff had an interesting theory but the implementation was going to take some doing.

Again, I was ahead of the curve. I had been accepted into a doctorial program that was yet to be developed. In the meantime I would take the normal courses with the Master's students. The school was called the Graduate School of Management. The "Behavioral Science" faculty convinced the dean that it should operate on a "Pass-Fail" system. They did not believe competition between students for grades was healthy. Also, students were mature enough that the second year they should be allowed to develop their own independent study program supervised by a faculty advisor. In addition the first year courses could be exempted by passing a Pre-Test. It was an innovative experiment headed for a clash with traditional Business School philosophy. The program was attractive to me. I was forty-five years old and not interested in sitting in a class listening to a professor regurgitate what he had read or learned in a research project. I wanted to find out why some businesses were successful and why so many failed.

If it had been Harvard Business School, I would have been looking for something else to do. I looked at the textbooks for Accounting, Economics, and Finance. They didn't look too difficult so I decided to try the Pre-Testing route. I would cram for two days, and then take the test. I used my tried and true method of preparing for exams: determine what in the material is important and if I were the instructor, "what questions would I ask?" In all of my undergraduate work I did not take any of these courses. I passed all three exams. In Economics I took the exam with three students who majored in economics in their undergraduate studies. The Economics Professor told me I made the highest score of those taking the Pre-Test. I guess there is no substitute for OJT ("On the Job Training").

In 1972 I was invited to present a paper at the annual meeting of the Institution of Gas Engineers in London. I was given the freedom to select my own topic. I flew to London and on May 18th gave my presentation, which I called Change and Exchange in International Gas Supply. The paper developed life cycle theory for national energy industries and individual energy firms. It showed high energy consumption was related to the standard of living and the relationship between per capita energy consumption and Gross National Product. In the discussion I posed the question; *"If thirteen percent of the world's population is consuming fifty percent of the world's energy, what does this mean, in terms of developing nations, of the energy resources in their location? Either a great quantity of new energy has to be found or there are going to serious problems of the reallocation of the energy that currently is available."* The paper created a huge amount of interest and later I was told that as a result of my paper the British Gas Industry instituted a premium fuel policy for natural gas in the UK. Looking back with energy problems of oil supply due to the increasing requirements of China and India, it appears the paper was prophetic.

Vanderbilt had an Honor Code and I was elected by the student body to be the Chairman of the Honor Council. One of the faculty members teaching computer programming brought charges against two students for cheating on a final exam. The two students were black and I knew we had a difficult task. When the Council held its hearing, we bent over backwards to make sure there could be no charges of discrimination. However, the evidence was indisputable. The papers were identical in every respect. The students were found guilty and expelled. Much later the students sued Vanderbilt for discrimination and I was on the witness stand for a day testifying in Federal Court. They lost their case.

Before I realized it, two years had slipped by. I decided I might as well qualify for a Master's Degree since I had completed all of the course work and my independent study program was approved. I elected to receive a degree in Business Management. For the first time in my college careers, I walked down the aisle and received my diploma without having it mailed to me.

Two of the students who graduated, Eduardo Vasconcellos and Jacques Marcovitch, were from Brazil. The summer of 1973 a seminar was held at Electrobraz to discuss assistance to the Sao Paulo State Council of Technology and the Management Institute of the University of Sao Paulo. Professor Rodinelli and I made a presentation of how Vanderbilt could provide assistance. The result was an agreement to assist in the design and development of two seminars on research management to be offered between September and December. Brazil was experiencing balance of payments problems and had a need to improve the quality of their products for export. The recommendation was to institute a change in the research organizations from theoretical research to applied research to assist small and medium-sized firms in product development and improvement in product quality.

By fall of 1973 my savings were nearly depleted. My work in Brazil helped GSM obtain a contract with the State of Sao Paulo for further assistance. I was named a Research Fellow and started to receive a monthly salary from Vanderbilt. Things were starting to change at GSM. The faculty had divided into two camps, the Hard Science group and the Behavioral Science group. This presented a big problem for the student body. Which side to join? It became very difficult for the Doctorial Students because our program was designed to produce a product that was a mixture of the two types. We had to get support from each and they didn't agree.

At the same time Dean Ansoff was getting caught up in the turmoil. Any dean's main job is fundraising. The local business community did not agree with the dean's philosophy. They were not interested in change agents coming out of the school. They wanted worker bees to come in and do what they were told. The consequence was that Ansoff left the school and the Finance Professor became the Acting Dean. The Behavior Group began to lose favor and the school was on the way to become a traditional Business School. Finally the requirements for the doctorial qualifications were determined. Four other students were admitted.

Three qualification papers had to be researched and developed. I started working on mine immediately. Once again I was naïve as to what I was coming up against. I was to later learn that in the academic system, faculty progress is measured by research and publication of articles in reputable journals or books. One of my papers was titled Managerial Development in the Small Firm. I submitted it to the California Management Review. It was accepted for publication and appeared in the Fall 1974 issue.

I should have known, like in Stone & Webster, I was doing too good a job. Behind the scenes younger GSM faculty were writing and submitting papers and were getting rejections. Not long ago (almost forty years later) I Googled my name to see what would come up. I was surprised to see that my article was still being used in bibliographies of papers on small business life cycles. Strangely, back at GSM, the issue of the California Management Review with my article disappeared from the school library.

I read in the Nashville Banner newspaper Governor Winfield Dunn was forming a task force to study the state's energy problems. This was in response to a telegram the governor received from President Nixon emphasizing the national energy problem. I volunteered to serve on the committee and ended up helping write the Task Force report, Energy in Tennessee. The report was submitted to the Governor on November 19, 1973. It concluded that the threat of an energy crisis was real and one of the recommendations was the establishment of a state energy office to serve as a focal point for energy matters in Tennessee.

On October 6th Egypt and Syria attacked Israel, starting the fourth Arab-Israel war. On October 8th OPEC's (the Oil Cartel) negotiations with the major oil companies to revise oil prices failed. On October 17th the OPEC Oil Ministers agreed to use oil as a weapon to influence the West's support of Israel and recommended an embargo against non-complying states. By November 5th an oil embargo was in effect. On December 12th I received a letter from the Taskforce Chairman, Ed Thackston, thanking me for my service on the committee. He wrote,

> I especially appreciate your efforts in helping to write and assemble the report. If it had not been for your help, the energy crisis might have been over by the time I could have completed the report.

In early March of 1974 I received a call from the Governor's Office and was told the governor wanted to talk to me. He said Tennessee was facing an energy crisis and he needed someone to come in and coordinate the state activities. He did not ask my political affiliation. He was very business-like. He said, "This needs a professional approach and I can see from your background you are a professional. You tell me what you need to do the job and if it's reasonable I'll do everything I can to see you get it." The governor presented me with a challenge. Solving the state's energy problems looked more interesting than trying to get a dissertation proposal approved by a split personality faculty at Vanderbilt. I accepted the governor's offer.

On March 11, 1974 the governor created the State Energy Office by Executive Order and I was appointed the director. Unlike the task force report recommendation, the office was not located in the Department of Economic and Community Development; it was directly within the office of the governor. Often opportunity comes disguised as a problem. The path of least resistance is to ignore it or let someone else deal with it. Doing nothing is a choice. It is easy to watch what is happening. Solving problems involves some risk. The choice to be a doer is made by risk takers. The satisfaction comes with the doing.

29

Energy Conservation for Tennessee and the U.S.

My first day as Director of the Tennessee Energy Office started out from scratch. After signing all of the necessary papers, I was on my own. I had no office, not even a chair! Within a few days I had a secretary, a young woman named Beth Jones. I told her, "You are going to be a secretary, but now our job is to create an office." We located office space in the Capitol Hill Building and arranged for the lease. Next, we went to the place that stored used furniture not needed by other state government departments.

A list was made of the new things we would need: movable walls, file cabinets, chairs, telephones, etc. I was surprised at how fast word got around that I would be hiring staff. I was besieged with calls from people that had friends or relatives looking for a job. I felt no strong reason to hire anyone because of political connections. I needed professional staff that were attracted by the challenge and wanted to help solve the serious problems the State was facing. I created an organization plan, job descriptions and requirements for each position. I learned from experience the place to eliminate personnel problems was upfront.

I was tough in interviews. I tried to convince applicants they wouldn't want to work for me. I said, "If you are looking for work in an intense, challenging environment, this might be the place for you.

You will not be told when to come to work or when to go home. You will be given problems to solve. If it takes staying late or coming in on Saturdays, that will be up to you. I will only ask you to get the job done efficiently and in a timely manner. However, if you are looking for a place to hang your hat eight to five and draw a pay check, this is not the place for you." I was looking for three types of people: those with technical, business, and legal backgrounds and experience. I wanted doers, not talkers or thinkers.

It wasn't long before I assembled a good staff of engineers, lawyers, and MBAs. I received a gift when a young woman, Claudia Viken, walked in who had been a newspaper reporter. She became my contact person with the media and handled all press releases from the office. I had more women and minorities on my staff than any other group in state government. Bernie Yomtov, an MBA from Vanderbilt, was given responsibility for research and later became my speechwriter. I also had three attorneys.

One of these was an exception to my rule of not hiring someone on the basis of a telephone call from an influential person. When Sam Bartholomew, a prominent Nashville attorney, called and recommended Tracy Swartschild, I listened. Tracy had just graduated from Vanderbilt Law School and had to wait another year until his wife finished Law School before moving back home to Virginia. He proved to be a worthy addition to our staff. I inherited Leon Guthrie and three other government employees who were allocating thirty percent of the state's petroleum products on an emergency basis.

Our first project was a small brochure, *Tips for Saving Gasoline! from Governor Winfield Dunn.* It was quickly copied by the State of Virginia down to the Tennessee three stars on the Piggy Bank. I was a panelist at the Southern Governor's Conference in Atlanta in May. Next, we started planning the first Governor's Conference on Energy Conservation. This took place on September 5th, 1974 co-sponsored by the National Federation of Independent Business. The keynote address was given by Frederick Dent, the Secretary of the U.S. Department of Commerce. This set the pattern for similar conferences held throughout the country. Governor Dunn was surprised when the president of NFIB presented him with the "Distinguished Service Award." We followed the Governor's Conference with a series of Regional Workshops throughout the state: Columbia, Cookeville, Chattanooga, Jackson, Nashville, Memphis, and Knoxville. I was the speaker before six other groups in November and December. In the first quarter of 1975, I was the featured speaker at eight other Engineering, Educational, and Business organization meetings. September through December of the year I was a guest on fourteen radio programs and appeared on four TV programs. The first quarter of 1974 I was on five radio programs and one TV station. I developed a very good relationship with all of the members of the media. I understood their need for a good story and tried to give them one. I was honest and forthright and never tried to avoid answers to tough questions. They appreciated the fact that in most of my presentations I used quotations from literature to illustrate my points.

As an example, when I was the speaker at the "Energy Conservation Regional Workshop" at the Chattanooga Choo Choo, I remarked extemporaneously that I noted as I came into the hotel a number of gas lights that burned twenty-four hours a day. I said it reminded me of the experience I had in Indiana when I researched the old gas production fields, which were now depleted. How tourists came on excursion trains to see the gas burning at the wells. I then quoted Emily Dickinson's verse *"My candle burns at both ends."*

I spoke the language of writers when I was with them, I spoke the language of engineers when I was with them, and I spoke the language of businessmen when I was with them. Communications is important and it was the keystone of my message in trying to convince people they should conserve energy. It was working. A letter from an Assistant Vice President at Baptist Hospital on January 17, 1975 said,

> By participation in the workshop and by careful study of the EPIC Manual, our organization has achieved significant reductions in electrical consumption (thirty-nine percent).

The need for energy conservation became more important and unique when in the fall of 1974 a nationwide coal strike occurred. It was a double whammy for the State of Tennessee. Seventy-eight percent of the electricity generated by TVA was fueled by coal. The TVA stockpiles of coal were down to a forty-five-day supply. The United Mine Workers contract for supply of bituminous coal expired on November 12th. TVA and the State of Tennessee could face the prospect of Blackouts and Brownouts. The problem in Tennessee was more acute than in other states because the average electric consumption in the state was double that of the national average because of the large number of homes which used electricity for heating. It was a critical situation so I met with TVA staff to see what their contingency plans were for rationing or allocation of electric power. I was shocked to learn they had no plans.

They said they might use rolling blackouts to conserve power. They had not thought through that there were hospitals and individuals on life support systems that would be cut off. Even a temporary cut-off could be a matter of life and death. The energy office started recommending that electric consumers help by reducing their thermostats to sixty-eight degrees to help reach the TVA goal of twenty percent reduction. The situation was serious since a reduction of ten percent by TVA could result in the laying off of one worker out of every three.

In October of 1974 a plan was proposed to operate the schools only four days a week in the event of continued energy shortages. School officials said that a four-day school week would not affect the quality of education. In October The Governor met with one hundred sixty power representatives who asked for help in the energy crunch. They were afraid of massive lawsuits in the event they were not able to fulfill contracts because of a power shortage. The governor told them the state did not have the authority to institute mandatory energy conservation measures. All the State Energy Office could do was encourage people to conserve energy voluntarily.

In late October I was asked to be a speaker at a transportation seminar at the University of Tennessee in Knoxville. *The Memphis Press Scimitar* carried the headline,

ENERGY DIRECTOR RAPS INEFFICIENT U.S. CARS.

The article continued,

> "Suppose, instead of contributing $6.5 billion a year to the bank accounts of oil-producing nations, we spent that sum on research to provide a more efficient, equally comfortable, means of individual transportation than the internal combustion automobile? Could we design a vehicle capable of moving twenty miles on a gallon of gasoline, or the equivalent in some other energy form? I find it incredible if we could not."

Looking back, does this sound familiar? Was it was prophetic?

A controversy arose in November when TVA still had no firm plans for allocation if and when their coal supply was diminished. At a conference I recommended that TVA request the facilities at Oak Ridge reduce their electricity consumption. The governor was disappointed that the voluntary conservation of electricity by TVA had only produced a four percent reduction. Oak Ridge was consuming fifteen percent of TVA's output. My view was the Oak Ridge facility had a ten to fifteen year stockpile of nuclear warfare materials and a five-year stockpile of nuclear materials used by citizens. It reasonably could reduce electric use for a short while to help alleviate the energy crisis.

My suggestion created a maelstrom of comments from critics and politicians. The governor came under fire and was required to say that the suggestion was mine and not his. The controversy pointed out the seriousness of the situation and the failure of many to develop plans for the "What if?" question. What if energy rationing became a reality? The alternative was for TVA to cut off power to industrial customers. Oak Ridge might continue operations, but the citizens of Tennessee would have power in their homes, but no paycheck because they would be out of work. An editorial in the Harriman News called for my resignation because closing of the AEC plant would create economic chaos in their area. Nobody wanted to recognize the consequences if TVA ran out of coal. The outcome was AEC promised to cut plant electricity use sixty percent to help ease the TVA power shortage.

In November 1974 a new governor was elected in Tennessee. Ray Blanton, a Democrat, would replace Winfield Dunn in January 1975. I was not a political person and was not concerned about the outcome of the election. Naively I believed the energy problems of the nation and in Tennessee were so severe that they transcended political partisanship. I continued to fight the battle for energy conservation of all fuels. When the new governor took office, I requested a meeting. I knew he was busy with transition and I was not concerned when I received no response.

One Friday evening I received a telephone call at my home from a reporter in Knoxville. He told me that he had just attended a press conference in Knoxville where the Governor stopped on his way back to Nashville from Washington, D.C. The issues of energy problems arose and the governor made the statement he was looking for someone to advise him on energy problems. "But Governor, you have a Director of the State Energy Office, Carroll Kroeger," a reporter said.

"Yes, but I'm going to get rid of him." the governor replied.

"I wanted you to know about it before it appears in tomorrow's newspapers," the reporter told me. I was glad I always had good relations with the media.

I thanked him for the information. The following Monday morning I called Vivian into my office and told her I wanted to hold a press conference as soon as possible. I called the staff together and told them what had happened. I was not going to wait for the governor to "get rid of me." I was submitting my resignation effective that date. I thanked them for all of their hard work and told them they could be proud of having been responsible for developing some of the first energy conservation programs in the country. At the press conference I announced my resignation. I said since the governor had never responded to my requests for meeting with him I did not feel I could effectively carry out the duties of my office. If he no longer wanted me to work for him, all he had to do was ask me in private and I would have submitted my resignation. Since he did not have the common courtesy to do that and had announced to the press he was going to get rid of me, I was responding in like manner. I was submitting my resignation effective that day.

I served as Director from March 11, 1974 to March 1, 1975, ten days less than a year. Looking back, energy conservation methods now in use throughout the nation were established in less than a year. Carl Brown, a law clerk in the office, wrote in his letter of resignation,

> Energy policy is not a simple matter to administer. And against that backdrop you stood engaged on a dozen energy fronts. Yet, despite the pressure, despite the long hours, despite the inherent difficulties, you remained a professional and there is no higher compliment in my vocabulary. Your availability, your sense of perspective—never sacrificing the big picture to the day to day exigencies, your imagination, your uncompromised dedication to the staggering task at hand, your sensitivity to employee needs, and your purposeful calm set an example which was not lost on me. It made working under you a joy and a challenge. Thank you for making it such a rich and meaningful experience.

I was about to learn a lesson in hardball politics. The governor immediately told all of the staff of the Energy Office that if he learned any of them had lunch with me or even had a private telephone conversation with me they would be fired. Although I have no proof, I believe the word went out that anyone giving me employment would be in trouble. There was a new set of rules in state government. Our son, who was the Director of Personnel for the Department of Economic and Community Development, was visited by two members of the governor's staff and given five names and told to put them on the payroll and see that they got paid effective the first of the year. When he replied that their request was against the law, he was told, "We didn't ask for a legal opinion. Do what you are told." He immediately went into his office and wrote out his resignation. Postscript to the story: near the end of his term, Governor Blanton, his brother, and his legal advisor were indicted and sent to Federal prison in disgrace for selling pardons and paroles.

In the meantime I was looking for something interesting to do. I began to receive calls from across the state encouraging me to seek the presidential appointment to the TVA Board of Directors. I had become very familiar with their operations and thought there were ways to improve their operations. A controversy was arising about their nuclear power program. The chairman asked Governor Dunn and I to fly down to visit the Browns Ferry Nuclear plant. It was clear on the plane he wanted to convince us to support his program. My Navy training had educated me about nuclear physics and nuclear safety measures. He said that MIT had made a statistical study and concluded that the possibility of a nuclear failure was better than the possibility of getting hit by lightning, I was not impressed. My reply was "Mr. Chairman, if I'm concerned about getting hit by lightning, I don't go out in a thunder storm. If you build a nuclear power plant near my home, there's no place my wife and children can go if you have a meltdown."

I made application for the appointment with the Presidential Personnel Office. I was told I had the most impressive resume they received. I visited the congressional offices and received letters of support from a bi-partisan group of more than twenty-five U.S. senators. I had support from all of the Environmental Groups in Tennessee because I had opposed the nuclear program on economic grounds. In my meetings with TVA Planners I looked at their assumptions and discovered two fallacies: the assumption that the price relationship between coal and "yellow cake" fuel would remain the same in future years, and, more importantly, they did not contract for fuel supply for each plant and that contracts had no firm price guarantee.

On Sunday March 16, 1976 I received the endorsement of the Chattanooga Times newspaper and the support of many others. I was told by the Presidential Personnel Office that three names had been submitted to President Ford. Announcement was made that the president had appointed James Hooper of Mississippi. Investigative reporters started checking him out. His business career was questionable. His wife being a National Committee Woman for the Republican Party could have been a factor in his appointment. Mr. Hooper failed to get confirmation by the Senate.

President Ford had to make a second appointment. In June 1976 he selected Thomas Longshore from Birmingham, Alabama to be his second nominee. Mr. Longshore's qualifications were in question and he also failed to be confirmed by the Senate. This was a "learning experience" for me in how political systems work. Neither of the two candidates had any real energy experience and failed to receive Senate confirmation.

TVA's nuclear program failed for economic reasons. They sold a billion dollars worth of bonds to finance the construction. If you drive by Hartsville, Tennessee, you can see the cooling towers that were built for a "Nuclear Park." The power plants were never completed. It does not give me pleasure to want to say "I told you so." If I had become a member of the TVA Board, could I have made a difference? I'll never know, but I know I would have tried! Today the nation still receives most of its oil from the Middle East and there is talk of the need for "Energy Independence." Consumers in Tennessee are being asked to conserve electric use because of the environmental impact of coal emissions from coal fired generating plants. As they say, "It's déjà vu all over again."

30

Two Ways to Lose a Million Dollars

One of the great lessons in life is learning how to overcome adversity. When I left the Tennessee Energy Office, I found a job in 1975. Third National Bank had a new president. When I asked him for help, he referred me to a member of the bank's board of directors. His name was Joe Davis and he had become wealthy in the coal business. Joe was a super tennis player at Montgomery Bell Academy and later at Vanderbilt. After college he worked for a Mr. Potter, learning the coal business. After ten years he branched out on his own and over time developed a coal property in Kentucky with a unit train operation, which became the highest coal producing mine in the country. Mapco got a new president who decided to transform it into an energy company. It was formed as "Mid America Pipeline Company" to transport petroleum products from the Gulf refineries to the upper Midwest. Mapco negotiated with Joe to acquire his coal business through a tax-free exchange of stock.

The bank president said that the market value of Joe's stock was over forty million dollars. All of his financial eggs were in one basket and he needed to diversify his holdings. I went to work for Joe at eighteen thousand dollars a year, but the carrot was that when he acquired new businesses I would manage them for him. It developed into an interesting job. When the word gets out that you have money, all kinds of people come out of the woodwork with proposals they want you to finance. I took on the responsibility of screening all of these proposals.

Joe already was involved with Jim Stewart, in a partnership taking over a contract from a company in Florida to build fifty miles of the Pan-American Highway through the jungles of Panama. Most of the proposals I looked at were scams or pipe dreams. Many were owners of drilling rigs who wanted financing to drill wells for oil in locations they knew would strike oil but not enough to make production economically feasible. They would make their money drilling the wells. Joe was ultra conservative. He wanted to get back into the coal business, so I had to learn the coal business.

I joined the American Coal Association and studied all of their books. We looked at coal properties all of the way from Oklahoma to West Virginia. It was an interesting exercise. However, each time we arrived at a point for Joe to sign an agreement, he would back off. Things started going wrong with the project in Panama. A group of road builders from Tennessee had been engaged to do the work in Panama. They knew how to build roads and bridges in Tennessee but had no experience out of the country. This turned out to be a fatal flaw. Joe asked me to go to Panama to see what the problems were.

I flew to Panama City and was flown to a base camp in the middle of the jungle. It was halfway between Panama City and the border of Columbia. It had to be self-sufficient with barracks for the workers, and a commissary to provide them with food. Several things were evident. First, none of the Tennesseans spoke Spanish, nor were they interested in trying to learn. Second, they didn't know in Panama there was a five-month rainy season. The jungle was a rain forest and you couldn't do construction work during the rainy season. The contract had a penalty clause if the job was not completed on time.

The Tennessee contractors didn't understand the Spanish culture and couldn't get their equipment and replacement parts cleared through Panama customs. When I asked the Job Superintendent about the problems, he said, "These damn Panamanian workers are lazy and won't work." Under Panamanian law at least half of the work force had to be local labor. I got a driver and jeep to take me out to a job site. We stopped at a location where a crew of workers were standing and not working. When I asked for the one in charge in Spanish, they perked up. One came up, smiled, and it was clear he was happy to see a "gringo" who spoke Spanish. The crew was supposed to be building the concrete abutments for culverts to drain water under the roadbed.

They would dig out the dirt, put the plywood forms in place, and wait for the concrete to be poured. They would have to wait until the concrete set before they could move the forms to a new location. They had dug out places for the next sets but didn't have enough forms. All they needed was more plywood to make more forms!

The project was losing twenty-five thousand dollars a month on the commissary and they didn't know why. They sold tickets to the workers who would turn one in when they went to the commissary for each meal. The person collecting the tickets was supposed to destroy them. Instead, he was putting them in his pocket and reselling them. Knowing the culture of the country you are trying to work in is essential! I returned to Nashville and gave my report to Joe. There was no way to save the project. It was too far gone. The result was that Joe lost a million dollars and Jim Stewart lost a million dollars

After that Joe became even more "gun-shy." It became clear he was wary of getting involved in acquiring other businesses. There was no incentive for me to remain with Davis Coal and no reason for Davis Coal to keep me on the payroll. We agreed to come to a parting of the ways. Lesson Number One—be careful doing business in a foreign country if you don't speak the language, understand the culture, and know local people you can trust. It's not easy to accept losing a million dollars. It's even harder to make a million dollars. What makes the difference between a business that is successful and one that fails? It's a question that has lasted over time. If there was an easy answer, everyone would be running a successful business. It's the same question about being successful in life. The answers probably are similar.

Fast forward to 1982. I was sitting at my desk at Belmont School of Business when a student walked in and said, "I've decided you should be my partner in a tax and duty free business."

"Really," I said, "and what makes you think I should be your partner?"

He smiled and said, "Because I'm from Greece and my parents started the duty free business there. I think there is an opportunity here in the United States to do the same thing. You are the only one around here who has had international business experience and the understanding to make it work." Other students came to me with business ideas and I did not take this one seriously.

"Where do you think it would be possible to start this business?" I asked.

"In Buffalo, New York," he said, "there is a good border crossing into Canada and no duty free business is located there."

"Okay," I said, "put together a business plan and I'll look at it."

Usually after that kind of a conversation the student would go away and I would never see them again. However, in about a week he was back with a plan. He had photos of the location, with cost estimates for a building and equipment. They totaled almost five hundred thousand dollars. "Where do you think we would get the money to do this?" I asked. "I don't have five hundred thousand dollars. Do you have five hundred thousand dollars?" He said he thought we could go to a bank and borrow it. "A banker is not going to loan a half million dollars to a college student and professor just because they think they can start a new business," I told him.

"What would they require to make such a loan?" he asked.

"A going business concern that has a proven earnings record," I told him.

"Okay," he said, "I'll look for one"

I thought that was the end of that and forgot about him. In about two weeks he was back. "There is one in upper New York State at the border that has been in business for many years. It has four owners who are getting up in years and I think they might be willing to sell. I've talked to one of them and he would like to meet us."

"You meet with him and tell him I would have to see the last five years of their financial statements before I would be willing to meet with him," I told him. Again he went away and once again he was back with the financial reports for a company called "Champlain Tax and Duty Free." I looked them over and was surprised. It was a business with a huge profit margin. "What do they want for this business?" I asked.

"Ten million dollars, but they will sell it for three million down and hold the paper on the remaining seven to be paid back to them over ten years." Some quick calculations made it look like it might work. We made arrangements for the meeting.

We went to Champlain, New York one weekend, met one of the owners, and inspected the property. It was unique. The firm owned five acres at the border crossing of Interstate 10, the main highway from New York to Montreal. It was the only business in the country to actually own the land at the border crossing on which the duty free shop was located. It looked like it might be an acquisition that would work. "We will have to put together a business plan and see how the numbers look," I said.

We crunched numbers and came up with a business plan. We took it to a bank in Nashville and they looked at it. Their answer was "No." We went to the office of J.C. Bradford Stock Brokers and they said "No." It was clear there were two problems; people in Nashville didn't understand the tax and duty free business and it was too far away for them to be interested. We approached a venture capital firm in New York City. They said if they looked at it they would have to have a controlling interest in the business. We weren't willing to turn the business over to someone else who would make all of the business decisions. We were going to have to find someone who understood the duty free business and was in international business.

"Do you know anyone who might help us find a bank?" he said.

I thought and said, "I might, but it is not going to be easy. If we got a loan, it would be highly leveraged. It would be very unusual to get someone to do it for us without our having any money in it." I thought about the Finance Director of the British Gas Corporation. He might know a Merchant Bank in London we could talk to. I called him and he agreed to make an introduction. To make a long story short, after long, difficult negotiations we got the loan.

We got a lawyer in Nashville who represented us on a contingency arrangement. He arranged for a lawyer in New York who charged us ten thousand dollars. Grace borrowed it at a Nashville Bank. When it was final, Citibank, which represented the London bank, had one hundred thousand dollars withdrawn from our bank account for services they rendered for the London Bank. We owed the Nashville lawyers twenty-five thousand dollars for their services. We took over management of the operation. In order to pay off the debt we would have to increase sales ten percent a year. Taking inflation into account, it looked like we could do it.

We came up with some innovative ideas. Tour buses would stop occasionally and their passengers were good customers. If we could get all of the tour buses to stop, we would be in good shape. Why not sell them tax and duty free diesel oil for their buses? If they could save money for their bus, they would stop at our shop. The passengers would have to get off the bus while we were refueling it. We made arrangements with CITGO and were in business!

We moved to Montreal, leased an apartment on Nun's Island, and enjoyed the summer. The city has great restaurants and we found adjusting to a bi-lingual culture no problem. We tried to speak French and were accepted with no problems. When the weather turned cold, we bought winter clothing and tried to adjust. We went to a hockey game and found it interesting and somewhat exciting. It got really cold, twenty below zero. It's not safe to stay out in the cold in that kind of weather. You can get frostbite very easy.

At Christmas Grace and I looked at each other and said, "What are we doing here?" We packed up, got in our car, and returned to Nashville. Several months later we got notification from the New York State Government to cease selling tax and duty free gas and diesel oil. It happened to the previous owners when they opened the shop to sell normal merchandise. They fought it through the New York courts and won. It looked like we would have to do the same thing to sell tax and duty free gas and oil. While we were looking at the problem, another thing happened that changed everything.

There was a huge change in the exchange rate between the U.S. and Canadian dollar. Most of our customers were Canadian who came over into New York State on vacation or to go shopping. The Province of Quebec launched a campaign to get their citizens to stay home and not spend their money in the United States. Our business took a nose dive. The change in exchange rate was the same as increasing the price of our merchandise forty percent. Over the next year we reached a point where we could no longer make the payments on the bank loan and the payments to the former owners.

I stopped taking a salary to try and help the financial situation. It was not enough. We had to file for bankruptcy. It's not pleasant to fail in business. Sometimes it is because of your mistakes. In the case of "Kroeger & Smith Management Consultants" in New Jersey, it was because we thought we had a product that everyone would buy. We were ahead of our time and wrong. With Champlain Tax & Duty Free we were so highly leveraged there was no room for error. Nobody could have foreseen such a change in the exchange rate, but it happened. I was wrong and blinded in thinking that we could make it work. If things had gone right, I would be a multi-millionaire.

Greed can blind you and it clouded my judgment. My partner went back to Greece and because I had given a personal guarantee, I was faced with the problem of paying the Nashville Law firm the twenty-five thousand dollars owed by the company. It took me five years to pay it off. Lesson Number Two: if you start a new business, plan for things to go wrong. Have a plan "B" and a plan "C." Make sure you have enough capital in reserve to weather a financial storm.

Do you learn something from failure? Certainly! Ask any football coach. He will tell you that a team learns more from losing a close game than they do when they trounce another team. You learn from making mistakes. That's what is called experience. You adjust, make changes, and try to get better. The coach of the Green Bay Packers, Vince Lombardi, said, "It's not that you get knocked down. It's whether you get back up again." There is no substitute for persistence in life. Winners never quit and quitters never win!

Lesson Number Three: choose a business partner carefully. The quickest way to lose a friend or relative is to loan them money or go into business with them. There are no problems as long as things are going well. The problems come if the business becomes highly successful or goes down the tubes. Too much money or no money creates a parting of the ways. There are exceptions. I've had business partners three times. Two were failures. The success was with my wife Grace. It succeeded because of the huge amount of trust we had in each other. Failure was not a choice for us. We took big risks and both worked our bottoms off twelve hours a day, seven days a week to make the business succeed.

31

You Can't Stop Students from Cheating

Working for Joe Davis in the coal business did not go well and I was looking for a job again. The president of Third National Bank in Nashville had been helpful in getting the job with Joe, so I asked him to help me again. He picked up the phone and called the Chancellor of Belmont University and arranged an appointment. Belmont was a small school located near Vanderbilt, which before the war had been Ward-Belmont, a fashionable girl's finishing school. The main building was Belmont Mansion, a historic Pre-Civil War plantation house. Finishing schools did not survive after World War II and in the 1950s it was taken over by the Southern Baptist Convention and turned into Belmont College.

My meeting went well and he suggested I talk with the Dean of the School of Business, Howard Wells. A few days letter I met with the Dean. He introduced me to some of the faculty, and told me I would like Dr. Jay Selleck because we had similar backgrounds. Selleck was not a pure academic; he was teaching because he liked to teach. He had an extensive business background having worked for Avco (an aircraft manufacturing firm) and currently was part owner of a company that made safety equipment that turned off machines if a worker's hands got near where they could be injured by the machinery. He also was a Lt. Colonel in the Tennessee National Guard.

Many of the faculty had practical business experience. Lawrence Glover taught accounting and was a CPA with his own business. Robert Mulloy had extensive experience in the music business. Belmont developed a unique niche in "Music City USA" and was the only school in the country offering a degree in music business. It looked like a perfect fit and the Dean gave me an application to fill out for employment. I waited for more than a week without any return call from the dean and called Jay Selleck to see what was going on. "I think you better come to my office," he said. We made an appointment and when I entered his office he closed the door and smiled.

"What's going on?" I asked.

He chuckled and said, "The dean is in a quandary and doesn't know what to do. He wants to hire you but has a problem with your application."

"What's the matter?"

"You remember there is a question which says, 'Do you consume alcoholic beverages?'"

"Sure, I answered it truthfully," I said. "In moderation. You know I'm not an alcoholic, but Grace and I have a glass of wine occasionally."

"That's the problem. The dean asked the chancellor a hypothetical question if someone didn't give a firm 'No' to that question could he hire them. The Chancellor said he couldn't. So Howard doesn't know what to do."

"I tried to tell the truth," I said. "I don't want to be a hypocrite."

"Okay," said Jay, "we're going to solve the problem. Here's another application. I want you to fill it out and when you get to that question say 'No.'"

"But that will not be the truth," I said.

"Look," he said, "we have a faculty member who is an alcoholic. Everybody knows it because sometimes at commencement he is so drunk he can hardly walk in the procession. This application is only to protect someone's rear end if you should embarrass the school."

Selleck looked me straight in the eye. "Do you have a drink in your hand right now?"

"No," I replied.

"Then write 'No' as your answer. I'll take the application to the dean. His problem will be resolved and you can start work here." Teaching at Belmont was fun. The dean started me out at night on American Management Association courses. The students were full-time employees who wanted to improve their job skills. I was rewarded after teaching a course for Administrative Assistants when a middle aged woman called to say that after completing the course, she had been promoted from Executive Secretary to Administrative Assistant. Next I taught a daytime course "Introduction to Business" My time in law school at Indiana University in Indianapolis provided background for me to start teaching "Business Law" and Selleck asked me to take over the courses he had been teaching in "Personnel Management" and "Business Policy and Corporate Strategy." I was attracted to get my MBA at Vanderbilt because Dean Igor Ansoff was nationally known as the expert in Corporate Strategy. It was a natural fit for me to take over. Jay said because it was a case study course taught like Harvard Business School, there was a big job to grade the papers. He would pick out the three or four best students from the class and make them graders. So I followed his method.

A problem arose when some of the students in the class complained that the graders were not consistent. Some did not grade as hard as others. I decided the solution was for me to do the grading. The first time I did it I was surprised. Four of the papers were exactly the same! I wrote a big fat zero on each of them and the next class meeting announced what I had discovered and that if it happened again the culprits would be expelled from the class. After class, one of the students came and said he did the work and the others copied from him. I told him he was as guilty as they were and not to allow anyone to copy his work again. The next one was a tall basketball player. I closed the door to my office because he started shouting at me. "You're not fair," he said. "Everyone knows that copying was allowed in this course. You didn't warn us you didn't allow cheating in your class."

I was shocked. A student was telling me it was okay to cheat in this Baptist school. "Well, now you have been warned," I told him, "and you better not try it again in any of my classes." A short time later two students knocked on my office door. "Mr. Kroeger," they said, "We want to thank you for what you did in class today. We do our own work and don't think it's fair if others copy and get away with it." They went on to say that they thought the school should have an Honor Code and asked if I would support them if they made an appointment with the chancellor to request adoption of an Honor Code. I couldn't believe the school didn't have one. I attended four schools: Washburn, Nebraska State, Rice, and Vanderbilt. Each had an Honor Council and Code. In fact, at the Graduate School of Management at Vanderbilt, I served as Chair of the Honor Council.

I was at a school without an Honor Code and students who wanted to have one. How could I refuse? I told them they had my full support and would be happy to go with them to try to convince the administration to adopt one. The day arrived and we met with the chancellor and the dean of students. The students gave their presentation. The chancellor leaned back in his chair and said, "Here we go again. This comes up about every two or three years. Students are going to cheat. You can't stop them." The dean of students joined in. "You can't stop it, and besides, if we had an Honor Council, sometime a student would be found guilty and they would want to expel them. I would have to deal with their parents and try to explain it."

The meeting was over and I couldn't believe that a Baptist School would condone cheating in its classes. From then on, the first day of my classes each semester I announced the rules for my class. I didn't allow cheating. There were consequences for bad behavior. Anyone that tried it in my class would be tossed out. If they didn't like my rules, they could withdraw from my classes. Now, the first day, was the time to do it. I did not know what would happen after that, but I knew cheating was wrong. Every exam I took in college I had to sign the honor pledge "I have neither given nor received any aid on this exam."

The results were surprising. My classes could only hold forty students. From that time on, at registration the registrar had to cut off enrollment to my classes because of the demand. Anyone who thinks young people don't appreciate rules and structure is wrong. There are boundaries that make it possible for civilized people to live together peacefully. Good behavior deserves to be rewarded. All should understand there are consequences for bad behavior. Something can be done about cheating and bad behavior. The best time for young people to learn this is at home and, if necessary, in college.

I look back and I probably was an exception. One of the problems in our educational system is reflected in the words of the dean of students. High school principals and college administrators are afraid of parents and a lawsuit. That day I spent testifying in Federal Court for the Vanderbilt Honor System is a good example. It's much easier to look the other way than to fight for what is right. One of the real challenges in life is deciding whether to take the path of least resistance or fight for what is right.

There are times when you are a teacher that something happens that makes it all worthwhile. It happened to me the summer of 1980. I was sitting in my office when the telephone rang and a male voice said, "Professor Kroeger, I'm in town and I'd like to take you to lunch." We arranged to meet at a restaurant nearby and my curiosity was aroused. Why would a former student want to buy me lunch? I arrived at the restaurant and was surprised to see a tall young man in a Navy Officer's uniform. On his chest was a pair of bright gold pilot's wings. Then it hit me! Over a year ago this student had knocked on my office door and asked for advice. He said that Dr. Selleck had suggested he talk to me because I had been a Navy officer and might be able to help him.

"I have a big problem," he said. "I've passed the requirements to get into the Navy flight program and all I have to do is finish my degree."

"That doesn't sound like a problem to me," I said.

"You don't understand, I have to pass the course in Mathematical Analysis. If I don't pass this course, I don't graduate and I don't get into the Navy program. If I take the course this summer at Tennessee State, can I transfer the credits to Belmont?"

"Why don't you just take the course here at Belmont?" I asked.

"I have a personality conflict with the Math teacher," he said.

"You have a huge problem," I said. "He is the head of the Math Department and has to approve transfer credits. If he thinks you went to Tennessee State to avoid him or because you think it will be easier there, he won't approve the transfer."

"What am I going to do?" he said furtively.

"How bad do you want to fly a Navy plane?" I asked.

"More than anything in this world, I'd do anything that's not illegal or immoral to fly."

"Then you have no choice," I said. "You must make an appointment with the Math teacher, eat humble pie, and tell him what you just told me. Tell him you need his help. Say you will do whatever he tells you as long as it's legal and moral. If you have to get down on your knees and beg, do it."

"I can't do that, it's too hard for me."

"If you are going to let your ego stand in the way of reaching your dream, then forget it," I said. "If you think this is hard, you don't know what hard is. I went through thirty-one months of Navy Officer Training. Math was my poorest subject, so I can sympathize with you. But if you think this is hard, the Navy program will be ten times harder! They will push you to the limits of your mental and physical endurance. They will force you to do mental and physical things you think you won't be able to do. The Navy flight program is an elite program. They will test you and do everything they can to make you quit. If there's the slightest possibility you might quit when you get into a tough situation, they will weed you out. They only want people who, when faced with an impossible task, say without hesitation, 'No problem, I can do that!' You might as well find out now whether you are a quitter!"

"I don't know if I can do it," he said, getting up to leave.

"It all depends on how bad you want to fly that Navy plane," I told him. I don't recall seeing him after that. I was busy teaching my courses in Personnel Management, Business Law, Business Policy, and Corporate Strategy. It was only when I walked into the restaurant I recognized him. He had changed, his posture was straight, and he had filled out physically. He looked handsome in his Navy Ensign's uniform. The gold wings on his chest told the story. He walked over, grasped my hand firmly, and said, "I want to thank you for your advice. You were right when you told me what I had to do to get through Math Analysis. But you lied to me!"

"What did I say that wasn't true?" I asked.

"You said the Navy program would be ten times harder than my going to talk to my Math teacher. It wasn't ten times harder, it was a hundred times harder, but I didn't quit!" We had a nice lunch and talk. He was home on leave and soon would go on for further training to learn how to fly multi-engine planes. I congratulated him for his perseverance and told him I was a little envious. My dream at one time was to wear those gold wings. I knew the price he paid to earn them. He was one of the Navy's elite and had every right to be proud.

He thanked me again, we shook hands, and I returned to my office at Belmont. I never saw him again. But his call and that lunch will remain to the end of my days. It's the kind of thing that makes being a teacher worthwhile. After teaching for five years at Belmont, I applied for tenure. When the Chancellor asked the Business School Dean what the students thought of me, he said, "They think Mr. Kroeger is hard, but he is fair."

32

Building a Nashville Business Incubation Center

We moved back to Nashville and I stopped taking a salary from the Tax and Duty Free business. I was looking in the "help wanted" section of The Tennessean and noticed that Tennessee State University was looking for a director of a new organization called "Growth Enterprises, Inc," which was to manage the operations of "The Nashville Business Incubation Center." It sounded interesting so I sent in an application. Later I was called in for an interview. The concept was innovative. The idea was to provide below market cost of leasing space for entrepreneurs to start a new business, help acquire the managerial know-how, and become independent within two to three years.

The project was a joint venture between Tennessee State University (TSU) and The Tennessee Valley Authority (TVA). TSU would provide the land for a new building to be constructed and TVA would provide the funding. A third organization would be created, a not-for-profit company to be called Growth Enterprises, Inc. The latter would be given a contract by TSU to manage the operation of the Incubation Center. A short time after the interview I received a call from TSU and was told I had been selected for the job.

It was just like the Tennessee Energy Office all over again. I didn't have a chair to start with. TSU agreed to provide a temporary office and Jenny Lemons as an assistant. The new eighteen thousand square-foot building was under construction across the street at 10th and Charlotte, but would not be finished for several months. It was designed to house ten start-up or existing businesses. My job was to take this idea from concept and build it into a going operation. The first order of business was to recruit a board of directors of local business men and women. It wasn't an easy assignment. Many declined or suggested someone else.

One of those was Phil Bredesen, who had become a successful owner of a HMO Health business. (He later became Mayor of Nashville and a two term Governor of the State.) Phil was intrigued by the concept and agreed to serve on the new board. Others recruited were: Sam Bartholomew, partner of a Nashville Law firm, Wayne Oldham, a successful owner of a number of Wendy's franchises, Bob McNeilly, a Vice President of First American Bank, and several others. The center opened for business on Thursday, April 26, 1986. It was marked by the planting of an oak tree in the grass near the entrance. The tree was to emphasize the center's theme "From Acorns to Mighty Oaks."

The first problem we encountered was the building had been designed to house light manufacturing type businesses. This type of business required a large amount of startup capital and we could not find any to go into the Incubation Center. We had to revise the requirements for entry. TSU had been traditionally a school for minorities. If we were to recruit minority entrepreneurs and help them become successful business owners, they would not be able to raise the capital for a light manufacturing business. The result was that the businesses we were going to be housing in the building were going to require air conditioning. We had to go through two bureaucracies in order to get approval, both TVA and TSU. That took most of the summer. We also had to go through the same process when we ordered the furniture for our office.

I was blessed to get Jennie Lemons as my assistant. She knew how to thread through the maze of the State University system. She knew the gatekeepers and those in the unofficial positions of power. She had an MBA from TSU, and was the widow of a prominent black doctor. The next thing on my agenda was to enlist the help of the local media to get the word out and inform the community about the project. It was one of the first in the country and a pilot project. The organizational structure was strange. I knew from the start there would be problems because I would have to answer to three different bosses: TSU, TVA and the new board of directors. This was not an ideal situation from an organization design standpoint. The TVA representative was Ken Looney. Dr. Otis Floyd was the interim President of TSU.

Slowly people began to come in wanting to start new businesses. Most didn't have a clue other than an idea or a dream. Of course none of them had any startup capital. They thought "that was what we did, give them the money!" None of them had heard of a business plan, let alone how to develop one. The best one I interviewed wanted to quit his job and be in the office janitorial business. He already had the necessary equipment; brooms, mops, pails, and cleaning materials. He had been moonlighting and built enough satisfied clients that he couldn't work his fulltime job and moonlight too. He was ready to take the risk and be in business for himself. I approved his application.

As time progressed, the best applicants turned out to be individuals who had started sometimes in their home or a small space. They wanted to grow their business and we offered them that possibility. A good example was "Christie Cookie Company." Christie started his business in his kitchen, eventually opened a retail shop on Main Street in Nashville. He couldn't continue mixing cookie dough and baking the cookies in his kitchen. He was the first successful business to come into and eventually leave the center. By October of 1986 we were still seeking clients. Lillian Coleman, of Elim Inc., a small package shipment company, signed a lease. Over a period of time she was joined by Carpets of Art, a commercial flooring operation, a general contractor, GEM Construction, John Carnes, a commercial photographer, ADTECH productions Inc, a manufacturer of computer systems, HI-TECH LABS, Inc., a designer and manufacturer of electronic products, and Gil Williams Productions, a commercial photography and video production company. The center reached eighty percent capacity in May 1987.

May 13–14th, I presided over the Tennessee Business Incubation Conference at the Sheraton-Nashville Hotel in Nashville. Things were settling down into a business operation. I spent much of my time promoting the idea of Incubation Centers. On December 14, 1987 I received a Certificate of Appreciation from the Nashville Minority Business Development Center for my support of minority economic development. As a result of our promotional efforts one of our tenants, HI-TECH LABS, was named as one of the "100 Ideas for New Businesses" in the December 1987 issue of Venture Magazine. In March 1988 I was asked to serve as a judge for the WLAC/AM and Sovran Bank Fifty Thousand Dollar New Business Grant. The award was presented at a banquet on April 22, 1988 at Chancellor's in the Vanderbilt Plaza Hotel.

The center achieved international prominence on May 27th when it was visited by a delegation of ten Economists from the Soviet Union as a part of the USA-USSR Seminar on Regional Economic and Planning. June 20th I received a letter from Dr. Mary Beth Pudup from the University of West Virginia, a member of the American delegation. It read in part,

> Because the visit to Nashville was the last item on the Soviet's literary, I had feared they would be tired and already thinking about home by the time we arrived. How wrong I was! The US Seminar delegates, including myself, had been telling the Soviets all along about the importance of small business and local initiatives in local community growth. But the whole thing remained an abstraction until the delegation visited the Incubation Center. Witnessing the small business center made them true believers. As one of the delegates himself remarked to you, the work you do is exactly the sort of thing the Soviets wish to experiment with. The visit to the Incubation Center made a valuable contribution in the success of the entire field trip.

In August I agreed to present a portion of the conference on Rural Small Business Incubation Centers at the Rural Revitalization Conference at UT Martin. In early December the Chairman of the Board of Directors called me on the telephone and invited me to go to lunch. It was Friday and we went to one of the most expensive restaurants in Nashville. After lunch he told me what a super job I had done, but he said, "It's time for a new face and I would like to have your resignation on Monday."

I was shocked. "What have I done wrong?" I asked.

"Nothing, you've done a wonderful job, but it's time for someone else to take over the operations of the Incubation Center," he said. I was hurt. If I had been told that I had screwed up, I could have accepted his request. It didn't seem fair and it took me a long time to get over it.

Looking back, I understand. It was time for a "caretaker" type of person, one to maintain and perpetuate the operations. They no longer needed a "creator/builder." Upon reflection it's easy to see why a new face was needed. I was not a caretaker. My entire career I had been a change agent or an entrepreneur. In Indiana I was not content because I was not a "caretaker" personality. At Washington Natural, in Germany, in Britain and Spain I was happy because I was a "change agent." I was a "creator/builder" at the Tennessee Energy Office and at the Nashville Business Incubation Center. The time would have come for me to realize it was time for me to move on.

The Chairman of the Board did what Governor Ray Blanton did. He fired me! I did what I told the woman in Seattle to do. I put my ego back together said, "Nobody is ever going to do this to me again," and I did what I was good at doing. I started a new business with my wife. It is not easy to be out of work, especially when you believe it has nothing to do with how well you have done your job. It's easy to think it's not fair. The normal thing is to not want to take any risks and keep on doing what you have always done. However, life is not fair and it doesn't do any good to sit around feeling sorry for yourself. It doesn't help for the government to keep giving people unemployment checks. The only thing that does help is for each person to get up off their butt and go find some work like my father did during the "Great Depression."

Tom Brokaw called some of these people the "Greatest Generation." The reason was they were the product of the "Great Depression." They learned how to cope with and overcome adversity. There are great lessons to be learned from failure. It was wrong for the Behavioral Scientists to change the grading system at Vanderbilt to Pass/Fail. There is nothing wrong with competition. It's a competitive world. Learning how to overcome failure and adversity is more important than stroking someone's self esteem. The sooner educators learn this the better our children will be able to meet the challenges of this new century.

33

Good Looks—Curse Or a Blessing?

From the beginning I was told I was special. An older brother died in childbirth and my mother had a very hard time delivering me. The doctor told her she could not survive trying to have another child, so I was special to both my mom and dad. It never occurred to me that I was different until much later. It was only after changing jobs three times that it dawned on me it wasn't the people in the company's behavior that was the problem. The problem was me! Everyone was satisfied with the way things were. I thought there were better ways of doing things. As Pogo said, "We have met the enemy and he is us!"

I have been different in many other ways, which I never fully understood. Our Creator made each of us different from all others. It's as if he breaks and throws away the mold after each of us is born. If you study your ancestry, you begin to see why. The farther back you go, the bigger the tree gets. As I was growing up, I was told, "You are a good looking young man." It did not register with me that I had been endowed with what some call "good looks." I grew up as an only child and I learned to be very independent. I developed what some psychologists would call a desire for "personal space." In other words, I have never been a "hugger." In fact, I'm a "loner."

That doesn't make me conceited. It means personal relationships are not trivial for me. Experts say we form our opinion of someone within the first few seconds we see them. They call this "first impressions." When I was growing up, I was told how I looked was important. In business they say it is very important. When you go for that interview, you should look your very best. If you watch TV commercials, you get the impression that the first glance makes a difference. Sometimes it's called "love at first sight." I had some Navy buddies that fell in love with every good-looking girl they saw.

I became aware that girls were attracted to me. Not all girls, of course; the ones I was interested in didn't give me the time of day. Fortunately I was very naïve as far as relationships with members of the opposite sex were concerned. A very aggressive girl taught me how to kiss and put my hand on her bra when we were in high school. I was shocked when she got married and told me that it did not have to change our relationship. Another girl in high school tried to seduce me and fortunately I resisted because I wanted to join the Navy and be a fighter pilot. Later I learned that she had been impregnated by another boy who didn't want to marry her.

When I was at Rice a very attractive blond told my roommate, Bob Smader, she thought I was conceited. If I gave that impression, it was not because I was conceited; it was because I was afraid for anyone to get too close to me. I created an invisible wall. Two secretaries tried to seduce me. The first was in Indiana. Her approach was subtle. Frank Sinatra had a hit record at that time, "All the Way." She looked me and said she was ready to go "All the Way." Later, at Christmas she gave me the Glenn Miller recording of "In the Mood." She was in the mood but I wasn't. I remembered what Arthur Elliott said about getting in the employees' "drawers."

The other secretary was in London. She was twenty-eight and said she was a virgin but ready to have sex. She didn't want to have a baby so she said she had started taking the pill. Her problem was that the only men she was interested in were already married. She said she had a Trust Fund worth a half a million pounds. At the exchange rate of that time, it was worth about one and a half million dollars. A nice dowry! That comment passed right over my head. When she learned that Artie Shaw's band was one of my favorites, she gave me his album "Any Old Time." The lyrics say, "Any old time you want me, I'll be there."

I was forty years old, married with two children, and again I remembered what Arthur Elliott said. A short time later she got married and left the company. One of Grace's friends in Seattle looked at me as we were dancing and said, "I'm going to seduce you!" Another of Grace's friends in Indiana loved to dance the jitterbug with me and one Christmas gave us a set of sheets and pillowcases. She handed them to me and said, "When you put your head on this, think of me."

I realize there are some men who would not consider this a problem. However, it can be if you have a value system and take your marriage vows seriously. In Europe the wives of two of my bosses made overtures to me. At every company party one kept asking me to dance with her. It was clear her marriage was in trouble. She later left and went back to the States and got a divorce. The other said, "We have to stop meeting this way." Flirting may give the ego a boost, but sometimes it can lead to more serious things. Fooling around with the boss's wife is "taboo," "verboten"! It is not a good way to enhance your career!

I've had another problem to compound the situation. I've always looked younger than my years. That used to irritate me when I was in the Navy and couldn't buy a glass of beer without showing an ID. It created a problem in business, because I wanted to be successful not because of how I looked but because of my hard work and performance. I must admit it hasn't been as bad as I have grown older. I've discussed this problem with my daughter Sheryl because she has the same problem. Not long ago, one morning at the supermarket as I was checking out, a lady came up behind me and said, "I'd go home with you anytime to have breakfast!" At a concert Grace and I attended, Grace went across the room to talk with a friend and a strange woman came up and said, "My name is Margaret, don't you remember me, I live in Morningside?" Sheryl said to me, "It's not safe for you to go out alone. Are women always hitting on you?" Sheryl has the same problem. She is a beautiful woman. I say that not as a proud father, but as a matter of fact. When she walks into a room, she turns heads. She said to me, "It's hard to handle. A lot of times I wish I were ugly." That is a terrible thing for a woman to say but I can understand it. I had a handsome student at Belmont say to me one time, "I don't understand it, when I go out on a date, the girls want to take their clothes off."

So, are good looks a blessing or a curse? Everyone is human and temptation is always lurking around the corner. I have not been immune. When I was recalled to the Navy in 1951 my ship anchored one hundred yards off the beach at Cannes on the French Riviera. The crew went bananas because they had never seen young women in bikinis. You couldn't get your hands on a pair of binoculars because they all were taken. An invitation was issued to some of the officers to attend a dance given by the Franco-American Club. I didn't have anything better to do so I went.

There was a bevy of French girls available for dancing. One was a really good dancer. I asked her to dance and we spent the rest of the evening dancing. The Navy provided transportation to take the girls home. When the Jeep arrived at her house, she turned and said, "When will I see you again?" I didn't reply so she said, "I'm at the Beach California every afternoon," and went into her house. Sometime later I was on liberty and found myself close to the beach "California." I stopped by and she was there. We had a light lunch and she took me to meet her family.

She was staying with an uncle and aunt who owned the house. The aunt was a beautiful woman and her uncle was a movie producer. They all lived in Paris and came south to the Riviera for the summer months. I told them I was married and had a young son. It didn't seem to bother Nadine. I gave her a copy of the 1950 Anthology of American Verse, which contained a poem I wrote when I was at Rice. When her family learned I was interested in writing, they insisted in taking me to meet the mother of the famous Antoine de Saint Exupery, author of The Little Prince. His mother lived in a villa in the mountains overlooking the Mediterranean. Unfortunately, when we arrived, she was not home.

Nadine gave me two books in French. One was all about Paris and inscribed, "To help you find your way coming back." The second was a French-English Dictionary inscribed, "To help you ask your way back." She was honest and forthright. "I want to be married and have a family." She did not seem to be bothered by the fact that I was married and had a son. The last evening before my ship left, we went to Juan les Pins to a dance where Sidney Bechet and his band were playing. He was the first notable jazz saxophonist and played a straight soprano saxophone. It was a wonderful night of listening and dancing to New Orleans Style Jazz like "Tin Roof Blues" and "Wildcat Blues." When we said goodbye, she put her arms around my neck and kissed me. The next day the Capricornus weighed anchor and we steamed away toward Naples. I never saw her again. If I had been a bachelor with no family obligations, I would have gone to Paris to look for her!

You have to have trust for a marriage to succeed. In today's world we are besieged with commercial advertising dripping with sex. Young teenage girls say to their parents they want to have plastic surgery to enhance the size of their breasts, to reduce the size of their nose and change almost any part of their bodies. It seems that regardless of what we have been given we want to change it. My question is "Why?" If anyone thinks it's fun to have members of the opposite sex ogling you, then think again.

In 2005 I joined The USS Capricornus Association, a group of former members of the crew from World War II to the end of 1960. I was the only member from the time of the Korean Conflict. The group has a reunion every year to get together and shoot the bull with old shipmates. Not long ago the Chairman forwarded an e-mail to me from a man asking if anyone remembered a Chief Petty Officer who was on the ship in 1951 when it was with the Sixth fleet in the Mediterranean. Since I was the only member on the ship at that time the e-mail was sent to me for a response. This Petty Officer died a few years ago and this person in France was trying to learn more about him. It turned out this man's mother had met the sailor in Southern France, fell in love with him, and they had an affair.

After the ship left, the girl found she was pregnant, but didn't try to get in touch with the sailor because she knew he was married and had two children. This fifty-nine-year-old Frenchman was trying to learn something about his biological father. I did not know him and was sorry to not be able to provide any information. I thought, *How sad!* Here was a son who never had the pleasure of knowing his father, a dad without the opportunity to play baseball or football with his son, a woman with the responsibility of raising a child without the help of a father. I thought, *How lucky I was when I resisted the temptation.* I'm glad there is no middle-aged man or woman in Paris wondering what their American biological father was like.

The consequences of temptation go far beyond the few minutes of physical pleasure that sex can give! There are enough temptations in life to resist without the burden of being so physically attractive everyone is staring at you. Even worse, telling you they are going to try and seduce you! There are times when it can be an advantage. If you want to be a TV anchor, a movie star, or a pop singer, it can be an asset. There are some professions where good looks can be an advantage. The secret is to not be fooled into thinking that's all it takes. That's why there are dumb blond jokes.

A combination of good looks with hard work and character are the tools for success. If image is the most important thing in your life, get over it! Image is fleeting! Grace and I have fun watching TV and discerning which politician, or which TV personality is wearing a hairpiece or a wig, or which one has had a facelift? If you look closely, you can tell how foolish they look. Who are they trying to fool? For the most part they are fooling themselves! If you watch the TV commercials closely, you begin to understand what's going on. There are all kinds of products you can buy to try to make you look younger.

Fortunes are being made selling these products. The reality is that everyone ages and gets older; it doesn't matter how hard you try or what you do, you are going to get older. You can save a lot of money by learning how to grow old gracefully. There's an old saying you shouldn't judge anything by its cover. It's true. With maturity comes an understanding that looks are superficial whether good or ugly.

In the important things in life they don't matter. In a life or death situation it doesn't matter whether your brain surgeon is handsome or not. If you are in the military or law enforcement, the thing that matters is character. Can you depend on your partner when the going gets tough? It's true everywhere, especially; in marriage, in business partnerships, in friends. Oprah Winfrey said, "A true friend walks in when everyone else walks out." There is no substitute for trust.

Navy Seals distilled it down to "You don't lie, you don't steal, and you don't cheat. Your personal reputation and that of your unit are sacred." The important relationships in life are built upon trust. Once broken, trust is hard to repair. Are good looks a blessing or a curse? The reality is they are insignificant in the overall scope of life. They are worth only what you do with them. Beauty is temporary regardless of how hard you may try to preserve it. The important things like character endure and are lasting.

If you were given physical good looks, be thankful. If you weren't, be thankful because it's what is in your heart that matters. Try to cultivate those things that will last. If you have good looks, learn how to manage them in a positive manner. If you don't have good looks, be thankful, you don't have to deal with the curse. If you have the right value system, you don't need them to be successful in life.

A short time ago, Grace and I attended a conference in New Orleans. A young man turned to us and said, "I just wanted to tell you what a handsome couple you are." To me it was the nicest compliment. Both Grace and I are in our eighties. We have been married more than sixty years. Our hair is white with age, but our hearts are full of love for each other and mankind.

34

The True Value of Education and Experience

There are several myths that have existed for decades. When I was growing up, my parents drilled into me that I had to get an education; it was the key that opened the doors of opportunity. I proceeded to get the education required to open the doors. First was the high school diploma. It opened the door to enlist in an elite Navy officer training program. Second was the college degree. I ran into the glass ceiling when my supervisor told me, "You've gone as far as you can go without a college degree." I went back to college for a year, got the piece of paper, later became a "Chartered Engineer," and never used any of the high-powered math courses I was required to take.

Our daughter was admitted into Vanderbilt University Engineering School without a high school diploma because she was able to successfully pass the Freshman Engineering Math Course. When I attended the Graduate School of Management at Vanderbilt to earn a Master's degree, I was able to avoid taking the courses in Accounting, Economics, and Finance by passing pre-tests. Why then are we told we must have the education and experience required for certain jobs? There are professions that you need special training: medical doctors, attorneys, etc.

In most work you learn the job by doing. You don't learn to ride a bicycle, ski, snowboard, skate board, ice or roller skate by reading a book. You have to fall a few times before you learn how to keep your balance. I'm reminded of a conversation I had when we lived in Seattle. I had a neighbor, Ernie Bagley, that worked for a public utility different than the one I worked for. On weekends we sometimes would get together and compare notes. He, like me, had changed jobs several times. He said, "They always told me, 'Ernie, you don't have enough experience,' so I went out and got some. Now they tell me, 'Ernie, you've got too much experience.' What I wasn't to know is where was I when I was just right?"

It was when I was teaching Personnel Management at Belmont that I began to get an understanding of how things work. In the business world I never had much use for the people in the Personnel Departments. In my opinion they were not too swift. To make their jobs easy they create the glass ceilings for jobs when they write the job descriptions. Rarely do they do personal interviews. Most of the time if they do, it is after the candidate had submitted a resume and survived a battery of tests.

Glass ceilings are created to help make the employment decision easy. They are weeding out tools that have little to do with whether a person can do the job. One of the reasons is that the decision maker rarely has the understanding of people to tell if they have the intangible qualities that make a good employee. These qualities are: do they get to work on time (do they wait for the last bus)? Are they a fast learner (do they have to be told how to do something more than once)? Can they see work that needs to be done or do they have to be told what to do (do they have personal initiative)? When they apply for a job, are they looking for a job or work (as my wife said, "Do you need a worker")? If they encounter a problem, how do they react? Do they try to find a solution or do they stop and wait for someone else to solve it?

I learned the best way to solve personnel problems was to do it on the front end in the interview. I was tough when I said, "If you are looking for work, then this is the place for you. If you are just looking for a place to get a paycheck, then go someplace else." Our educational system has been using the same methods for the last century. Many of the so-called "educators" have never had a real job. They do not consider their purpose is to prepare young men and women to go out into the workplace, survive, and earn a living. This is true throughout the system. When I was in college, we observed that there was a natural process of attrition. Many students would start out in engineering. When that became too hard, they would change their majors to mathematics. If that became too hard, they would change to arts and science courses.

I am sorry to say that the best and brightest did not become teachers. It was the direct opposite. There is a good reason why there is a shortage of math and science teachers. First, those who had natural aptitude for math and science can make more money as engineers and scientists. Most of those who became teachers took the path of least resistance, the easiest courses. Until teachers of the hard, difficult courses get paid more than other teachers, there will not be many good ones.

This behavior has permeated our higher educational system as well. I can speak from experience because I attended five colleges and universities and I taught for five years in a college where I earned tenure. With the exception of technical schools, very few teachers have worked in the real world. They live in what is called a "normative" world. Their world is a theoretical "the way things ought to be" world. Typical of this attitude is my experience with a young professor who didn't like my "descriptive" world dissertation proposal and told me I should take some more economics courses. I had a colleague at Belmont who once made the remark "This would be a pretty good job if we didn't have to deal with the students." What did he think he was getting paid for?

When our daughter was attending Vanderbilt, she had two roommates. Both were majoring in psychology. When they graduated, they discovered they were not prepared to enter the work force. No one in the faculty bothered to tell them they needed at least a Master's degree in order to get a job as a social worker. One who went through on a scholarship could only find employment as a file clerk in Atlanta. The other was more fortunate. Her father was the president of Exxon. He sent her to Catherine Gibbs Secretary School in New York to gain the skills to be employable. Many educators don't care what the job market is for graduating students. They are more interested in preserving their own jobs.

When looking for employment, great emphasis is placed upon experience. This is the "worker bee" attitude. What does "experience" really mean? The interest is not in what you can do; it's on what you have done. In other words, we want to keep on doing what we have been doing. If a Personnel Director looked at my resume, they probably would conclude that I couldn't hold a job because I changed jobs every three years. But if they looked closely, they would find that each move was up the career ladder assuming more and more responsibility.

This was the attitude when my boss Jim Gary said to me, "You haven't done that job before." My reply was, "That's why I want it." Grace and I met it in another form when we tried to buy our first car. Commercial Credit Corporation said, "They have never had any credit before." Fortunately, the car company sales person said, "You have to start sometime." It comes down to a matter of trust. In this case, trust that we were honest and would pay back the loan. In the case of Jim Gary, trust that I was competent and would do the job.

What do we mean when we say "trust"? We really are talking about a value system. An employer is looking for someone who is reliable and will not lie, cheat, or steal. Does that sound familiar? Try Governor Huckabee's book, *Do the Right Thing*. How do you measure trust? It's not easy in a written examination. If you are astute and have a good understanding of people, you can do it better in a personal interview. Because my wife, Grace, is a people person and has worked in the public so much, she is good at it. Years ago when you needed a loan you went to your local banker who knew you and your family. He knew from experience whether you were trustworthy. Today we try to do it remotely through mathematical formulas called "Credit Scores." Which do you think is the most accurate?

Another way of observing trust is to watch what happens in big companies. When an executive gets promoted, most of the time he wants to take his executive secretary with him. It has nothing to do with how she looks. It's because he knows he can depend on her and trust her. It's the same with other employees. In very large firms everyone is on a team. You may be on a team whether you know it or not. I learned this in Spain when Paul Temple told me he was leaving Esso. When his mentor, Bill Stott, who had been on the board of directors of Jersey Standard, resigned, Paul knew his future was limited.

What do we mean when we talk about "experience"? Is this a good measure of future performance? It depends on what we are looking for. There are different kinds of jobs that require different types of work. If the job is to keep on doing things the way they have always been done, then experience in maintaining the status quo is important. In the past this was the norm. However, in a new world of global economy and rapidly changing technology, experience is not relevant. I used to tell my students at the Belmont School of Business, if they learned anything, it should be how to solve problems. I guarantee if you say in a job interview that you are a problem solver that's what most employers are looking for.

When Ernie Bagley asked the question "Where was I when I was just right?" he was asking a profound question. There are times when your experience has no value. When I came home from work in Rhode Island and saw my unemployed next-door neighbor sitting on his rear end on the porch drinking beer, I didn't feel sorry for him. I didn't feel sorry because I remembered when my dad was unemployed during the "Great Depression" and looking for work. He didn't sit on his rear end feeling sorry for himself. He went out and found work doing something different than he had ever done before, wherever he could find it in Iowa, Wisconsin, Michigan, or Indiana.

My neighbor, on the other hand, said, "I'm a pipe fitter." There was no work for pipe fitters so he sat like a toad feeling sorry for himself. Some readers may think what I say cruel. I make no apologies. I know what it's like to be out of work. It has happened to me several times. It is degrading and hard to adjust to the loss of self-esteem. In our society we are judged by the work we do. However, it is not the job of government to find us work or to pay us for not working. It is up to us to do what my dad did. If your experience is no longer relevant, learn a new skill and move on. We live in a changing world. People are no longer interested in buying buggy whips!

When the president of the Third National Bank in Nashville looked at my resume and said, "You're too powerful for Nashville, you need to go to New York or Houston," he was telling me I was overqualified for any job in Nashville. In his opinion, like Ernie Bagley, I had too much experience and education. What do you do when you have too much education or experience? There is no way you can get rid of it.

When I was growing up, I had a hard time understanding the difference between the way things should be and the way things are. My mother tried to tell me I had to accept the way things are. I was not willing to do that. At Vanderbilt I was interested in why some businesses were successful and some failed. The answer was in the study of the life cycle of the firm. Firms go through different periods of change. They require different management styles and personalities. In the beginning they need risk takers I call "creator/builders." In the middle they need "caretakers." In later stages they require a "surgeon/mortician" who either cuts out the dead wood and saves the business or shuts it down.

Looking back, I was not a caretaker. I was always looking for a better way to do things. Most public utility operations are routine and need only caretakers. The operation of the Business Incubation Center reached a stage where they didn't need my creative/building skills. They needed a caretaker. It was time for me to move on. I should have known it.

I worked in Gas Public Utilities when they were making a dramatic change in their supply from manufactured to natural gas. In Seattle, Washington, New Zealand, Australia, West Germany, Belgium, Britain, and Spain, I was a change agent and didn't know it. I was wise enough to recognize when the operations were going to become routine and would require maintenance. Jim Gary told me when I was leaving, "Because of your forward planning, we can go a year without replacing you."

Looking back, there are three kinds of people: thinkers, talkers, and doers. Rarely is there a combination: thinker-talker, thinker-doer, or talker-doer. Most rare is a combination of all three. One time I was introduced to the major shareholder of a gas company. He was with his son-in-law who opened his mouth. His father-in-law said to him, "Shut up and listen, you might learn something!" Everyone needs to figure out where they fit in. Thinkers should be working in research. Talkers should be in Marketing. Doers should be forming new businesses or making changes in existing businesses. Each person should learn what they are comfortable in doing.

If you look around, you can see many people who are not happy in what they are doing. This is tragic. We spend more time in our work than we do in anything else. I am reminded of an experience I had in Seattle. I inherited a woman when I took over the Distribution Department. It was clear she didn't like her job and thought minimum performance was okay. What was worse was that she was keeping others from doing their work. I called her in and told her I was terminating her. She broke down in tears and said, "What am I going to do?" I told her to go home and after she put her ego back together to do some soul searching. Ask "What do I really like to do?" "What am I good at?" When she had the answers, go out and find a job doing what she liked to do. Two months later she stopped by my office. "I want to thank you," she said with a smile. "I hated your guts for firing me, but you forced me to do what I should have done. It took me a while to know what I'm good at. I've found a job I love. I would not have done it if you hadn't forced me to. Thank you again!"

Most people are afraid to risk jumping off the cliff into the unknown. What is the answer to the question "Where was I when I was just right?" The answer is "Now!" It doesn't matter whether you have the required education and experience. What matters is "Can you do the job?" If a glass ceiling impedes your way, do as my German friend Otto Baeder said. "Find a way over, under, or around the problem." Break through the ceiling. Be persistent. Find a way to bypass the Human Resource barriers. Find a way to get an interview with the decision maker and say, "I can do the job and solve your problems."

Be a risk taker. Say, "You can't afford to turn me down. I'll work a month without pay to prove I can do the job!" I have a daughter-in-law who did not go to college. She has worked her way up in different health care organizations by doing the job. She was interviewed for a job as executive secretary for one of the top doctors in the best hospital in Nashville. The job required a degree and computer skills. She called me and said she had the interview the next day, but was concerned because the job description required experience in the use of a computer program called "Power Point." I knew she was a quick learner and told her not to worry; if she got the job, I would teach her how to use "Power Point." She impressed the doctor in the interview and he hired her. He didn't care that she didn't have a college degree. He was convinced she could do the job. When she filled out the final paper work, the person processing the papers said, "I don't understand what this means where it asks for your degree. You put 'OJT.' What does that mean?" She smiled and said, "On the Job Training."

She got the job, learned how to use "Power Point," and has received a promotion to Administrative Assistant. (This job also is supposed to require a degree.) Over the last twenty years, more and more people have gone to college. A college degree no longer means what it did at one time. Almost every college now offers a MBA. Today there are college graduates looking for a job. Why? Because the educational system has not looked at the job market to learn what jobs are needed. Not every job should require a college degree. There are and will be plenty of occupations which pay good wages that do not require a college education. A revolution is coming in education. Programs are being developed for self-learning. The global economy is going to be a harsh teacher but people who have confidence and are willing to work will survive.

35

Starting a Successful New Business

When I put my ego back together after leaving the Nashville Incubation Center, I decided nobody was going to do that to me again. I looked at possibilities for Grace and me to start a new business. She had a real estate license since 1978 and while I was at the Center passed her broker's exam. Why not go into the real estate business? I took the exam and got my Affiliate Broker's license, and took enough training courses to earn the GRI (Graduate Real Estate Institute) designation. I did some number crunching on costs of opening an office. It was going to be jumping off another cliff. Entrepreneurs are risk takers. It's the only way that new businesses get started.

We learned about RE/MAX International. It was a new national franchise operation and an office had opened in Nashville. We had to find a niche in the business and it wasn't going to be easy. There were about three thousand agents in the Greater Nashville area. Five old line real estate firms controlled most of the business. Anyone you knew either had a relative or a friend in the business. Many agents operated by "winging it." That is, they didn't operate in a businesslike manner. How could we distinguish Grace from all of the other agents out there? Didn't they all do the same thing? RE/MAX looked like the best choice. They already had name recognition and a national network.

Nashville was starting to change. Many of the old line family members had passed on and the new generations weren't interested in being caretakers for the old family business. They were starting to sell to investors or firms from out of state. Large national companies were starting to locate regional offices in Nashville and move people in from out of state. The business community and the music industry were starting to work together to attract tourists. The Chamber of Commerce was launching a national ad campaign about "Music City U.S.A." The only problem with RE/MAX was it required paying a thousand dollars a month desk fee. It was designed for top producers who already had established themselves with enough business they could pay the fee. The attraction was that the agent could retain one hundred percent of the commissions they earned after paying the desk fee. It was as close to being in business for yourself as possible but with some advantages.

With credit cards in hand we joined the RE/MAX organization. We decided the niche for us was executive relocation. The existing firms had the listings for most of the homes for sale. They didn't worry about buyers. The adage was "You must have listings to survive in real estate." If you had the listings, buyers would come. Grace had one advantage over everyone else. She had packed up her family and moved all over the country and to and from five foreign countries. She understood the problems and concerns of a wife and family moving into a new and strange place.

We put together one of the first "Relocation Packages" in Nashville. It contained information about schools, taxes, churches, driver's licenses, etc. We also developed a package for children we called "Nashville is Fun for Kids." It was full of information about parks, sports, and all of the places children would be interested in. The next thing was to get wired into the RE/MAX national network. We registered to attend the California State RE/MAX Convention in San Diego. I designed and we printed a brochure about Grace and her real estate services. I studied TV commercials and determined they had two elements: a headline to grab your attention and a "hook" for you to remember. We coined a headline with a double entendre: *"Grace doesn't fiddle around."* This would tie in with the Chamber's national ad campaign with the hook *"For Music City U.S.A. Referrals call 'Amazing Grace.'"* We then adopted a fiddle as a logo.

When we arrived in San Diego, everyone at the convention couldn't believe we had come so far to be with them. Grace passed out business cards and pamphlets to everyone. Business firms were starting to move from California to Tennessee and we came home with three referrals. Next we went to the Chamber of Commerce and subscribed to a service that provided us with the names and addresses of everyone who sent letters to the Chamber asking for information about Nashville. There were several hundred a month. We sent them a letter offering to send them a free relocation package.

An advantage of the RE/MAX organization was they had panels of Top Producers who were willing to share information of how they did it. These were men and women who were selling millions of dollars worth of real estate each year. One advertised that he sold a house a day! They had no qualms about sharing information because we were not going to be competing with them. We learned the new marketing tool was "Personal Promotion." Under the old scheme the real estate firms did the advertising and advertised the firm. Under the RE/MAX system the agent paid for all advertising, so why not advertise the agent?

When we returned to Nashville, we looked at how real estate firms were advertising. Each company had ads with photos of houses they had listed for sale. If you were interested in buying a house, you called the agent. In other words, you were calling the agent for the seller. Who represented the buyer? Nobody! About this time we learned of a new organization called the "Real Estate Buyer's Agent Council." A new concept was developing, agents representing the interests of buyers. Grace attended the classes and became the twenty-seventh in the country to earn the "ABR" Accredited Buyer's Representative designation. (Today there are more than fifty thousand ABRs) There was a nice magazine published in color on slick paper called Homes and Land. Since we had no listings for sale, how could we start advertising? If we couldn't advertise houses, we would advertise Grace. We decided this would be where we would start the first personal promotion in Nashville. We paid for a half-page ad, which had a big fiddle in it with Grace's photo. It said, *"Grace Doesn't Fiddle Around! Buying or Selling a House in Music City U.S.A.? Call 'Amazing Grace' Kroeger."*

The ad created a firestorm in Nashville. All of the old time agents were shocked. They said, "You can't do that. You must advertise houses." The publisher of the magazine had no problem; he was happy to take our money. Grace started getting referrals from around the country representing buyers. In addition, we decided we didn't want other agents knowing in advance what our marketing plans were going to be. The easiest way to do that was not go into the office. We invested in equipment and started working out of our home. Today that is called a "home office." We were one of the first to arrange with the Multiple Listing Service to have what was called a "Dumb Terminal." This was before personal computers and allowed us to tie directly into the MLS service by telephone line just like the company office. We bought our own copy machine and fax machine. It wasn't long before we were as well equipped in our home as in the company office.

Grace and I worked as business partners and our personalities meshed in business the same as in our marriage. Her strengths were my weaknesses and vice versa. She loved being with people and didn't like paper work. I did all of the marketing and paperwork. I paid the bills and we ran it like a business. We weren't in it as a hobby or part-time job. It was a full time going business concern. Grace started getting RE/MAX Awards. In 1992 she became eligible for the Certified Residential Specialist (CRS) designation and for the first time became a member of the RE/MAX 100% Club. This meant she earned over one hundred thousand dollars in commissions during the year. Each year we attended the RE/MAX International Convention in: Las Vegas, or Orlando. We paid a hefty fee to have a personal promotion booth, which I manned. Each year we tried to come up with a clever gimmick we could give away with Grace's name and telephone number for people to take home with them. These cost a lot of money but brought good returns in referrals. We looked for things that would have "shelf life," that is, something that people could use in their business each day. One year it was a nice paperclip holder. Another time it was a brushed brass covered address book.

It wasn't long before "Amazing Grace" became known throughout the RE/MAX organization. One time Grace's broker attended a regional broker's meeting in North Carolina. He came back to Nashville and told Grace the first person he met asked when he said he was from Nashville, "Do you know 'Amazing Grace'?" It has been several years since we have advertised, but people still call her "Amazing Grace!" Grace was inducted into the coveted "RE/MAX Hall of Fame." She had earned over a million dollars in commissions. At one convention one of the top producer women from Atlanta approached me and said, "How can you work with your wife? My husband is retiring and I asked him to come in the business with me and he refused." My answer was simple. "I don't have a big ego. For over twenty-five years she helped me become successful in my career. Now it's her turn."

Grace has won many awards in Real Estate. We flew to San Francisco where she was one of the nine charter members of REBAC (Real Estate Buyers Agent Council) that received their "Hall of Fame" Award. She was in the distinguished company of the founder and owner of RE/MAX International. Grace received the Greater Nashville Association of Realtors "Life Member Award of Excellence" in 1996. Probably the thing she is most proud of was when she was appointed by Governor Don Sundquist to serve a five-year term as one of the five Commissioners of the Tennessee Real Estate Commission. This is the body that sets the standards and oversees the licensing of real estate agents for the State of Tennessee. Grace worked hard to improve the professionalism and ethics of the real estate industry in the state during her term.

Changes continued in the real estate business. Executive relocation became big business. We were fortunate to have been ahead of the curve. Some might say "at the right place at the right time." Grace was successful because of her special expertise and hard work. Opportunists saw the possibility of getting a piece of the action and formed "Relocation Companies." These contracted with employers to take the responsibility for their employee's relocation. The deal was they could reduce the firm's costs by charging the real estate agent a referral fee of thirty to thirty-five percent of what they earned from the transaction. The result was to not allow the employee any say in whom they would work with in their move to buy or sell their house. The inevitable happened, a decline in service, because when the monetary incentive was reduced, the quality of service declined.

Grace found it was no longer worthwhile to work referrals. Another trend started in the real estate business. Large national firms started buying up small local builders and hiring agents to represent them for new home sales. They developed their own relocation packages and started advertising to attract prospective buyers directly bypassing the Buyer's agents. Only sophisticated buyers would know that the agent at the model home was working only in the interest of the builder. For about the last ten years Grace and I said, "There is something terribly wrong with Real Estate and the Mortgage Business." It started when people began buying homes with no money down. We said, "This is crazy. If there is a downturn in the economy or any of these people get sick and lose their jobs, they have no equity in the property. They will just move out and walk away from the loan. Someone will be left holding the bag for the bad loan." We said the same thing about all of the new homes being built in the Spring Hill,

Tennessee area. This is where the General Motors Auto plant was located. Things can change. There was no guarantee that General Motors would always manufacture cars at the Spring Hill Plant. Whenever we expressed our concern, it fell on deaf ears. Once again there is no satisfaction in being a prophet. The attitude was "Let the good times roll!"

Unfortunately, the real estate bubble burst and GM shut down the Spring Hill Plant. There are consequences for everything that happens. As the saying goes, "You can deal with small problems as they occur or you can let them accumulate and deal with a huge problem later on." As time went by, we decided it was time to slow down. We formed our own real estate company "Magnolia Realty Company." We did not want the responsibility for other agents. We would be a two-person company and take only the business we wanted.

We have a list of hundreds of families we sold homes to. We kept in touch with them on birthdays, anniversaries, etc. They call us if and when they need information about real estate and want to sell their home. We've had a challenging, fun, and rewarding career in real estate. Grace was the first to have her photo on her business card, the first to do personal promotion, the first to specialize in executive relocation, one of the first to have a home office, one of the first to have a home connection to the MLS Service, and one of the first to specialize as a Buyer's Agent. To this day everyone calls her "Amazing Grace."

Afterward—A Look in the Rearview Mirror

The first most important turning point of my life was when I enlisted in the Navy. It forced me to develop the left side of my brain. It pushed me to the limits of my physical and mental abilities. I developed discipline and confidence. When I received my Navy commission, I was sure I could do anything, so I went out and did it.

The second most important turning point was when Grace agreed to marry me (after only knowing me for six weeks). It was a gift from God. She not only jumped off a cliff; she dove off into the Grand Canyon! When we left Nashville, we had forty dollars, two suitcases with our clothes and a dream. I was blessed. She was willing to leave her home, friends, and family and follow me all over the world. Grace still has *"beauty or charm, a pleasing quality or manner, a sense of what is right and proper."* "Amazing Grace" is not just a real estate slogan. It is a description of the characteristics of her life!

"Regrets, I have a few," as the song says in "I Did It My Way." I regret the times I said or did things that made tears come to my wife's eyes. I regret there were times I put my career before my family. I regret I never was able to overcome my mother's prejudice. Life is a series of choices. As Yogi Berra said, *"When you come to a fork in the road, take it!"* The tendency is to look for the path of least resistance. That's the well-trod path. If you choose to take the less traveled one, there's no limit to where it can take you!

LaVergne, TN USA
06 April 2011

223070LV00004B/123/P

9 781609 768195